Mountain Bike

AMERICA™

VIRGINIA

SECOND EDITION

Contact

Dear Readers:

Every effort was made to make this the most accurate, informative, and easy-to-use guidebook on the planet. Any comments, suggestions, and/or corrections regarding this guide are welcome and should be sent to:

Outside America™
c/o Editorial Dept.
300 West Main St., Ste. A
Charlottesville, VA 22903
editorial@outside-america.com
www.outside-america.com

We'd love to hear from you so we can make future editions and future guides even better.

Thanks and happy trails!

Mountain Bike AMERICA™

VIRGINIA

SECOND EDITION

An Atlas of Virginia's
Greatest Off-Road Bicycle Rides

by Scott Adams

The
Globe
Pequot
Press

Guilford, Connecticut

Published by
The Globe Pequot Press
P.O. Box 480
Guilford, CT 06437
www.globe-pequot.com

Produced by
Beachway Press Publishing, Inc.
300 West Main St., Ste A
Charlottesville, VA 22903
www.beachway.com

Mountain Bike America™ is a trademark of Beachway Press
Publishing, Inc.

Editorial Assistance given by Stefon Eickoff, John Boyle,
Ryan Croxton, and Byrd Leavell III

Virginia Highlands Trail Network courtesy of John Boyle

Cover Design Beachway Press

Photographer Scott Adams

Maps designed and produced by Beachway Press

Find Outside America™ at **www.outside-america.com**

*Cover Photo: Peering through the trees along the Slacks Trail
near Sherando Lake at the rolling hills of the Blue Ridge
Mountains.*

**Library of Congress Cataloging-in-Publication Data
is available.**

ISBN 0-7627-0704-6

Manufactured in the United States of America
Second Edition/First Printing

Acknowledgments

 special thanks to all the folks who have ever supported my efforts and desires to get to this point. It goes without saying that I would be hard-pressed to manage my ideas and dreams without all of the regular and unending encouragement, extra helping hands, and borrowed elbow grease from those around me and from those who believe in me. Thanks.

Scott Adams

owledgmer

Table Of

Contents

Preface

TRAIL OBSTACLES:

Rocks, Roots, Trees and...Politics?

Mountain Bike America: Virginia will help you find new trails. Other books on bicycling (and a lot of trial and error) will help you to develop the skills to ride those new trails. Still other books will show you how to fix your bike when you get a flat tire on those trails. But what do you do when your favorite trails get closed to bikes? Well, there's no book to remedy that, really. It all depends on you.

Well, not quite. You see—it depended on you. When trails close and bikes are banned, chances are the "problem" had already existed for a while. Maybe a few cyclists had been rolling carelessly past hikers on the trail, frightening them. Or maybe a few cyclists had been riding muddy trails, damaging them. Or maybe the "problem" was that a vocal opponent of mountain bikes had been bending the park management's ear for the past year, worrying them. And finally, because management hadn't heard from bikers, management just gave in.

You see, if some people have their way, mountain bikes will be restricted to pavement, private property, rail trails, and ski resorts in the off-season. Such people often get their understanding of our pastime from sensational television ads or magazine depictions of fearless teenagers engaged in death-defying feats. Sometimes, though, these people form their opinions based on a dangerous experience or a negative encounter on a trail. Fear motivates people. Scare someone today, even by accident, and your trail gets closed tomorrow.

Keeping Trails Open

Trail etiquette is a big part of the answer—the preventive solution. Just ask the International Mountain Bicycling Association (IMBA). Sure, the official IMBA "Rules of the Trail" are important. But simple courtesy, basic caution, and a little empathy for other trail users are the real requirements. In the long haul, they are more important than your bike gear, than your bike clothes—more important even than your bike. After all, a mountain bike isn't very useful if there isn't any place to ride it.

The second simple step to keep trails open is to join together with other cyclists. Join your local mountain bike club or association so your head gets counted and your voice gets heard. Besides, it's often a great way to meet other riders and learn about trails before they're published in a book or a magazine. A year's membership rarely costs more than twenty dollars, the cost of a bike tire. You'll find it's well worth it.

CLUBS

In Virginia, there are a few principal mountain bike groups that make a real diference. In Eastern Virginia it's the Eastern Virginia Mountain Bike Association (EVMBA). In Central Virginia it's a club called Mountain Bike Virginia. In Northern Virginia, the Mid-Atlantic Off-Road Enthusiasts (MORE) handle things very well all the way into Maryland and D.C. In the Western Virginia, Mountain Bike Virginia and other trail groups keep things in order. All of these clubs are known for keeping trails open. For leading great rides. For building new trails and maintaining old ones. For rais-

ing money for parks. For educating riders. And, well—for giving mountain bikers a good name.

Better than Lincoln Logs

And if you think breaking a sweat in the woods on your bike is fun, then working on trails might be more fun than you think. Who needs Erector Sets, Lincoln Logs or Legos, when you can build or maintain a real trail? Constructing a new treadway—or fixing an old one—will leave you with a sense of satisfaction that you can't buy in a bike shop. Skeptical? Call one of these local clubs and try it once. It's that simple. And it's fun.

IMBA

Speaking of simple, how much did your bike cost? And your helmet? And the bike rack for the car? Add it up, and think about it. Then consider writing out a check for the relatively paltry sum of twenty dollars to the International Mountain Bicycling Association (IMBA). IMBA is the national voice for mountain bikers, and twenty dollars gets you membership for a year—and helps support their effort to keep trails and land open to mountain bikers across the nation.

20-20-20

Twenty dollars to your local mountain bike group, twenty dollars to IMBA, and twenty hours a year as a trail volunteer. That's the recipe for access. That's the formula for keeping trails open and healthy. That's the ticket for preserving your fun. You've got the book and the bike. Time to do the rest.

This fine guide not only reveals some of the best shared-use trails around, but makes clear one crucial fact: cyclists' continued access to trails depends upon their courtesy toward hikers and equestrians and their willingness to help maintain those trails. The information in this book, and that message, is the key to some great riding!

Andy Carruthers

Andy Carruthers is one of the region's core mountain bike advocates, working diligently and successfully to keep local trails accessible to cyclists. Many thanks should go to him and all the volunteers who work to keep our trails open and healthy.

Introduc

A note from the folks behind this endeavor...

We at Outside America look at guidebook publishing a little differently. There's just no reason that a guidebook has to look like it was published out of your Uncle Ernie's woodshed. We feel that guidebooks need to be both easy to use and nice to look at, and that takes an innovative approach to design. You see, we want you to spend less time fumbling through your guidebook and more time enjoying the adventure at hand. At any rate, we hope you like what you see and enjoy the places we lead you. And most of all, we'd like to thank you for taking an adventure with us.

Happy Trails!

Welcome to the new generation of bicycling! Indeed, the sport has evolved dramatically from the thin-tired, featherweight-frame days of old. The sleek geometry and lightweight frames of racing bicycles, still the heart and soul of bicycling worldwide, have lost much ground in recent years, unpaving the way for the mountain bike, which now accounts for the majority of all bicycle sales in the U.S. And with this change comes a new breed of cyclist, less concerned with smooth roads and long rides, who thrives in places once inaccessible to the mortal road bike.

The mountain bike, with its knobby tread and reinforced frame, takes cyclists to places once unheard of—down rugged mountain trails, through streams of rushing water and thick mud, across the frozen Alaskan tundra, and even to work in the city. There seem to be few limits on what this fat-tired beast can do and where it can take us. Few obstacles stand in its way, few boundaries slow its progress. Except for one— its own success. If trail closure means little to you now, read on and discover how a trail can be here today and gone tomorrow. With so many new off-road cyclists taking to the trails each year, it's no wonder trail access hinges precariously between universal acceptance and complete termination. But a little work on your part can go a long way to preserving trail access for future use. Nothing is more crucial to the survival of mountain biking itself than to read the examples set forth in the following pages and practice their message. Then turn to the maps, pick out your favorite ride, and hit the dirt!

WHAT THIS BOOK IS ABOUT

Within these pages you will find everything you need to know about off-road bicycling in Virginia. This guidebook begins by exploring the fascinating history of the mountain bike itself, then goes on to discuss everything from the health benefits of off-road cycling to tips and techniques for bicycling over logs and up hills. Also included are the types of clothing to keep you comfortable and in style, essential equipment ideas to keep your rides smooth and trouble-free, and descriptions of off-road terrain to prepare you for the kinds of bumps and bounces you can expect to encounter. The major provisions of this book, though, are its unique perspectives on each ride, it detailed maps, and its relentless dedication to trail preservation.

Without open trails, the maps in this book are virtually useless. Cyclists must learn to be responsible for the trails they use and to share these trails with others. This guidebook addresses such issues as why trail use has become so controversial, what can be done to improve the image of mountain biking, how to have fun and ride responsibly, on-the-spot trail repair techniques, trail maintenance hotlines for each trail, and the worldwide-standard Rules of the Trail.

Each of the 48 rides is complete with maps, photos, trail descriptions and directions, local history, and a quick-reference ride information guide including such items as trail-maintenance hotlines, park schedules, costs, local bike stores, dining, lodging, entertainment, and alternative maps. Also included at the end of each regional section is an "Honorable Mentions" list of alternative off-road rides (70 rides total).

It's important to note that mountain bike rides tend to take longer than road rides because the average speed is often much slower. Average speeds can vary from a climbing pace of three to four miles per hour to 12 to 13 miles per hour on flatter roads and trails. Keep this in mind when planning your trip.

MOUNTAIN BIKE BEGINNINGS

It seems the mountain bike, originally designed for lunatic adventurists bored with straight lines, clean clothes, and smooth tires, has become globally popular in as short a time as it would take to race down a mountain trail.

Like many things of a revolutionary nature, the mountain bike was born on the west coast. But unlike Rollerblades, purple hair, and the peace sign, the concept of the off-road bike cannot be credited solely to the imaginative Californians—they were just the first to make waves.

The design of the first off-road specific bike was based on the geometry of the old Schwinn Excelsior, a one-speed, camel-back cruiser with balloon tires. Joe Breeze was the creator behind it, and in 1977 he built 10 of these "Breezers" for himself and his Marin County, California, friends at $750 apiece—a bargain.

Breeze was a serious competitor in bicycle racing, placing 13th in the 1977 U.S. Road Racing National Championships. After races, he and friends would scour local bike shops hoping to find old bikes they could then restore.

It was the 1941 Schwinn Excelsior, for which Breeze paid just five dollars, that began to shape and change bicycling history forever. After taking the bike home, removing the fenders, oiling the chain, and pumping up the tires, Breeze hit the dirt. He loved it.

His inspiration, while forerunning, was not altogether unique. On the opposite end of the country, nearly 2,500 miles from Marin County, east coast bike bums were also growing restless. More and more old, beat-up clunkers were being restored and modified. These behemoths often weighed as much as 80 pounds and were so reinforced they seemed virtually indestructible. But rides that take just 40 minutes on today's 25-pound featherweights took the steel-toed-boot- and-blue-jean-clad bikers of the late 1970s and early 1980s nearly four hours to complete.

Not until 1981 was it possible to purchase a production mountain bike, but local retailers found these ungainly bicycles difficult to sell and rarely kept them in stock. By 1983, however, mountain bikes were no longer such a fringe item, and large bike manufacturers quickly jumped into the action, producing their own versions of the off-road bike. By the 1990s, the mountain bike had firmly established its place with bicyclists of nearly all ages and abilities, and now command nearly 90 percent of the U.S. bike market.

There are many reasons for the mountain bike's success in becoming the hottest two-wheeled vehicle in the nation. They are much friendlier to the cyclist than traditional road bikes because of their comfortable upright position and shock-absorbing fat tires. And because of the health-conscious, environmentalist movement of the late 1980s and 1990s, people are more activity minded and seek nature on a closer front than paved roads can allow. The mountain bike gives you these things and takes you far away from the daily grind—even if you're only minutes from the city.

MOUNTAIN BIKING INTO SHAPE

If your objective is to get in shape and lose weight, then you're on the right track, because mountain biking is one of the best ways to get started.

One way many of us have lost weight in this sport is the crash-and-burn-it-off method. Picture this: you're speeding uncontrollably down a vertical drop that you realize you shouldn't be on—only after it is too late. Your front wheel lodges into a rut and launches you through endless weeds, trees, and pointy rocks before coming to an abrupt halt in a puddle of thick mud. Surveying the damage, you discover, with the layers of skin, body parts, and lost confidence littering the trail above, that those unwanted pounds have been shed-permanently. Instant weight loss.

There is, of course, a more conventional (and quite a bit less painful) approach to losing weight and gaining fitness on a mountain bike. It's called the workout, and bicycles provide an ideal way to get physical. Take a look at some of the benefits associated with cycling.

Cycling helps you shed pounds without gimmicky diet fads or weight-loss programs. You can explore the countryside and burn nearly 10 to 16 calories per minute or close to 600 to 1,000 calories per hour. Moreover, it's a great way to spend an afternoon.

No less significant than the external and cosmetic changes of your body from riding are the internal changes taking place. Over time, cycling regularly will strengthen your heart as your body grows vast networks of new capillaries to carry blood to all those working muscles. This will, in turn, give your skin a healthier glow. The capacity of your lungs may increase up to 20 percent, and your resting heart rate will drop significantly. The Stanford University School of Medicine reports to the American Heart Association that people can reduce their risk of heart attack by nearly 64 percent if they can burn up to 2,000 calories per week. This is only two to three hours of bike riding!

Recommended for insomnia, hypertension, indigestion, anxiety, and even for recuperation from major heart attacks, bicycling can be an excellent cure-all as well as a great preventive. Cycling just a few hours per week can improve your figure and sleeping habits, give you greater resistance to illness, increase your energy levels, and provide feelings of accomplishment and heightened self-esteem.

BE SAFE—KNOW THE LAW

Occasionally, even the hard-core off-road cyclists will find they have no choice but to ride the pavement. When you are forced to hit the road, it's important for you to know and understand the rules.

Outlined below are a few of the common laws found in Virginia's Vehicle Code book.

- **Bicycles are legally classified as vehicles in the state of Virginia.** This means that as a bicyclist, you are responsible for obeying the same rules of the road as a driver of a motor vehicle.
- **Bicyclists must ride with the traffic—NOT AGAINST IT!** Because bicycles are considered vehicles, you must ride your bicycle just as you would drive a car—with traffic. Only pedestrians should travel against the flow of traffic.

3

- **You must obey all traffic signs.** This includes stop signs and stoplights.
- **Always signal your turns.** Most drivers aren't expecting bicyclists to be on the roads, and many drivers would prefer that cyclists stay off the roads altogether. It's important, therefore, to clearly signal your intentions to motorists both in front and behind you.
- **Bicyclists are entitled to the same roads as cars (except controlled-access highways).** Unfortunately, cyclists are rarely given this consideration.
- **Be a responsible cyclist.** Do not abuse your rights to ride on open roads. Follow the rules and set a good example for all of us as you roll along.

THE MOUNTAIN BIKE CONTROVERSY

Are Off-Road Bicyclists Environmental Outlaws?
Do We have the Right to Use Public Trails?

Mountain bikers have long endured the animosity of folks in the backcountry who complain about the consequences of off-road bicycling. Many people believe that the fat tires and knobby tread do unacceptable environmental damage and that our uncontrollable riding habits are a danger to animals and to other trail users. To the contrary, mountain bikes have no more environmental impact than hiking boots or horseshoes. This does not mean, however, that mountain bikes leave no imprint at all. Wherever man treads, there is an impact. By riding responsibly, though, it is possible to leave only a minimum impact—something we all must take care to achieve.

Unfortunately, it is often people of great influence who view the mountain bike as the environment's worst enemy. Consequently, we as mountain bike riders and environmentally concerned citizens must be educators, impressing upon others that we also deserve the right to use these trails. Our responsibilities as bicyclists are no more and no less than any other trail user. We must all take the soft-cycling approach and show that mountain bicyclists are not environmental outlaws.

ETIQUETTE OF MOUNTAIN BIKING

When discussing mountain biking etiquette, we are in essence discussing the soft-cycling approach. This term, as mentioned previously, describes the art of minimum-impact bicycling and should apply to both the physical and social dimensions of the sport. But make no mistake—it is possible to ride fast and furiously while maintaining the balance of soft-cycling. Here first are a few ways to minimize the physical impact of mountain bike riding.

- **Stay on the trail.** Don't ride around fallen trees or mud holes that block your path. Stop and cross over them. When you come to a vista overlooking a deep valley, don't ride off the trail for a better vantage point. Instead, leave the bike and walk to see the view. Riding off the trail may seem inconsequential when done only once, but soon someone else will follow, then others, and the cumulative results can be catastrophic. Each time you wander from the trail you begin creating a new path, adding one more scar to the earth's surface.

4

- *Do not disturb the soil.* Follow a line within the trail that will not disturb or damage the soil.
- *Do not ride over soft or wet trails.* After a rain shower or during the thawing season, trails will often resemble muddy, oozing swampland. The best thing to do is stay off the trails altogether. Realistically, however, we're all going to come across some muddy trails we cannot anticipate. Instead of blasting through each section of mud, which may seem both easier and more fun, lift the bike and walk past. Each time a cyclist rides through a soft or muddy section of trail, that part of the trail is permanently damaged. Regardless of the trail's conditions, though, remember always to go over the obstacles across the path, not around them. Stay on the trail.
- *Avoid trails that, for all but God, are considered impassable and impossible.* Don't take a leap of faith down a kamikaze descent on which you will be forced to lock your brakes and skid to the bottom, ripping the ground apart as you go.

Soft-cycling should apply to the social dimensions of the sport as well, since mountain bikers are not the only folks who use the trails. Hikers, equestrians, cross-country skiers, and other outdoors people use many of the same trails and can be easily spooked by a marauding mountain biker tearing through the trees. Be friendly in the forest and give ample warning of your approach.

- *Take out what you bring in.* Don't leave broken bike pieces and banana peels scattered along the trail.
- *Be aware of your surroundings.* Don't use popular hiking trails for race training.
- *Slow down!* Rocketing around blind corners is a sure way to ruin an unsuspecting hiker's day. Consider this—If you fly down a quick singletrack descent at 20 mph, then hit the brakes and slow down to only six mph to pass someone, you're still moving twice as fast as they are!

Like the trails we ride on, the social dimension of mountain biking is very fragile and must be cared for responsibly. We should not want to destroy another person's enjoyment of the outdoors. By riding in the backcountry with caution, control, and responsibility, our presence should be felt positively by other trail users. By adhering to these rules, trail riding—a privilege that can quickly be taken away—will continue to be ours to share.

TRAIL MAINTENANCE

Unfortunately, despite all of the preventive measures taken to avoid trail damage, we're still going to run into many trails requiring attention. Simply put, a lot of hikers, equestrians, and cyclists alike use the same trails—some wear and tear is unavoidable. But like your bike, if you want to use these trails for a long time to come, you must also maintain them.

Trail maintenance and restoration can be accomplished in a variety of ways. One way is for mountain bike clubs to combine efforts with other trail users (i.e. hikers and equestrians) and work closely with land managers to cut new trails or repair existing ones. This not only reinforces to others the commitment cyclists have in caring for and maintaining the land, but also breaks the ice that often separates cyclists from their fellow trailmates. Another good way to help out is to show up on a Saturday morning with a few riding buddies at your favorite off-road domain ready to work. With a good attitude, thick gloves, and the local land manager's supervision, trail repair is fun and very rewarding. It's important, of course, that you arrange a trail-repair outing with the local land manager before you start pounding shovels into the dirt. They can lead you to the most needy sections of trail and instruct you on what repairs should be done and how best to accomplish the task. Perhaps the most effective means of trail maintenance, though, can be done by yourself and while you're riding. Read on.

ON-THE-SPOT QUICK FIX

Most of us, when we're riding, have at one time or another come upon muddy trails or fallen trees blocking our path. We notice that over time the mud gets deeper and the trail gets wider as people go through or around the obstacles. We worry that the problem will become so severe and repairs too difficult that the trail's access may be threatened. We also know that our ambition to do anything about it is greatest at that moment, not after a hot shower and a plate of spaghetti. Here are a few on-the-spot quick fixes you can do that will hopefully correct a problem before it gets out of hand and get you back on your bike within minutes.

• **MUDDY TRAILS.** What do you do when trails develop huge mud holes destined for the EPA's Superfund status? The technique is called corduroying, and it works much like building a pontoon over the mud to support bikes, horses, or hikers as they cross. Corduroy (not the pants) is the term for roads made of logs laid down crosswise. Use small-and medium-sized sticks and lay them side by side across the trail until they cover the length of the muddy section (break the sticks to fit the width of the trail). Press them into the mud with your feet, then lay more on top if needed. Keep adding sticks until the trail is firm. Not only will you stay clean as you cross, but the sticks may soak up some of the water and help the puddle dry. This quick fix may last as long as one month before needing to be redone. And as time goes on, with new layers added to the trail, the soil will grow stronger, thicker, and more resistant to erosion. This whole process may take fewer than five minutes, and you can be on your way, knowing the trail behind you is in good repair.

LEAVING THE TRAIL. What do you do to keep cyclists from cutting corners and leaving the designated trail? The solution is much simpler than you may think. (No, don't hire an off-road police force.) Notice where people are leaving the trail and throw a pile of thick branches or brush along the path, or place logs across the opening to block the way through. There are probably dozens of subtle tricks like these that will manipulate people into staying on the designated trail. If executed well, no one will even notice that the thick branches scattered along the ground in the woods weren't always there. And most folks would probably rather take a moment to hop a log in the trail than get tangled in a web of branches.

OBSTACLES IN THE WAY. If there are large obstacles blocking the trail, try and remove them or push them aside. If you cannot do this by yourself, call the trail maintenance hotline to speak with the land manager of that particular trail and see what can be done.

We must be willing to *sweat for* our trails in order to *sweat on* them. Police yourself and point out to others the significance of trail maintenance. "Sweat Equity," the rewards of continued land use won with a fair share of sweat, pays off when the trail is "up for review" by the land manager and he or she remembers the efforts made by trail-conscious mountain bikers.

RULES OF THE TRAIL

The International Mountain Bicycling Association (IMBA) has developed these guidelines to trail riding. These "Rules of the Trail" are accepted worldwide and will go a long way in keeping trails open. Please respect and follow these rules for everyone's sake.

1. *Ride only on open trails.* Respect trail and road closures (if you're not sure, ask a park or state official first), do not trespass on private property, and obtain permits or authorization if required. Federal and state wilderness areas are off-limits to cycling. Parks and state forests may also have certain trails closed to cycling.
2. *Leave no trace.* Be sensitive to the dirt beneath you. Even on open trails, you should not ride under conditions by which you will leave evidence of your passing, such as on certain soils or shortly after a rainfall. Be sure to observe the different types of soils and trails you're riding on, practicing minimum-impact cycling. Never ride off the trail, don't skid your tires, and be sure to bring out at least as much as you bring in.
3. *Control your bicycle!* Inattention for even one second can cause disaster for yourself or for others. Excessive speed frightens and can injure people, gives mountain biking a bad name, and can result in trail closures.
4. *Always yield.* Let others know you're coming well in advance (a friendly greeting is always good and often appreciated). Show your respect when passing others by slowing to walking speed or stopping altogether, especially in the presence of horses. Horses can be unpredictable, so be very careful. Anticipate that other trail users may be around corners or in blind spots.
5. *Never spook animals.* All animals are spooked by sudden movements, unannounced approaches, or loud noises. Give the animals extra room and time so they can adjust to you. Move slowly or dismount around animals. Running cattle and disturbing wild animals are serious offenses. Leave gates as you find them, or as marked.
6. *Plan ahead.* Know your equipment, your ability, and the area in which you are riding, and plan your trip accordingly. Be self-sufficient at all times, keep your bike in good repair, and carry necessary supplies for changes in weather or other conditions. You can help keep trails open by setting an example of responsible, courteous, and controlled mountain bike riding.

7. *Always wear a helmet when you ride.* For your own safety and protection, a helmet should be worn whenever you are riding your bike. You never know when a tree root or small rock will throw you the wrong way and send you tumbling.

Thousands of miles of dirt trails have been closed to mountain bicycling because of the irresponsible riding habits of just a few riders. Don't follow the example of these offending riders. Don't take away trail privileges from thousands of others who work hard each year to keep the backcountry avenues open to us all.

THE NECESSITIES OF CYCLING

When discussing the most important items to have on a bike ride, cyclists generally agree on the following four items.

- **HELMET.** The reasons to wear a helmet should be obvious. Helmets are discussed in more detail in the Be Safe—Wear Your Armor section.
  - **WATER.** Without it, cyclists may face dehydration, which may result in dizziness and fatigue. On a warm day, cyclists should drink at least one full bottle during every hour of riding. Remember, it's always good to drink before you feel thirsty—otherwise, it may be too late.
    - **CYCLING SHORTS.** These are necessary if you plan to ride your bike more than 20 to 30 minutes. Padded cycling shorts may be the only thing preventing your derriere from serious saddle soreness by ride's end. There are two types of cycling shorts you can buy. Touring shorts are good for people who don't want to look like they're wearing anatomically correct cellophane. These look like regular athletic shorts with pockets, but have built-in padding in the crotch area for protection from chafing and saddle sores. The more popular, traditional cycling shorts are made of skin-tight material, also with a padded crotch. Whichever style you find most comfortable, cycling shorts are a necessity for long rides.
      - **FOOD.** This essential item will keep you rolling. Cycling burns up a lot of calories and is among the few sports in which no one is safe from the "Bonk." Bonking feels like it sounds. Without food in your system, your blood sugar level collapses, and there is no longer any energy in your body. This instantly results in total fatigue and light-headedness. So when you're filling your water bottle, remember to bring along some food. Fruit, energy bars, or some other forms of high-energy food are highly recommended. Candy bars are not, however, because they will deliver a sudden burst of high energy, then let you down soon after, causing you to feel worse than before. Energy bars are available at most bike stores and are similar to candy bars, but provide complex carbohydrate energy and high nutrition rather than fast-burning simple sugars.

BE PREPARED OR DIE

Essential equipment that will keep you from dying alone in the woods:
- SPARE TUBE
- TIRE IRONS—See the Appendix for instructions on fixing flat tires.
- PATCH KIT
- PUMP

- MONEY—Spare change for emergency calls.
- SPOKE WRENCH
- SPARE SPOKES—To fit your wheel. Tape these to the chain stay.
- CHAIN TOOL
- ALLEN KEYS—Bring appropriate sizes to fit your bike.
- COMPASS
- FIRST-AID KIT
- MATCHES
- GUIDEBOOK—In case all else fails and you must start a fire to survive, this guidebook will serve as excellent fire starter!

To carry these items, you may need a bike bag. A bag mounted in front of the handlebars provides quick access to your belongings, whereas a saddle bag fitted underneath the saddle keeps things out of your way. If you're carrying lots of equipment, you may want to consider a set of panniers. These are much larger and mount on either side of each wheel on a rack. Many cyclists, though, prefer not to use a bag at all. They just slip all they need into their jersey pockets, and off they go.

BE SAFE—WEAR YOUR ARMOR

While on the subject of jerseys, it's crucial to discuss the clothing you must wear to be safe, practical, and—if you prefer—stylish. The following is a list of items that will save you from disaster, outfit you comfortably, and most important, keep you looking cool.

- HELMET. A helmet is an absolute necessity because it protects your head from complete annihilation. It is the only thing that will not disintegrate into a million pieces after a wicked crash on a descent you shouldn't have been on in the first place. A helmet with a solid exterior shell will also protect your head from sharp or protruding objects. Of course, with a hard-shelled helmet, you can paste several stickers of your favorite bicycle manufacturers all over the outer shell, giving companies even more free advertising for your dollar.
- SHORTS. Let's just say Lycra cycling shorts are considered a major safety item if you plan to ride for more than 20 or 30 minutes at a time. As mentioned in The Necessities of Cycling section, cycling shorts are well regarded as the leading cure-all for chafing and saddle sores. The most preventive cycling shorts have padded "chamois" (most chamois is synthetic nowadays) in the crotch area. Of course, if you choose to wear these traditional cycling shorts, it's imperative that they look as if someone spray painted them onto your body.
- GLOVES. You may find well-padded cycling gloves invaluable when traveling over rocky trails and gravelly roads for hours on end. Long-fingered gloves may also be useful, as branches, trees, assorted hard objects, and, occasionally, small animals will reach out and whack your knuckles.
- GLASSES. Not only do sunglasses give you an imposing presence and make you look cool (both are extremely important), they also protect your eyes from harm-

ful ultraviolet rays, invisible branches, creepy bugs, dirt, and may prevent you from being caught sneaking glances at riders of the opposite sex also wearing skintight, revealing Lycra.

- **SHOES.** Mountain bike shoes should have stiff soles to help make pedaling easier and provide better traction when walking your bike up a trail becomes necessary. Virtually any kind of good outdoor hiking footwear will work, but specific mountain bike shoes (especially those with inset cleats) are best. It is vital that these shoes look as ugly as humanly possible. Those closest in style to bowling shoes are, of course, the most popular.

- **JERSEY or SHIRT.** Bicycling jerseys are popular because of their snug fit and back pockets. When purchasing a jersey, look for ones that are loaded with bright, blinding, neon logos and manufacturers' names. These loudly decorated billboards are also good for drawing unnecessary attention to yourself just before taking a mean spill while trying to hop a curb. A cotton T-shirt is a good alternative in warm weather, but when the weather turns cold, cotton becomes a chilling substitute for the jersey. Cotton retains moisture and sweat against your body, which may cause you to get the chills and ills on those cold-weather rides.

OH, THOSE CHILLY VIRGINIA DAYS

If the weather chooses not to cooperate on the day you've set aside for a bike ride, it's helpful to be prepared.

- *Tights or leg warmers.* These are best in temperatures below 55 degrees. Knees are sensitive and can develop all kinds of problems if they get cold. Common problems include tendinitis, bursitis, and arthritis.

- *Plenty of layers on your upper body.* When the air has a nip in it, layers of clothing will keep the chill away from your chest and help prevent the development of bronchitis. If the air is cool, a polypropylene long-sleeved shirt is best to wear against the skin beneath other layers of clothing. Polypropylene, like wool, wicks away moisture from your skin to keep your body dry. Try to avoid wearing cotton or baggy clothing when the temperature falls. Cotton, as mentioned before, holds moisture like a sponge, and baggy clothing catches cold air and swirls it around your body. Good cold-weather clothing should fit snugly against your body, but not be restrictive.

- *Wool socks.* Don't pack too many layers under those shoes, though. You may stand the chance of restricting circulation, and your feet will get real cold, real fast.

- *Thinsulate or Gortex gloves.* We may all agree that there is nothing worse than frozen feet—unless your hands are frozen. A good pair of Thinsulate or Gortex gloves should keep your hands toasty and warm.

- *Hat or helmet on cold days?* Sometimes, when the weather gets really cold and you still want to hit the trails, it's tough to stay warm. We all know that 130 percent of the body's heat escapes through the head (overactive brains, I imagine), so it's important to keep the cranium warm. Ventilated helmets are designed to keep heads cool in the summer heat, but they do little to help keep heads warm during rides in sub-zero temperatures. Cyclists should consider wearing a hat on extremely cold days. Polypropylene Skullcaps are great head and ear warmers that snugly fit over your head beneath the helmet. Head protection is not lost. Another option is a helmet cover that covers those ventilating gaps and helps keep the body heat in. These do not, however, keep your ears warm. Some cyclists will opt for a simple knit cycling cap sans the helmet, but these have never been shown to be very good cranium protectors.

All of this clothing can be found at your local bike store, where the staff should be happy to help fit you into the seasons of the year.

TO HAVE OR NOT TO HAVE...
(Other Very Useful Items)
Though mountain biking is relatively new to the cycling scene, there is no short-age of items for you and your bike to make riding better, safer, and easier. We have rummaged through the unending lists and separated the gadgets from the good stuff, coming up with what we believe are items certain to make mountain bike riding easier and more enjoyable.

- **TIRES.** Buying yourself a good pair of knobby tires is the quick-est way to enhance the off-road handling capabilities of your bike. There are many types of mountain bike tires on the mar-ket. Some are made exclusively for very rugged off-road ter-rain. These big-knobbed, soft rubber tires virtually stick to the ground with unforgiving traction, but tend to deteriorate quickly on pavement. There are other tires made exclusively for the road. These are called "slicks" and have no tread at all. For the average cyclist, though, a good tire somewhere in the middle of these two extremes should do the trick.
- **TOE CLIPS or CLIPLESS PEDALS.** With these, you will ride with more power. Toe clips attach to your pedals and strap your feet firmly in place, allowing you to exert pressure on the pedals on both the downstroke and the upstroke. They will increase your pedaling effi-ciency by 30 percent to 50 percent. Clipless pedals, which liberate your feet from the traditional straps and clips, have made toe clips virtually obsolete. Like ski bindings, they attach your shoe directly to the pedal. They are, however, much more expensive than toe clips.
- **BAR ENDS.** These great clamp-on additions to your original straight bar will provide more leverage, an excellent grip for climbing, and a more natural position for your hands. Be aware, however, of the bar end's propensity for hooking trees on fast descents, sending you, the cyclist, airborne.
- **FANNY PACK.** These bags are ideal for carrying keys, extra food, guidebooks, tools, spare tubes, and a cellular phone, in case you need to call for help.
- **SUSPENSION FORKS.** For the more serious off-roaders who want nothing to impede their speed on the trails, investing in a pair of suspension forks is a good idea. Like tires, there are plenty of brands to choose from, and they all do the same thing—absorb the brutal beatings of a rough trail. The cost of these forks, how-ever, is sometimes more brutal than the trail itself.

- **BIKE COMPUTERS.** These are fun gadgets to own and are much less expensive than in years past. They have such features as trip distance, speedometer, odometer, time of day, altitude, alarm, average speed, maximum speed, heart rate, global satellite positioning, etc. Bike computers will come in handy when following these maps or to know just how far you've ridden in the wrong direction.

TYPES OF OFF-ROAD TERRAIN

Before roughing it off road, we may first have to ride the pavement to get to our destination. Please, don't be dismayed. Some of the country's best rides are on the road. Once we get past these smooth-surfaced pathways, though, adventures in dirt await us.

- **RAILS-TO-TRAILS.** Abandoned rail lines are converted into usable public resources for exercising, commuting, or just enjoying nature. Old rails and ties are torn up and a trail, paved or unpaved, is laid along the existing corridor. This completes the cycle from ancient Indian trading routes to railroad corridors and back again to hiking and cycling trails.
    - **UNPAVED ROADS.** These are typically found in rural areas and are most often public roads. Be careful when exploring, though, not to ride on someone's unpaved private drive.
        - **FOREST ROADS.** These dirt and gravel roads are used primarily as access to forest land and are kept in good condition. They are almost always open to public use.
        - **SINGLETRACK.** Singletrack can be the most fun on a mountain bike. These trails, with only one track to follow, are often narrow, challenging pathways through the woods. Remember to make sure these trails are open before zipping into the woods. (At the time of this printing, all trails and roads in this guidebook were open to mountain bikes.)
        - **OPEN LAND.** Unless there is a marked trail through a field or open space, you should not plan to ride here. Once one person cuts his or her wheels through a field or meadow, many more are sure to follow, causing irreparable damage to the landscape.

TECHNIQUES TO SHARPEN YOUR SKILLS

Many of us see ourselves as pure athletes—blessed with power, strength, and endless endurance. However, it may be those with finesse, balance, agility, and grace that get around most quickly on a mountain bike. Although power, strength, and endurance do have their places in mountain biking, these elements don't necessarily form the framework for a champion mountain biker.

The bike should become an extension of your body. Slight shifts in your hips or knees can have remarkable results. Experienced bike handlers seem to flash down technical descents, dashing over obstacles in a smooth and graceful effort as if pirouetting in Swan Lake. Here are some tips and techniques to help you connect with your bike and float gracefully over the dirt.

Braking

Using your brakes requires using your head, especially when descending. This doesn't mean using your head as a stopping block, but rather to think intelligently. Use your best judgment in terms of how much or how little to squeeze those brake levers.

The more weight a tire is carrying, the more braking power it has. When you're going downhill, your front wheel carries more weight than the rear. Braking with the front brake will help keep you in control without going into a skid. Be careful, though, not to overdo it with the front brakes and accidentally toss yourself over the handlebars. And don't neglect your rear brake! When descending, shift your weight back over the rear wheel, thus increasing your rear braking power as well. This will balance the power of both brakes and give you maximum control.

Good riders learn just how much of their weight to shift over each wheel and how to apply just enough braking power to each brake, so not to "endo" over the handlebars or skid down a trail.

GOING UPHILL—Climbing Those Treacherous Hills

- *Shift into a low gear* (push the thumb shifter away from you). Before shifting, be sure to ease up on your pedaling so there is not too much pressure on the chain. Find the gear best for you that matches the terrain and steepness of each climb.
- *Stay seated.* Standing out of the saddle is often helpful when climbing steep hills with a road bike, but you may find that on dirt, standing may cause your rear tire to lose its grip and spin out. Climbing requires traction. Stay seated as long as you can, and keep the rear tire digging into the ground. Ascending skyward may prove to be much easier in the saddle.
- *Lean forward.* On very steep hills, the front end may feel unweighted and suddenly pop up. Slide forward on the saddle and lean over the handlebars. This will add more weight to the front wheel and should keep you grounded.
- *Keep pedaling.* On rocky climbs, be sure to keep the pressure on, and don't let up on those pedals! The slower you go through rough trail sections, the harder you will work.

GOING DOWNHILL—
The Real Reason We Get Up in the Morning

- *Shift into the big chainring.* Shifting into the big ring before a bumpy descent will help keep the chain from bouncing off. And should you crash or disengage your leg from the pedal, the chain will cover the teeth of the big ring so they don't bite into your leg.
- *Relax.* Stay loose on the bike, and don't lock your elbows or clench your grip. Your elbows need to bend with the bumps and absorb the shock, while your hands should have a firm but controlled grip on the bars to keep things steady. Steer with your body, allowing your shoulders to guide you through each turn and around each obstacle.

- *Don't oversteer or lose control.* Mountain biking is much like downhill skiing, since you must shift your weight from side to side down narrow, bumpy descents. Your bike will have the tendency to track in the direction you look and follow the slight shifts and leans of your body. You should not think so much about steering, but rather in what direction you wish to go.
- *Rise above the saddle.* When racing down bumpy, technical descents, you should not be sitting on the saddle, but standing on the pedals, allowing your legs and knees to absorb the rocky trail instead of your rear.
- *Drop your saddle.* For steep, technical descents, you may want to drop your saddle three or four inches. This lowers your center of gravity, giving you much more room to bounce around.
- *Keep your pedals parallel to the ground.* The front pedal should be slightly higher so that it doesn't catch on small rocks or logs.
  - *Stay focused.* Many descents require your utmost concentration and focus just to reach the bottom. You must notice every groove, every root, every rock, every hole, every bump. You, the bike, and the trail should all become one as you seek singletrack nirvana on your way down the mountain. But if your thoughts wander, however, then so may your bike, and you may instead become one with the trees!

WATCH OUT!
Back-road Obstacles

- **LOGS.** When you want to hop a log, throw your body back, yank up on the handlebars, and pedal forward in one swift motion. This clears the front end of the bike. Then quickly scoot forward and pedal the rear wheel up and over. Keep the forward momentum until you've cleared the log, and by all means, don't hit the brakes, or you may do some interesting acrobatic maneuvers!
- **ROCKS.** Worse than highway potholes! Stay relaxed, let your elbows and knees absorb the shock, and always continue applying power to your pedals. Staying seated will keep the rear wheel weighted to prevent slipping, and a light front end will help you to respond quickly to each new obstacle. The slower you go, the more time your tires will have to get caught between the grooves.
- **WATER.** Before crossing a stream or puddle, be sure to first check the depth and bottom surface. There may be an unseen hole or large rock hidden under the water that could wash you up if you're not careful. After you're sure all is safe, hit the water at a good speed, pedal steadily, and allow the bike to steer you through. Once you're across, tap the breaks to squeegee the water off the rims.
- **LEAVES.** Be careful of wet leaves. These may look pretty, but a trail covered with leaves may cause your wheels to slip out from under you. Leaves are not nearly as unpredictable and dangerous as ice, but they do warrant your attention on a rainy day.
- **MUD.** If you must ride through mud, hit it head on and keep pedaling. You want to part the ooze with your front wheel and get across before it swallows you up. Above all, don't leave the trail to go around the mud. This just widens the path even more and leads to increased trail erosion.

Urban Obstacles

- **CURBS** are fun to jump, but like with logs, be careful.
- **CURBSIDE DRAINS** are typically not a problem for bikes. Just be careful not to get a wheel caught in the grate.
- **DOGS** make great pets, but seem to have it in for bicyclists. If you think you can't outrun a dog that's chasing you, stop and walk your bike out of its territory. A loud yell to Get! or Go home! often works, as does a sharp squirt from your water bottle right between the eyes.
- **CARS** are tremendously convenient when we're in them, but dodging irate motorists in big automobiles becomes a real hazard when riding a bike. As a cyclist, you must realize most drivers aren't expecting you to be there and often wish you weren't. Stay alert and ride carefully, clearly signaling all of your intentions.
- **POTHOLES,** like grates and back-road canyons, should be avoided. Just because you're on an all-terrain bicycle doesn't mean you're indestructible. Potholes regularly damage rims, pop tires, and sometimes lift unsuspecting cyclists into a spectacular swan dive over the handlebars.

LAST-MINUTE CHECKOVER

Before a ride, it's a good idea to give your bike a once-over to make sure everything is in working order. Begin by checking the air pressure in your tires before each ride to make sure they are properly inflated. Mountain bikes require about 45 to 55 pounds per square inch of air pressure. If your tires are underinflated, there is greater likelihood that the tubes may get pinched on a bump or rock, causing the tire to flat.

Looking over your bike to make sure everything is secure and in its place is the next step. Go through the following checklist before each ride.

- *Pinch the tires to feel for proper inflation.* They should give just a little on the sides, but feel very hard on the treads. If you have a pressure gauge, use that.
- *Check your brakes.* Squeeze the rear brake and roll your bike forward. The rear tire should skid. Next, squeeze the front brake and roll your bike forward. The rear wheel should lift into the air. If this doesn't happen, then your brakes are too loose. Make sure the brake levers don't touch the handlebars when squeezed with full force.
- *Check all quick releases on your bike.* Make sure they are all securely tightened.
- *Lube up.* If your chain squeaks, apply some lubricant.
- *Check your nuts and bolts.* Check the handlebars, saddle, cranks, and pedals to make sure that each is tight and securely fastened to your bike.
- *Check your wheels.* Spin each wheel to see that they spin through the frame and between brake pads freely.
- *Have you got everything?* Make sure you have your spare tube, tire irons patch kit, frame pump, tools, food, water, and guidebook.

15

Liability Disclaimer

Neither the publisher, the producer, nor the authors of this guide assumes any liability for cyclists traveling along any of the suggested routes in this book. At the time of publication, all routes shown on the following maps were open to bicycles. They were chosen for their safety, aesthetics, and pleasure, and are deemed acceptable and accommodating to bicyclists. Safety upon these routes, however, cannot be guaranteed. Cyclists must assume their own responsibility when riding these routes and understand that with an activity such as mountain bike riding, there may be unforeseen risks and dangers.

THE MAPS

1 Area Locator Map

This thumbnail relief map at the beginning of each ride shows you where the ride is within the state. The ride area is indicated with a star.

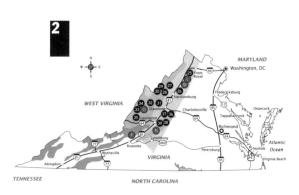

2 Regional Location Map

This map helps you find your way to the start of each ride from the nearest sizeable town or city. Coupled with the detailed directions at the beginning of the cue, this map should visually lead you to where you need to be for each ride.

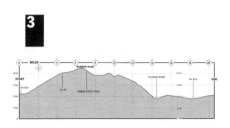

3 Profile Map

This helpful profile gives you a cross-sectional look at the ride's ups and downs. Elevation is labeled on the left, mileage is indicated on the top. Road and trail names are shown along the route with towns and points of interest labeled in bold.

MOUNTAIN BIKE VIRGINIA

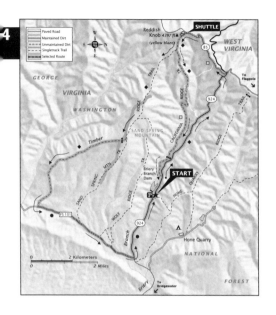

4 Route Map

This is your primary guide to each ride. It shows all of the accessible roads and trails, points of interest, water, towns, landmarks, and geographical features. It also distinguishes trails from roads, and paved roads from unpaved roads. The selected route is highlighted, and directional arrows point the way. Shaded topographic relief in the background gives you an accurate representation of the terrain and landscape in the ride area.

Ride Information *(Included in each ride section)*

📞 Trail Contacts:
This is the direct number for the local land managers in charge of all the trails within the selected ride. Use this hotline to call ahead for trail access information, or after your visit if you see problems with trail erosion, damage, or misuse.

🕐 Schedule:
This tells you at what times trails open and close, if on private or park land.

💲 Fees/Permits:
What money, if any, you may need to carry with you for park entrance fees or tolls.

Ⓝ Maps:
This is a list of other maps to supplement the maps in this book. They are listed in order from most detailed to most general.

Any other important or useful information will also be listed here such as local attractions, bike shops, nearby accommodations, etc.

e don't want anyone, by any means, to feel restricted to just the roads and trails that are mapped here. We hope you will have an adventurous spirit and use this guide as a platform to dive into Virginia's backcountry and discover new routes for yourself. One of the simplest ways to begin this is to just turn the map upside down and ride the course in reverse. The change in perspective is fantastic and the ride should feel quite different. With this in mind, it will be like getting two distinctly different rides on each map.

For your own purposes, you may wish to copy the directions for the course onto a small sheet to help you while riding, or photocopy the map and cue sheet to take with you. These pages can be folded into a bike bag, stuffed into a jersey pocket, or better still, used with the **BarMap** or **BarMapOTG** (see www.cycoactive.com for more info). Just remember to slow or even stop when you want to read the map.

5	Interstate Highway
8	U.S. Highway
3	State Road
CR 23	County Road
T 145	Township Road
FS 45	Forest Road
	Paved Road
	Paved Bike Lane
	Maintained Dirt Road
======	Unmaintained Jeep Trail
- - - -	Singletrack Trail
	Highlighted Route
	Ntl Forest/County Boundaries
	State Boundaries
	Railroad Tracks
	Power Lines
··········	Special Trail
	Rivers or Streams
	Water and Lakes
	Marsh

✝	Airfield	⛳	Golf Course
✈	Airport	🏃	Hiking Trail
🚲	Bike Trail	⛏	Mine
🚳	No Bikes	⚲	Overlook
🚣	Boat Launch	⊼	Picnic
)(	Bridge	P	Parking
🚌	Bus Stop	✕	Quarry
▲	Campground	((A))	Radio Tower
♨	Campsite	🧗	Rock Climbing
⛵	Canoe Access	▮	School
⊟	Cattle Guard	▰	Shelter
†	Cemetery	℘	Spring
⚑	Church	🏊	Swimming
⛪	Covered Bridge	♜	Train Station
⇀	Direction Arrows	✝	Wildlife Refuge
⛷	Downhill Skiing	🍇	Vineyard
⛩	Fire Tower	◆◆	Most Difficult
⛽	Forest HQ	◆	Difficult
🛺	4WD Trail	□	Moderate
⌶	Gate	●	Easy

Pennsylvania

MD   DE

West Virginia

Virginia

MOUNTAIN BIKE VIRGINIA

The Rides

1. Back Bay to False Cape
2. First Landing State Park
3. Great Dismal Swamp
4. Carrollton-Nike Park
5. Harwood's Mill
6. Newport News Park
7. Beaverdam Reservoir Park
8. Waller Mill Park
9. York River State Park
10. Petersburg National Battlefield
11. Pocahontas State Park
12. Belle Isle
13. Powhite Park
14. Poor Farm Park
15. Cumberland State Forest
16. Charlottesville Dirt Ride
17. Observatory Hill
18. Walnut Creek Park
19. Prince William Forest Park
20. Fountainhead Regional Park
21. Lake Accotink/Wakefield Park
22. Centreville Power Lines
23. Great Falls National Park
24. Middleburg Vineyard Ride

25. Elizabeth Furnace
26. Massanutten Mountain
27. Second Mountain ATV Trails
28. Blueberry Trail
29. Reddish Knob
30. Flagpole
31. North Mountain Trail to Elliot Knob
32. Williamsville Loop
33. Ellis Loop
34. Hidden Valley Recreation Area
35. Douthat State Park
36. Sherando Lake Loop
37. Big Levels
38. Henry Lanum Trail
39. Blue Ridge Dirt Ride
40. Potts Mountain
41. Brush Mountain
42. Mountain Lake
43. Mount Rogers Loop
44. Grayson Highlands State Park
45. Hidden Valley
46. Seven Sisters
47. New River Trail

48. Virginia Creeper Trail

Honorable Mentions

A. Ipswitch
B. Dogwood Dell
C. Hollywod Farm
D. Sugarloaf Mountain and The Waltons
E. James River State Park
F. Appomattox-Buckingham State Forest–Carter Taylor Trail
G. Prince Edward-Gallion State Forest
H. Burke Lake Park
I. South Run Power Lines
J. Difficult Run (Glade to Great Falls)
K. C&O Canal Ride
L. Duncan Hollow Trail
M. Edinburg Gap
N. South Pedlar ATV Trails
O. McDowell Battlefield Trail
P. North Mountain Trail
Q. Mountain lake MTB Trails
R. Poverty Creek
S. Fairy Stone State Park

George Washington National Forest

Jefferson National Forest

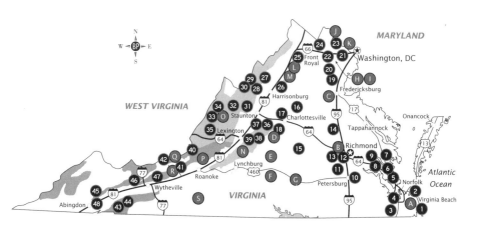

COURSES AT A GLANCE

1. Back Bay to False Cape

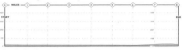

Length: 27 miles of open trails   **Time:** 1-4 hours
Nearby: Sandbridge, VA   **Difficulty:** Easy

2. First Landing State Park

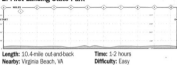

Length: 10.4-mile out-and-back   **Time:** 1-2 hours
Nearby: Virginia Beach, VA   **Difficulty:** Easy

3. Great Dismal Swamp

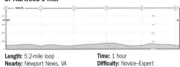

Length: 8.2-mile out-and-back   **Time:** 1 hour
Nearby: Suffolk, VA   **Difficulty:** Easy

4. Carrollton-Nike Park

Length: 2.5-mile loop   **Time:** 1 hour
Nearby: Smithfield, VA   **Difficulty:** Easy to moderate

5. Harwood's Mill

Length: 5.2-mile loop   **Time:** 1 hour
Nearby: Newport News, VA   **Difficulty:** Novice–Expert

6. Newport News Park

Length: 5.2-mile loop   **Time:** 1 hour
Nearby: Newport News, VA   **Difficulty:** Easy

7. Beaverdam Reservoir Park

Multiple Route Options

Length: 6+ mile trail system   **Time:** 1-2 hours
Nearby: Gloucester, VA   **Difficulty:** Easy to moderate

8. Waller Mill Park

Length: 4-5-mile loop   **Time:** 1 hour
Nearby: Williamsburg, VA   **Difficulty:** Difficult

9. York River State Park

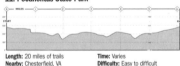

Length: 14.5 miles of MTB trails   **Time:** 2+ hours
Nearby: Williamsburg, VA   **Difficulty:** Easy to difficult

10. Petersburg National Battlefield

Multiple Route Options

Length: 6 miles of trails   **Time:** 1-2 hours
Nearby: Petersburg, VA   **Difficulty:** Easy to Moderate

11. Pocahontas State Park

Length: 20 miles of trails   **Time:** Varies
Nearby: Chesterfield, VA   **Difficulty:** Easy to difficult

12. Belle Isle

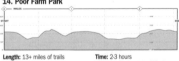

Length: 5+ miles of trails   **Time:** Varies
Nearby: Richmond, VA   **Difficulty:** Easy to difficult

13. Powhite Park

Multiple Route Options

Length: 8+ miles of trails   **Time:** Varies
Nearby: Richmond, VA   **Difficulty:** Moderate to difficult

14. Poor Farm Park

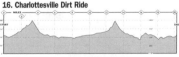

Length: 13+ miles of trails   **Time:** 2-3 hours
Nearby: Ashland, VA   **Difficulty:** Moderate to difficult

15. Cumberland State Forest

Multiple Route Options

Length: 40-50 miles of firest roads   **Time:** Varies
Nearby: Farmville, VA   **Difficulty:** Easy to moderate

16. Charlottesville Dirt Ride

Length: 20.3-mile loop   **Time:** 2-3 hour
Nearby: Charlottesville, VA   **Difficulty:** Moderate

Ride Profiles

17. Observatory Hill

Multiple Route Options

Length: 7+ miles of trails
Nearby: Charlottesville, VA
Time: Varies
Difficulty: Moderate to difficult

19. Prince William Forest Park

Multiple Route Options

Length: 8.2 miles of doubletrack
Nearby: Dumfries, VA
Time: Varies depending on route
Difficulty: Moderate

21. Lake Accotink/Wakefield Park

Length: 6.1-mile loop
Nearby: Annandale, VA
Time: 1 hour
Difficulty: Easy to difficult

23. Great Falls National Park

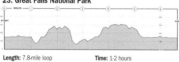

Length: 7.8-mile loop
Nearby: McLean, VA
Time: 1-2 hours
Difficulty: Moderate

25. Elizabeth Furnace

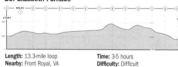

Length: 13.3-mile loop
Nearby: Front Royal, VA
Time: 3-5 hours
Difficulty: Difficult

27. Second Mountain ATV Trails

Length: 4.3-mile out-and-back
Nearby: Rawley Springs, VA
Time: 1-2 hours
Difficulty: Moderate

29. Reddish Knob

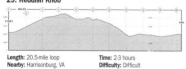

Length: 20.5-mile loop
Nearby: Harrisonburg, VA
Time: 2-3 hours
Difficulty: Difficult

31. North Mountain Trail to Elliot Knob

Length: 9.8-mile out-and-back
Nearby: Staunton, VA
Time: 2-3 hours
Difficulty: Difficult

18. Walnut Creek Park

Multiple Route Options

Length: 15 miles of trails
Nearby: Charlottesville, VA
Time: 2-3 hours
Difficulty: Moderate to difficult

20. Fountainhead Regional Park

Length: 4.5-mile loop
Nearby: Springfield, VA
Time: 1 hour
Difficulty: Moderate to difficult

22. Centreville Power Lines

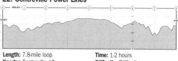

Length: 7.8-mile loop
Nearby: Centreville, VA
Time: 1-2 hours
Difficulty: Difficult

24. Middleburg Vineyard Ride

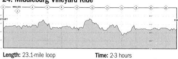

Length: 23.1-mile loop
Nearby: Middleburg, VA
Time: 2-3 hours
Difficulty: Moderate to difficult

26. Massanutten Mountain

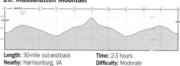

Length: 30-mile out-and-back
Nearby: Harrisonburg, VA
Time: 2-3 hours
Difficulty: Moderate

28. Blueberry Trail

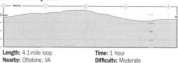

Length: 4.1-mile loop
Nearby: Ottobine, VA
Time: 1 hour
Difficulty: Moderate

30. Flagpole

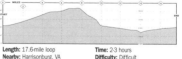

Length: 17.6-mile loop
Nearby: Harrisonburg, VA
Time: 2-3 hours
Difficulty: Difficult

32. Williamsville Loop

Length: 7.3-mile loop
Nearby: Flood, VA
Time: 2 hours
Difficulty: Moderate

COURSES AT A GLANCE

33. Ellis Loop

Length: 5.6-mile loop   **Time:** 1-2 hours
Nearby: Hot Springs, VA   **Difficulty:** Moderate

35. Douthat State Park

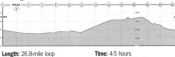

Length: 3.1-mile loop of 40+ miles   **Time:** 1 hour
Nearby: Clifton Forge, VA   **Difficulty:** Easy to Difficult

37. Big Levels

Length: 26.8-mile loop   **Time:** 4-5 hours
Nearby: Waynesboro, VA   **Difficulty:** Very difficult

39. Blue Ridge Dirt Ride

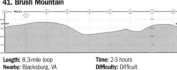

Length: 15.3-mile loop   **Time:** 2 hours
Nearby: Buena Vista, VA   **Difficulty:** Easy to moderate

41. Brush Mountain

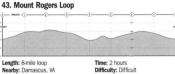

Length: 8.3-mile loop   **Time:** 2-3 hours
Nearby: Blacksburg, VA   **Difficulty:** Difficult

43. Mount Rogers Loop

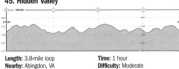

Length: 8-mile loop   **Time:** 2 hours
Nearby: Damascus, VA   **Difficulty:** Difficult

45. Hidden Valley

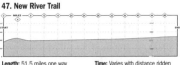

Length: 3.8-mile loop   **Time:** 1 hour
Nearby: Abingdon, VA   **Difficulty:** Moderate

47. New River Trail

Length: 51.5 miles one way   **Time:** Varies with distance ridden
Start: Pulaski, VA   **Difficulty:** Easy

34. Hidden Valley Recreation Area

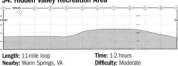

Length: 11-mile loop   **Time:** 1-2 hours
Nearby: Warm Springs, VA   **Difficulty:** Moderate

36. Sherando Lake Loop

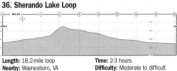

Length: 18.2-mile loop   **Time:** 2-3 hours
Nearby: Waynesboro, VA   **Difficulty:** Moderate to difficult

38. Henry Lanum Trail

Length: 5.3-mile loop   **Time:** 1-2 hours
Nearby: Buena Vista, VA   **Difficulty:** Difficult

40. Potts Mountain

Length: 8.6-mile loop   **Time:** 1-2 hours
Nearby: Roanoke, VA   **Difficulty:** Difficult

42. Mountain Lake

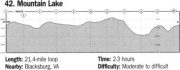

Length: 21.4-mile loop   **Time:** 2-3 hours
Nearby: Blacksburg, VA   **Difficulty:** Moderate to difficult

44. Grayson Highlands State Park

Length: 8-mile loop   **Time:** 2 hours
Nearby: Volney, VA   **Difficulty:** Difficult

46. Seven Sisters

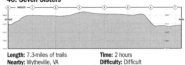

Length: 7.3-miles of trails   **Time:** 2 hours
Nearby: Wytheville, VA   **Difficulty:** Difficult

48. Virginia Creeper Trail

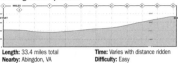

Length: 33.4 miles total   **Time:** Varies with distance ridden
Nearby: Abingdon, VA   **Difficulty:** Easy

Getting Around Virginia

Ⓑ AREA CODES

Virginia currently has five area codes: **540** serves Roanoke, western and northern Virginia excluding Arlington. **571** overlays with **703** to serve the Washington DC suburbs and Arlington area. **757** serves Hampton, Norfolk and southeastern Virginia. And **804** covers Richmond, Lynchburg and central Virginia.

ROADS

For current information on statewide weather and road conditions and closures, contact the Virginia Department of Transportation (VDOT) call the 24-hour HIGHWAY HELPLINE 1-800-367-ROAD (7623). (TTY users, call 1-800-432-1843) *www.vdot.state.va.us*

✈ AIRPORTS

Dulles International Airport (IAD) is 23 miles northwest of downtown Washington DC. **Ronald Reagan Washington National Airport** (DCA) is in nearby Alexandria. *www.metwashairports.com.* **Richmond International Airport** (RIC) is located 7 miles east of downtown Richmond. *www.flyrichmond.com.* **Norfolk/Virginia Beach International** (ORF) serves the Tidewater Region. *www.norfolkairport.com*

Other major airports in Virginia include **Roanoke Regional Airport** (ROA) *www.roanokeairport.com,* **Shenandoah Valley Regional Airport** (SHD) *www.flyshd.com,* Charlottesville Albemarle Airport (CHO) *www.cho-airport.state.va.us* and **Newport News-Williamsburg International** (NNW) *www.phf-airport.org.*

Most major airlines will carry your bicycle for a fee that varies between $50 and $90. However if you join the **League of American Bicyclists** (LAB) you can take advantage of their "Bikes Fly Free" program. For more information contact LAB at 202-822-1333 *www.bikeleague.org*

To book reservations online, check out your favorite airline's website or search one of the following travel sites for the best price: *www.cheaptickets.com, www.expedia.com, www.previewtravel.com, www.priceline.com, http://travel.yahoo.com, www.travelocity.com,* or *www.trip.com* just to name a few.

🚋 TRAIN

Compared to other states, Virginia is well served by **Amtrak**. All trains stop at Union Station in Washington DC. Amtrak carries boxed bikes for $12 (which includes a $7 fee for a box) to Alexandria, Richmond, Charlottesville, Petersburg, and Lynchburg.

The **Cardinal** offers by far the best Amtrak experience in Virginia. The train runs on Wednesday, Friday and Sunday between Washington and Chicago. Special bike racks on board allow roll on access to all stations for a $15 fee. The train stops at Manasses, Culpeper, Charlottesville, Staunton and Clifton Forge. The train is rarely full along this segment of the journey and the view from the lounge car is sublime.

Acela Regional Service serves, Richmond, Williamsburg and Newport News from New York and Boston several times a day. For more details, call 1-800-872-7245 or visit *www.amtrak.com* for more information.

VRE—Commuter rail service running weekdays along two lines from Fredericksburg and Manasses to Union Station. Some of these trains have cafe cars which have tiedowns for up to six bicycles. Call VRE at 1-800-RIDE-VRE to find out which trains carry bikes or visit *www.vre.org/cafecar.htm*.

Bus

Greyhound lines serves most larger towns and cities in Virginia along with Dulles Airport several times a day. Bicycles must be boxed and a $15 fee applies. Bike boxes are for sale for $10 at major terminals. *www.greyhound.com*

Local bikes on transit information for Virginia is located on the Internet at *www.bikemap.com/transit/va.htm*.

The Rides

Coastal

George Washington National Forest

Jefferson National Forest

MARYLAND

Washington, DC

Front
Royal

Fredericksburg

WEST VIRGINIA

Harrisonburg

Staunton

Charlottesville

Onancock

Tappahannock

Lexington

Richmond

Atlantic
Ocean

Lynchburg

Roanoke

Petersburg

Norfolk

Wytheville

VIRGINIA

Virginia Beach

Abingdon

TENNESSEE

NORTH CAROLINA

Virginia

Back Bay to False Cape

Ride Specs

Start: From the Back Bay Visitor Center
Length: 27.7 miles of trails
Approximate Riding Time: 1–4 hours
Difficulty Rating: Easy. Flat riding along the beach and dikes.
Trail Surface: Flat gravel packed roads, sandy trails, and beach
Land Status: National wildlife refuge and state park
Nearest Town: Sandbridge, VA
Other Trail Users: Hikers and campers
Canine Compatibility: Don't bring 'em. Pets are allowed in False Cape but not through Back Bay except in October—during the managed hunt.

Getting There

From Virginia Beach Waterfront: Travel east on Shore Drive (U.S. 60) until it turns right, becoming Atlantic Avenue. At 40th Street get in the right-hand lane. This is Pacific Avenue. Pacific Avenue becomes General Booth Boulevard after crossing Rudee Inlet Bridge. Go seven miles on General Booth Boulevard, then turn left on Princess Anne Road. Go 0.5 miles to the first light and turn left on Sandbridge Road. Take Sandbridge Road 5.6 miles, then turn right on Sandpiper Road. Follow Sandpiper Road 3.9 miles to Back Bay National Wildlife Refuge. The road ends at their parking lot. ***DeLorme: Virginia Atlas & Gazetteer:*** Page 35, C-7

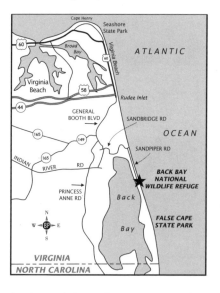

False Cape State Park, located on the southeastern tip of Virginia, is the least-visited park in the state of Virginia, averaging fewer than 25,000 visitors annually. However, False Cape isn't for everyone.

To get there, one must be willing to travel off-road by bicycle, foot, or boat at least 10 miles round-trip through the nearly 8,000 acres of Back Bay National Wildlife Refuge. There is no vehicular access to the park, and hardy adventurers must lug in their own food, shelter, and hefty cans of bug spray (False Cape is renowned for its large insect population).

The reward is one of the most isolated and unspoiled coastal environments on the East Coast.

Annually, hundreds of species of birds, including snow and Canada geese, tundra swans, and ducks, make this thin strip of Atlantic coastline their fall and winter home. River otters, white-tailed deer, mink, red and grey fox, muskrats, opossums, and raccoons also share this coastal habitat with a few of the non-native species such as nutria wild horses and feral pigs. Yes, pigs!

Seagulls will accompany you along the way.

Wild dunes and forests of loblolly pine, maple, and gnarled live oak grow right up to the persistent Atlantic surf, where sandpipers dodge the crashing waves and forage for meals in the sand. Farther out in the ocean, brown pelicans and osprey dive into the ocean in search of fish.

The adventure begins at Back Bay's visitor contact station, just south of the tiny coastal community of Sandbridge. Parking is plentiful, and the station is equipped with restrooms, a telephone, maps, and information about the area. And since no motorized vehicles are allowed past this point, there is no other logical alternative but to leave the car and unpack your bike. Water is in now available at the contact stations and first campsite, but cyclists should still carry plenty of liquid just in case.

The bike route starts on the east side of the visitor contact station and follows either the east or west dike south toward False Cape. Both dikes are topped with gravel and are well suited for cycling. Immediately before the Dune Trail, the two dikes split but reconnect at each of the three cross dikes on your way south.

The arrangement of the different dikes and cross dikes throughout the Back Bay Refuge form large areas of marsh and wetland into what is called an impoundment. Eight of these impoundments, or pools, exist in Back Bay. In fall and winter, the impoundments are filled, then planted with grass, plants, and other vegetation necessary as sustenance for the wintering birds and waterfowl this refuge serves to protect. Both the east and west dikes lead directly into False Cape State Park, and one or the other will be clearly designated for the journey through Back Bay.

Cyclists may also choose to ride the nine-mile route along the beach from the refuge to the North Carolina border. Be aware, though, that the best time is from two hours before low tide until two hours after, when there's plenty of hard, wet sand on which to ride. If you want to come back along the beach, be sure to keep an eye on the incoming tide.

Once you reach False Cape State Park you may find its coastal habitat very similar to Back Bay's—beautiful and unspoiled. There are numerous sights along the many miles of the park's bicycle routes, including the Wash Woods cemetery and church site, and False Cape's wildlife lookout tower (within a quarter-mile of Wash Woods)—a perfect place to view tundra swans and snow geese during the winter months.

At some point in the 19th Century, a small community called Wash Woods developed on what is now the state park. Most of its residents were farmers and fishermen who carried their small parcels of crops and fish across Back Bay by boat to sell on the mainland. However, amid heavy storms and a battering ocean, and the fatal blow of a massive hurricane in the early 1930s, Wash Woods did not survive. All that remains are a church's foundation and steeple and a small cemetery. Most other traces of the community have been covered by the blowing sands. The Wash Woods historical site is the southernmost point that bicycles are allowed.

In December 1994, Back Bay National Wildlife Refuge implemented a seasonal dike closure from November 1 to April 1. This effectively closes the only road-

Ride Information

🐾 Trail Contacts:
Back Bay National Wildlife Refuge
(757) 721-2412

False Cape State Park
(757) 426-7128

The False Cape State Park Tram is managed by the Back Bay Restoration Foundation.
(757) 426-3643

🕐 Schedule:
Back Bay dikes is closed from Nov. 1 to April 1. Beach to False Cape is open year-round. The Refuge is open daily from dawn to dusk. The Visitors contact station is open 8:00 a.m. to 4:00 p.m. *[Note: False Cape State Park and Back Bay National Wildlife Refuge are closed from the first Saturday through the second Saturday in October each year for the Game Management Program (Hunt).]*

💲 Cost:
$2.00 – Single visit permit (foot/bike)
$4.00 – Vehicles
Tram is $6 for adults and $4 for children age 12 and younger
Age 16 and younger – Free

💡 Local Events/Attractions:
Little Island City Park (swimming, surfing, fishing)

Virginia Marine Science Museum, located on General Booth Boulevard, is one of the top marine science museums in the nation.

Virginia Beach
(757) 425-FISH
www.vmsm.com

🛏 Accommodations:
False Cape State Park Camping - Camping is permitted year-round, but reservations are required. The camping areas are Barbour Hill Bay, Barbour Hill Ocean, False Cape Landing Bay and False Cape Landing Ocean. For camping information, contact the State Parks Reservation Center at 1-800-933-7275; in Richmond dial 225-3867.

🚲 Local Bike Shops:
Bike Rentals: Sandbridge Realty, on Sandbridge Road, approximately four miles from the Refuge.

🗺 Maps:
USGS maps: Knotts Island, VA, NC; North Bay, VA
ADC map: Tidewater road map
Back Bay National Wildlife Refuge trail map
False Cape State Park trail map

ways through its federal wildlife refuge to False Cape State Park. Officials at Back Bay felt hikers and bicyclists were disturbing the wintering waterfowl the refuge existed to protect. During these months visitors can take an electric tram from Little Island City Park, through the Refuge, and on to False Cape. The tram makes a round trip, picking up visitors at False Cape two hours after drop-off. However, the tram is not available to carry bicycles, so cyclists determined to arrive in False Cape State Park with two wheels during the winter months must pedal the 10-mile round trip along the beach.

MilesDirections

0.0 START at the Back Bay National Wildlife Refuge Visitor Contact Station. The bike trail starts on the east side of the visitors center. You will travel south along Back Bay's Interior Dike toward False Cape State Park.

0.2 The Interior Dike splits into east and west. Take either the East Dike or West Dike to False Cape, both of which are clearly designated.

Wet sand creates a hard surface on which to ride.

0.6 Begin passing Pool C, a large impoundment of marsh and wetland used for wintering birds and waterfowl. This and the other impoundments provide wildlife habitat year-round.

2.0 Reach the first cross dike. Continue south on either the East or West Dike. Begin passing Pool B.

2.5 Reach the second cross dike. Continue south on either the East or West Dike. Begin passing Pool A.

3.3 Reach the third cross dike and False Cape State Park. Regardless of which dike you were riding on, you will enter False Cape on the Barbour Hill Interpretive Trail, which forms a 2.4-mile loop. This is an interpretive trail, which passes the observation tower (overlook). The observation tower is great for viewing the barrier spit's unique wildlife in their natural environment. This road will lead you to the state park contact station.

4.25 From the Barbour Hill Beach Trail and the Visitors Contact Station, follow the Main Trail south toward False Cape Landing.

6.3 Reach False Cape Landing Trail. Continue straight on the Main Trail toward Wash Woods Historical Site.

7.5 Pass the Wash Woods Beach Trail (0.8 miles east to the Atlantic). Continue straight on the Main Trail.

7.8 Pass the Wash Woods Interpretive Trail (0.7 miles east to the Atlantic/0.1 miles west to the Wash Woods Environmental Education Center). Continue straight on the Mail Trail.

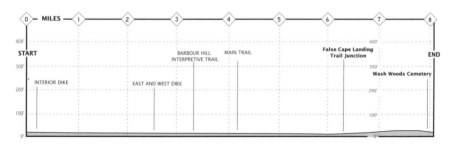

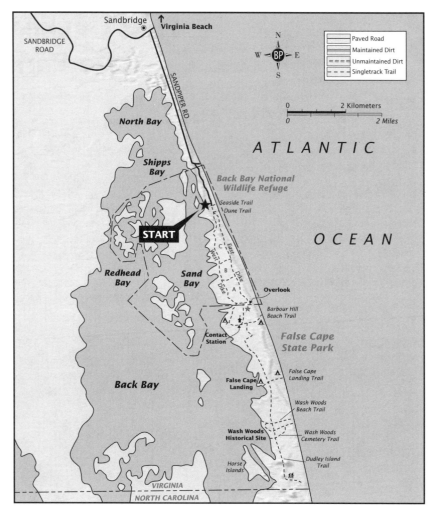

8.1 Turn left on the Wash Woods Cemetery Trail. Almost immediately you will come upon the old town of Wash Woods' cemetery and church site. Bicycles are not permitted beyond this point. You may walk the last two miles of this trail (Dudley Island Trail) to the North Carolina border.

Return to Back Bay along these different trails, mixing them differently for a different ride. Or ride along the beach all the way to

Back Bay for an unforgettable experience along a uniquely unspoiled coastline.

Helpful Mileage Information
5 miles – Back Bay to False Cape along the beach.
4 miles – False Cape to NC state line.
7.5 miles of rideable trails in Back Bay.
11.2 miles of rideable trails in False Cape.
27.7 miles – Total trails and beach open to bicycling.

First Landing State Park

Ride Specs

Start: From the Visitor Center

Length: 10.4-mile out-and-back

Approximate Riding Time: 1–1½ hours

Difficulty Rating: Easy. Relatively flat double-track

Trail Surface: Hard-packed dirt and sand

Land Status: State park

Nearest Town: Virginia Beach, VA

Other Trail Users: Hikers, joggers, campers, and dogs

Canine Compatibility: Good. Just be careful around the crowds of people who will be there in the warm months of the year.

Getting There

From I-64 at Newport News: *Approximately 100 miles from Richmond by way of I-64.* Take I-64 east across the Hampton Roads Bridge-Tunnel into Norfolk to U.S. 13. Exit I-64 to U.S. 13 and follow this to U.S. 60. Turn right on U.S. 60 and go approximately five miles to the park entrance on the right. Turn right into First Landing State Park and follow the entrance road to the visitor center. (Following U.S. 60 from I-64 also works, but there are dozens of stop lights along the way. It is, however, an ocean-view way to go.) ***DeLorme: Virginia Atlas & Gazetteer:*** Page 35, A-7

Pedaling along the Cape Henry Bike Trail. Hey folks! Where are your helmets?

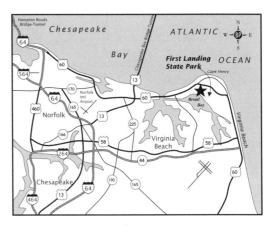

great ride for the family or the casual cyclist seeking an easy, relatively flat ride through a semitropical forest, complete with Spanish moss, bald cypress, lagoons, osprey, and the chicken turtle. Cyclists will pedal along the Cape Henry Trail, the park's only trail open to bikes. Be prepared for crowds, however, especially in the warm weather, as the park, named for the English settlers who first landed here in 1607 before reaching Jamestown, attracts over one million visitors a year.

You'll arrive at the state's most popular park along a narrow entrance road bordered by cypress swamps, high dunes, osprey, and the chicken turtle (an endangered species in Virginia, whose neck is nearly as long as its body). First Landing State Park attracts over one million visitors a year, but that's not merely due to its proximity to Virginia Beach or its famous boardwalk along the Atlantic Ocean. This national natural landmark has the distinction as the northernmost location on the East Coast where subtropical and temperate plants grow and thrive together. Warmed by Gulf Stream currents, the environment of this southeastern corner of Virginia is similar to that of more southern climates.

Garlands of Spanish moss hang from the thick branches of bald cypress, loblolly pine, osmanthus (wild olive trees), tall oak, beeches, and almost everything else standing above ground. If one spent enough time here, he or she too would be cloaked in the feathery garlands of moss.

"Early settlers called this area the great desert because they found its dense woods and swamps and huge sand dunes to be uninhabitable. Thousands of years ago the ocean lapped upon a shoreline about 50 miles west of here. As ocean and bay waters gradually receded, the wind and waves built a succession of sand dunes. As one row of dunes was being created, plant life was growing up on the one behind. Vegetation stabilized the shifting sand and the dunes became a permanent part of the landscape." Department of Conservation and Recreation.

Today some of those stabilized dunes reach 75 feet high and are among the highest natural points in Southeastern Virginia.

The Cape Henry Trail Bicycle Route is the only trail in the park open to bicycles, but it has something for everyone. All of the park's natural features, including the cypress swamp, salt marshes, old dunes, and The Narrows can be reached along this

Ride Information

📞 Trail Contacts:
First Landing State Park
(757) 412-2300

🕐 Schedule:
8:00 a.m. to dusk, year-round

💲 Fees/Permits
Parking fees at First Landing State Park
$3.00 on weekends
$2.00 on weekends
$1.00 during the off-season

❓ Local Information:
Virginia Beach Information Center

Chesapeake Bay Center

💡 Local Events/Attractions:
Old Cape Henry Lighthouse
http://us-lighthouses.org/oldcape.htm

Virginia Marine Science Museum
(757) 425-FISH
www.vmsm.com

🅿 Accommodations:
Eight campgrounds and 20 cabins for overnighters

🚲 Local Bike Shops:
Conte's Bikes & Fitness
Virginia Beach, VA
(757) 595-1333

HDK Cycles
Hampton, VA
(757) 827-0606

Oceanfront Bicycles
Virginia Beach, VA
(757) 425-5120

Bikes can be rented at the park's Bay Store located at the new Chesapeake Bay Center.

🅽 Maps:
USGS maps: Cape Henry, VA
ADC map: Tidewater road map
First Landing State Park trail map

hard-packed sand and dirt trail. The level terrain makes for very easy riding, so cyclists of all abilities will feel welcome here. If you're just visiting the area and don't bring your bike, there are dozens of bike rentals nearby.

In fact, you may want to start your ride just a few blocks west of the park at the Seashore Bike & Hobby Shop off U.S. Route 60 (where bike rentals are available). A paved section of the trail begins from the parking area next to this shop and leads you right into the park to the visitors center.

From the visitors center, follow the main trail left from the parking lot into the ocean breeze. Immediately, you will pass the bald cypress swamps, where thick-kneed cypress stretch out of the dark tannin-stained water through heavy Spanish moss.

Beyond the cypress swamps the trail resembles, more and more, old-growth forests of Virginia's past. Little has been done to change the landscape here since Seashore State Park, one of Virginia's first and oldest state parks, was established on June 15, 1936.

Once across 64th Street, the terrain changes a bit from the hard-packed sand and dirt that characterized the first section. Cape Henry Trail begins through some of the region's old dunes, developing into a looser surface of white sand. It then spans across a long wooden bridge over the salt marsh. Be sure to watch and listen for the osprey nesting in the trees high above the marsh.

The trail reaches its end at The Narrows, where a soda machine, bathrooms, and a cool place to rest await. Here you can watch shore fishermen cast their lines and boats navigate the channels to the ocean.

If you're interested in spending more time on the bike, take 64th Street east out of the park all the way to Virginia Beach. You can turn south and follow the boardwalk nearly 10 miles along the Atlantic coastline to Rudee Inlet before the bike route ends.

Boardwalk over the Salt Marsh.

Bald cypress stretch out of the cypress swamp under a canopy of Spanish moss.

MilesDirections

0.0 START at the First Landing State Park Visitors Center. From the visitors center parking lot, follow the Main Trail (Cape Henry Bicycle Trail) east toward the Atlantic Ocean.

0.1 Pass through the Bald Cypress Swamps. Cypress Trail is on the right. Osmanthus Trail is on the left. *Bicycles are not allowed on any trail but the main trail.*

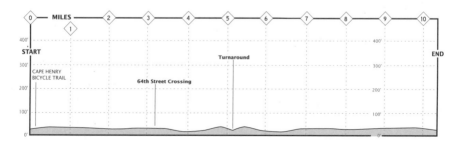

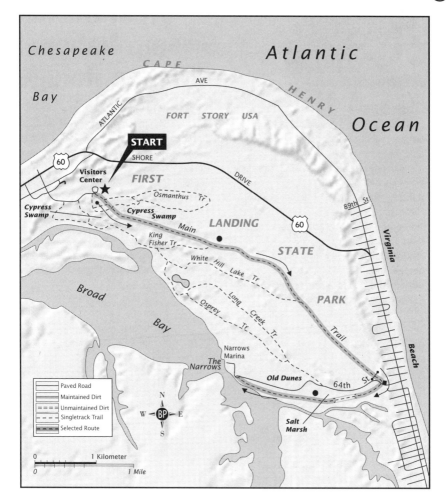

1.3 Pass King Fisher Trail on the right.

2.2 Pass White Hill Lake Trail on the right.

3.5 Cross 64th Street. There is a portable toilet in the parking lot before 64th Street. Once across the road, a wooden bridge carries you over a small cypress swamp. This bridge is part of the Main Trail. Continue along the Main Trail toward Broad Bay.

3.8 Bear left, continuing on the Main Trail. Pass over a long, wooden bridge spanning a salt marsh. Halfway across this bridge you can stop and sit on one of the viewing benches. This is a great spot to view the salt marsh

and some of its inhabitants, such as local osprey. Look for the osprey nests up in the trees growing from the salt marsh. Past this bridge, the trail becomes much sandier as it travels through some of the overgrown dunes along Broad Bay.

5.0 The Main Trail ends. Follow the paved drive a little further to The Narrows.

5.2 Reach The Narrows. There are restrooms and soda machines available here. Return to the visitors center along the same route.

10.4 Arrive back at your vehicle.

3

Great Dismal Swamp National Wildlife Refuge

Ride Specs

Start: From Washington Ditch Road
Length: 8.2-mile out-and-back; 140+ miles total
Approximate Riding Time: 1 hour along Washington Ditch Road
Difficulty Rating: Easy. Flat riding along a canal road.
Trail Surface: Hard-packed dirt/gravel canal roads
Land Status: National wildlife refuge
Nearest Town: Suffolk, VA
Other Trail Users: Hikers and photographers
Canine Compatibility: Dog friendly

Getting There

From I-664 out of Hampton and Newport News: Cross the Monitor-Merrimac Bridge-Tunnel south across Hampton Roads toward Portsmouth. Exit on VA 58, traveling west to Suffolk. Take the downtown Suffolk exit (Business 58/460/13). At the sixth stop light turn left onto Main Street (VA 13/32). At the 13/32 split follow VA 32 South. Follow the Great Dismal Swamp Refuge signs all the way to the Washington Ditch entrance. Parking available. *DeLorme: Virginia Atlas & Gazetteer:* Page 34, D-3

Lake Drummond's glassy surface is just 20 feet above sea level. This aged lake is at the heart of many of Dismal Swamp's legends and mysteries.

With over 140 miles of unpaved roads throughout this 109,000-acre wildlife refuge, the Great Dismal Swamp provides a variety of opportunities for off-road cyclists to explore one of the largest remaining wooded wetlands in the eastern United States. The Washington Ditch Road is just a small sampling, but certainly the most accessible route for cyclists interested in pedaling through the swamp's biological diversity to the mysterious and beautiful Lake Drummond.

When the full moon's pale light shines down upon the dark waters of the Great Dismal Swamp in just the right way, an ethereal lady in a white canoe is rumored to cruise soulfully across the still waters of Lake Drummond. Lake Drummond for some time was speculated to have been caused by what Native Americans described as a "firebird" falling to the ground. This account lead people to believe that a meteorite burned through the atmosphere and landed in the thick marsh, burying itself deep in the swamp before the resulting 3,100-acre crater filled with water. More recent theories, however, support that the lake was more likely formed after a large wildfire ravaged the swamp and burned its trees to the ground. The swampy waters filled in and thus prohibited new growth, leaving what is now a beautiful lake in the heart of the swamp.

The Great Dismal Swamp is also filled with lots of history. It was discovered by the first colonial governor of North Carolina, William Drummond, in the late 1600s while on a hunting trip, and is one of only two natural lakes in Virginia (Mountain Lake near Blacksburg is the other). Our first president, George Washington, dug huge ditches here in the 1760s, attempting to drain the swamp. Runaway slaves often hid in the swamp's endless wilderness to evade capture. In 1929, the canal was taken over by the U.S. Government for $500,000 from the Lake Drummond Canal and Water Company. Logging operations continued as late as 1976 deforesting the entire swamp at least once. And today, on the way to full recovery, tall cypress trees, black bears, bobcats, and long-legged egrets make this national wildlife refuge their home. The 109,000 acres of the Great Dismal Swamp within the refuge represent only a remnant of a swamp that once covered over one million acres. And even though this remnant has been altered numerous times by attempts to drain it, log it, and burn it, it is still one of the largest remaining wooded wetlands in the eastern United States.

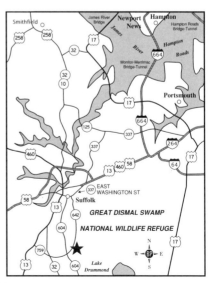

Washington Ditch Road is one of many canal roads within the refuge.

Its ancient primeval forests, lush greenery, vast wildlife, and unexplained mysteries make the Great Dismal Swamp unique and enchanting to all who navigate its broad wilderness, from Native Americans and early European settlers to modern-day explorers.

The canals built by George Washington still exist, and over 150 miles of unpaved roads open to bicycling currently crisscross through the refuge. The Dismal Swamp Canal, paralleling U.S. Route 17 on the refuge's east side, is the oldest man-made waterway still in use in the United States. Travelers can sail up this intracoastal waterway from Elizabeth City, North Carolina, to Portsmouth, Virginia.

MilesDirections

0.0 START from the parking lot at the Washington Ditch Road entrance.

1.1 Pass the ditch road on the left that heads due north. Take this to other routes.

4.1 Reach Lake Drummond. Return back to the parking area the way you came.

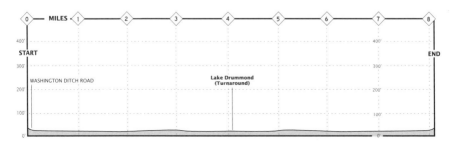

Hikers will love the one-mile interpretive Boardwalk Trail near the Washington Ditch Road parking area.

Unfortunately, this world-renowned natural area is one of the most remote and inaccessible wildlife refuge's in the country. For centuries, the only means of accessing the swamp had been either by foot or small boat—until recently. Many off-road cyclists have discovered the network of dirt roads in this 109,000-acre forested wetland to be excellent riding. However, there are few places to easily access any of the canal roads. Most of the refuge's dirt roads have no well-defined entrances, leaving cyclists to start on the refuge's western side, near Suffolk, and enter via the five-mile Washington Ditch Road. This road is the shortest trek to Lake Drummond and branches to many of the other dirt canal roads within the refuge (it is also one of the first monuments named after George Washington). Additionally, the one-mile, interpretive Boardwalk Trail from the parking area for the Washington Ditch Road into the thick-wooded refuge gives explorers a better perspective on the swamp, its inhabitants, and how the refuge is managed. The Jericho Lane entrance, also on the west side of the refuge closer to the town of Suffolk, offers additional access into the refuge.

The terrain is flat and the difficulty level is virtually nil, but pedaling through the swamp allows cyclists to witness more of the swamp's lush greenery and wealth of wildlife than by foot. This unusual and sometimes mystic national refuge is well worth all the time one can spend here.

Don't forget your bug spray when you come to visit the Great Dismal Swamp. Bugs and mosquitoes can become fierce and annoying during the hot and humid summer months.

Ride Information

ⓒ Trail Contacts:
Great Dismal Swamp National Wildlife Refuge
(757) 986-3705

Dismal Swamp Visitor/Welcome Center, North Carolina
(252) 771-8333

ⓞ Schedule:
Monday-Friday, 8:00 a.m.-3:30 p.m.
Closed all federal holidays

❓ Local Information:
There are numerous web sites with additional information about the Great Dismal Swamp. Simply type in "Great Dismal Swamp" on any search engine and you're bound to come across something good.

Suffolk News-Herald has an events listing and other great local information available online, *www.hamptonroadsmedia.com*

ⓠ Local Events/Attractions:
Planters Peanut Co. is located in downtown Suffolk.

ⓖ Local Bike Shops:
Bike West
Suffolk, VA
(757) 539-1820

Bay Bicycles
Portsmouth, VA
(757) 483-2818

Bike Line of Chesapeake
Virginia Beach, VA
(757) 497-7971

Great Bridge Cyclery
Chesapeake, VA
(757) 482-5149

Ⓝ Maps:
USGS maps: Suffolk, VA; Lake Drummond NW, VA; Corapeake, VA; Lake Drummond, VA; Deep Creek, VA

Carrollton-Nike Park

Ride Specs

Start: From the Carrollton-Nike Mountain Bike Trail trailhead just past the last parking area. The trail starts at the edge of the woods at the mountain bike trail sign, next to the bike rack and red trash can.

Length: 2.5-mile loop

Approximate Riding Time: 1 hour

Difficulty Rating: Easy to moderate. A good singletrack starter trail with a few log jumps and some rooty sections.

Trail Surface: Winding, level singletrack covered in a soft layer of pine needles with the occasional dip and root obstacles.

Land Status: County park

Nearest Town: Smithfield, VA

Other Trail Users: Hikers, dogs, and other park users

Canine Compatibility: Not bad. Plenty of water sources, but be careful of the paved trip back to the park entrance if you make this into a loop, and be aware of the crowds. As with most local parks, leashes are required.

Getting There

From Newport News/Hampton Roads: Cross the James River Bridge heading south on U.S. 17 toward the town of Smithfield. Less than two miles after crossing the bridge, turn right at the light onto Smith Neck Road (VA 669). Follow Smith Neck Road 1.7 miles to Titus Road (VA 668) Turn left on Titus Road and follow it back to VA 669. Turn left on VA 669 and drive 0.6 miles to the Carrollton-Nike Park Entrance. Travel to the very end of the Entrance Road to the last parking area. Just past this parking area at the edge of the woods is the trailhead.

From Norfolk and Virginia Beach: Follow U.S. 17 north toward Newport News and the James River Bridge. Cross over the Nansemond River, continuing to the James River Bridge. Soon after U.S. 17 joins with VA 32 and U.S. 258, turn left at the light onto Smith Neck Road (VA 669). From here, follow the direction above. *DeLorme: Virginia Atlas & Gazetteer:* Page 34, A-2

L ike a lot of regional parks, Carrollton-Nike is loaded with playing fields, baseball diamonds, jungle gyms, and lots of people (at least on nice weekends). Unique to this park, however, is its lengthy, wooded, singletrack mountain bike trail, built specifically for mountain bikers. Sure, anyone can use it, but its design suits off-road cyclists perfectly.

Admittedly, when I arrived here for the first time, I didn't have very high expectations. Afterall, the park is minutes from the James River Bridge, which crosses the mouth of the James just before it empties into Hampton Roads and then the Chesapeake Bay. Needless to say, the variety of terrain wasn't much to write home about. And when I saw all the soccer fields, the jungle gym, and the crowds of soccer league parents, I wondered if mountain biking would even be appropriate here. But my hesitation subsided the moment I discovered the trailhead, clearly labeled with a large Carrollton-Nike Mountain Bike Trail sign. As the trail lead me into the woods at the far end of the playing fields, my entire outlook began to change.

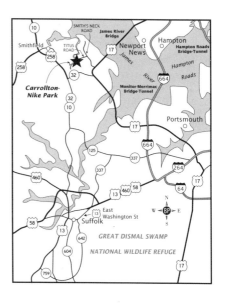

Much like the Marle Ravine Trail at York River State Park, the Harwood's Mill Trail near Newport News, or even the Dogwood Trail at Waller Mill, the mountain bike trail here at Carrollton-Nike was designed and is well maintained by local cyclists. Mountain Bike Virginia has done a superb job of creating a real off-road treasure in a place that might otherwise be considered not worth traveling to. And for local cyclists easing their way westward to harder and harder trails, the route that winds and weaves its way within the woods along the perimeter of the park and the playing fields is a perfect introductory singletrack course.

The trail hops into the woods at the far end of the parking area near the restrooms. Once you enter this stretch of

Scenery like this, overlooking Jones Creek, will stop just about anyone for a while.

woods between the marshes of Jones Creek and the playing fields, you'll probably forget about the soccer moms altogether, and for a couple of miles you'll be lost in a singletrack oasis of short ups and downs, creek crossings, tight, tree-hugging turns, and lots of great off-road riding. With the marshes of Jones Creek always present as a backdrop through the trees, your ride will be a delightful event through Virginia's scenic coastal environment.

The trail winds up taking you along the perimeter of one of the local working farms before spitting you out of the woods and back in eyesight of the park's playing fields. Once you pop out of the woods at this point, you'll be next to a set of radio towers on a dirt road that bisects the cultivated field (this working field alternates between peanuts and cotton). Travel up this dirt road to the paved Nike Park Road (VA 669), turn left, and head back up to the park entrance.

While you're here, pedal west from the parking area past the restrooms and check out the old missile bunkers. The bunkers are completely sealed shut today, but this 150-acre park used to be home to a Nike missile base run by the United States Army.

You could easily spend an hour or two riding along the Carrollton-Nike Mountain Bike Trail then tooling around the park's other foot trails watching wildlife and waterfowl in action on Jones Creek. So make sure to take the time to check out this marvelous singletrack mountain bike course and enjoy what other cyclists have created for our cycling pleasure.

Ride Information

📞 **Trail Contacts:**
Isle of Wight Parks and Recreation, Public Recreational Facilities Authority (804) 357-2291

Mountain Bike Virginia (mountain bike club) (804) 222-8006

🕐 **Schedule:**
8:00 a.m. to dark, year-round

🚻 **Facilities:**
Very nice restrooms are available during the park's operating hours. There are also drink machines near the restrooms.

❓ **Local Events/Attractions:**
A number of mountain bike races are held here each year. Call one of the trail contacts to learn more about the current year's race schedule.

🚲 **Local Bike Shops:**
Conte's Bikes & Fitness
Virginia Beach, VA
(757) 595-1333

The Open Road Bicycle Shop
Newport News, VA
(757) 930-0510

Colley Avenue Bike Shop
Norfolk, VA
(757) 622-0006
HDK Cycles, Hampton, VA, (757) 827-0606

Ⓝ **Maps:**
USGS maps: Benns Church, VA

MilesDirections

START from the Carrollton-Nike Mountain Bike Trail trailhead at the far end of the playing fields near the parking area. The trail is well blazed and easy to follow. And you won't have to worry about any spur trails or trail intersections that so often cause confusion. The trail is a fairly straightforward course through the woods in a confined area around playing fields, a working farm, and Jones Creek.

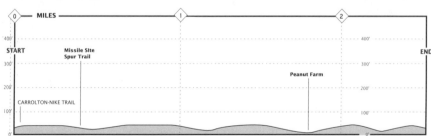

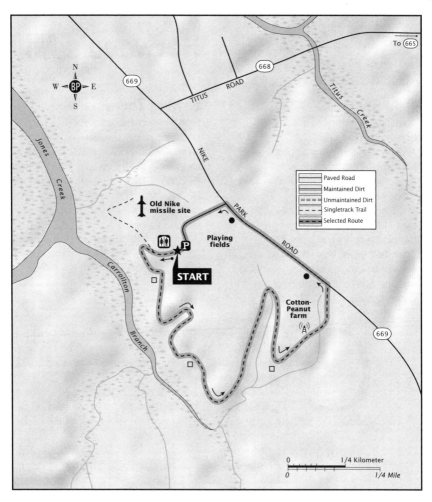

To (665)

668

669

TITUS ROAD

Titus Creek

NIKE

Jones Creek

↑ Old Nike missile site

PARK

ROAD

Playing fields

START

Carrollton

Branch

Cotton-Peanut farm

(('A'))

669

Paved Road
Maintained Dirt
Unmaintained Dirt
Singletrack Trail
Selected Route

N
W —●BP●— E
S

0   1/4 Kilometer
0   1/4 Mile

Harwood's Mill

Ride Specs

Start: From the Harwood's Mill
Length: 5.2-mile loop
Approximate Riding Time: 1 hour
Difficulty Rating: Novice to expert, with sections of flat, straight trails leading to twisting, obstacle-covered singletrack
Trail Surface: Twisting singletrack and dirt roads
Land Status: City park
Nearest Town: Newport News, VA
Other Trail Users: Equestrians and pedestrians may be encountered along the dirt roadways that connect each section of trail.
Canine Compatibility: Dog friendly

Getting There

From Newport News: Take I-64 to Exit 258 north on U.S. 17 (George Washington Memorial Highway). Follow U.S. 17 north for about four miles, then turn left on Oriana Road (VA 620). Cross over Harwood's Mill Reservoir and immediately turn left into the parking area for Harwood's Mill. The mountain bike trail starts across VA 620 from the parking area. *DeLorme: Virginia Atlas & Gazetteer:* Page 50, C-3

C yclists on the Virginia Peninsula, from Williamsburg to Newport News, have been diligently developing what can be considered excellent mountain biking routes in a region otherwise devoid of accessible off-road cycling terrain.

Far from the rugged landscape of the Appalachian Mountains or the peaks of Virginia's western highlands, mountain bikers in this Tidewater region have had to search far and wide for great places to ride. And if they couldn't find them, they created them.

The Harwood's Mill Mountain Bike Trail in Newport News Park and nearby Dogwood Trail at Waller Mill Park are evidence of the hard work and creative spirit of the many Eastern Virginia cyclists who developed these trails. Both trail systems combine heavily forested hilly terrain with winding, technical singletrack, guaranteed to challenge even the best off-roaders.

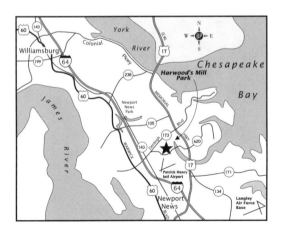

The trail system combines heavily forested hilly terrain with winding, technical singletrack, guaranteed to challenge even the best off-roaders. The narrow singletrack trails twist and turn throughout the trees so frequently that accidents would be inevitable without the control of a unidirectional traffic flow.

Harwood's Mill trail system begins on Oriana Road across from Harwood's Mill. The most

Heading out on the Expert trail—of course.

Ride Information

🌀 Trail Contacts:
Newport News Park
(757) 888-3333

Eastern Virginia Mountain Bike Association
(757) 722-4609

🕐 Schedule:
Open daylight to dark, year-round

❓ Local Information:
For a web site complete with local information, recreation, services, and more, go to the City of Newport News web site at *www.newport-news.va.us*

🚲 Local Bike Shops:
Conte's Bikes & Fitness
Virginia Beach, VA
(757) 595-1333

The Open Road Bicycle Shop
Newport News, VA
(757) 930-0510

Colley Avenue Bike Shop
Norfolk, VA
(757) 622-0006

HDK Cycles
Hampton, VA
(757) 827-0606

Oceanfront Bicycles
Virginia Beach, VA
(757) 425-5120

🅝 Maps:
USGS maps: Poquoson West, VA
ADC map: Virginia Peninsula road map

unique aspect of the Harwood's Mill Mountain Bike Trail is its categorized trail sections. Professionally beveled park signs head up each section of trail, marking them *Novice, Advanced,* or *Expert.* Wooden posts banded with their corresponding levels of difficulty guide the way on the trails; one white band = *Novice,* two yellow bands = *Advanced,* and three orange bands = *Expert.*

An important facet of this ride's unique character is its unidirectional trail. **One way only, please!** The trails twist and turn so frequently, much of the singletrack being incredibly narrow, that accidents would be inevitable without some control. Backtrack on the dirt roads if you wish to return to a particular section of singletrack.

The *Novice* section begins on relatively level terrain with a number of turns and twists through the trees—a good warm-up for things to come. The trail really doesn't begin to heat up, though, until you cross beneath the power lines to the trail's *Advanced* section. Tight, narrow turns weave around trees and logs, darting up and down the hills alongside the reservoir—beware of the many exposed roots along this section.

After finishing this section, you are rewarded with a leisurely ride along a forest road before heading toward the *Expert* trail. Don't be fooled by this rating, though. At no time will you plummet down vertical drops to an unknown fate or climb deadly walls of slippery rock! The *Expert* trail in Harwood's Mill was designed to challenge bike handling skills on flat terrain, and for this purpose, it is well suited. Tight corners, quick hills, obstacles, and pure singletrack make this as fun and challenging a section as any bombardier mountain bike ride in the land.

The rest of this roller coaster-like ride is back to the start by way of dirt forest roads. (Note the clear-cutting in the forested area surrounding you. Let's hope they spare the land around these trails.) As you follow the dirt roads toward Harwood's Mill parking area, you'll pass many of the trailheads for this mountain bike park. Jump back on the trails if you wish, but remember, it's a one-way route only. And don't forget to thank the Eastern Virginia Mountain Bike Association and Newport News Department of Parks and Recreation for this fabulous off-road mountain bike playground.

MilesDirections

0.0 START at Harwood's Mill on Oriana Road (VA 620). Cross Oriana Road to the Harwood's Mill Mountain Bike Trail. This is marked by a large sign at the start, detailing the rules of the trail. The first section of this trail is labeled "Novice" and is mostly easy

terrain. It's marked with a white band on wooden trailposts.

0.55 Turn right on the Dirt Road, heading north.

0.6 Turn right, back into the woods, continuing to follow the "Novice" singletrack trail.

0.7 Turn left on the Gravel Road that runs

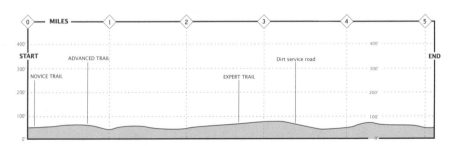

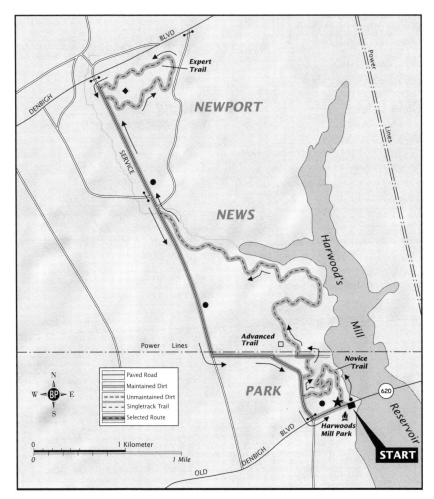

parallel with the power lines. Harwood's Mill Reservoir is down the road on the right.

0.8 Turn right at the "Advanced" trail sign, crossing beneath the power lines. This section is marked with two yellow bands and becomes quite a bit more difficult.

2.2 Leave the advanced trail and turn right on the Dirt Service Road. There is a sign at this point directing you 0.4 miles down the road toward the expert trail.

2.6 Turn right into the woods on the "Expert" trail (three orange bands). The Expert trail is not hilly or steep, rather very technical, with

obstacles laid across the trail at almost every turn.

3.4 Leave the "Expert" trail and turn left on the Dirt Service Road.

4.4 Turn left on the Gravel Road that runs parallel to the power lines.

4.6 Turn right on the Dirt Road, heading toward Oriana Road.

4.9 Turn left on Oriana Road. There is a dirt path on the other side of Oriana Road. Ride along this back to Harwood's Mill Park.

5.2 Reach Harwood's Mill Park.

6 Newport News Park

Ride Specs

Start: From the Information and Campsite Office
Length: 5.2-mile loop
Approximate Riding Time: 30 min.–45 minutes
Difficulty Rating: Flat, easy, wide, and scenic. A great place to come during lunch hour or on a lazy weekend.
Trail Surface: Hard-packed dirt
Land Status: City park
Nearest Town: Newport News, VA
Other Trail Users: Walkers, joggers, and occasionally equestrians
Canine Compatibility: Dog friendly

Getting There

From Newport News: Take I-64 to Exit-250 on Fort Eustis Boulevard (VA 105) heading east. Immediately turn left on Jefferson Avenue (VA 143) and cross over the City Reservoir. Go approximately one mile to Newport News Park's second entrance. Parking, toilets, information, telephones, and bike rental available at the Campsite Office and Information Center. *DeLorme: Virginia Atlas & Gazetteer:* Page 50, C2

For cyclists interested in an incredible journey through American history, this easy, off-road ride in Newport News Park is the perfect way to get started. Pedaling along a wide, dirt path through one of the nation's largest municipal parks, off-road cyclists will enjoy a peaceful wooded setting in an area that saw battle in two of this country's greatest wars.

The city of Newport News' Parks and Recreation Department has done much for its steadily growing number of local mountain bikers, culminating in some great trails and tours for off-road cyclists all along the Virginia Peninsula. One such example is Newport News Park in Newport News. As one of the nation's largest municipal parks, Newport News Park has plenty of potential for supporting bicycling, both on and off road.

This leisurely ride through Newport News Park features an easy, off-road loop in

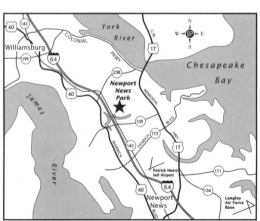

the peaceful setting of a wooded environment. The previous chapter discusses the challenges of winding singletrack trails along the Harwood's Mill Mountain Bike Trail in the southern portion of Newport News Park. Both rides, however different, are perfect examples of what Newport News, one of America's oldest cities, has done for mountain biking, one of America's newest sports.

Founded in 1619, Newport News has since become a major

This is a great family trail, smooth and flat for easy pedaling. Connect to the Battlefield Park and you've got a whole day of riding.

American seaport. Early on, however, this point on the Virginia Peninsula at the head of Hampton Roads was no more than the setting for a small English colony trying to establish itself in the "New World."

The city's name derives from the English sea captain Christopher Newport, who sailed from London in 1606 with an expedition of 100 men to settle and explore the New World. Newport and the renowned Captain John Smith landed at what would be named Jamestown on May 14, 1607—the first English colony in America. For those possibly confused, Plymouth, in Massachusetts, was the first English colony of families in the New World.

Captain Newport sailed back and forth from Jamestown to England throughout the years for both supplies and news from the homeland. Legend holds that when word spread Captain Newport was sailing back to the colonies, people would rush to the end of the peninsula to hear any news Newport brought back from their homes in England. In 1619, colonists on the peninsula officially adopted the name Newportes Newes for their small town in the New World.

Artillery that helped buy our independence in during the Revolutionay War.

Since Captain Newport's first landing at Jamestown, events on the Virginia Peninsula continued to shape America's destiny. In October 1781, rebel armies, under the command of General George Washington, battled with muskets and cannons to victory over the Redcoats on the fields at Yorktown, and American Independence was won from the British.

This independence, however, would not come without a price, and America would soon be at war once again—this time with itself. The land within the boundaries of today's Newport News Park once again soaked in the blood of American soldiers, only now it was brother against brother. On April 16, 1862, the violent thunder of Confederate and Union artillery echoed across the land in what was the first major Civil War engagement on the Peninsula. The Battle of Dam No.1, as it was called, cost both sides a combined total of more than 3,000 men killed, wounded, or missing. After this battle, both sides continued up the Peninsula toward Richmond, where they would meet again to clash in the Seven Days Battle at Richmond.

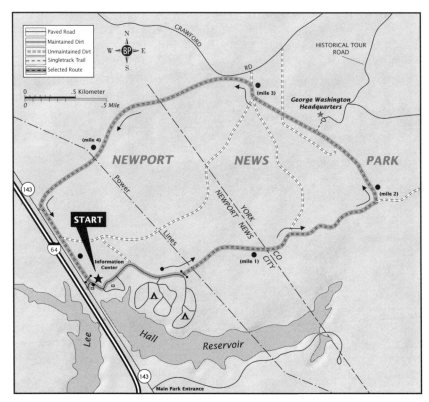

MilesDirections

0.0 START at the Campsite Office and Information Center. If you forgot your bike, you can rent one from the Information Center. Turn right on the Park Access Road, heading toward the camping areas.

0.5 Go through a gate. Continue on the Park Access Road.

0.6 Turn left on the Newport News Park Bicycle Trail. Go around the gate if it is closed. This trail is a hard-packed dirt road, and is almost completely flat.

2.4 Pass the dirt road on the right leading to George Washington's Headquarters.

4.6 Bear left at the gate, continuing on the Bike Trail. This last section runs alongside VA 143.

5.2 Reach the parking lot.

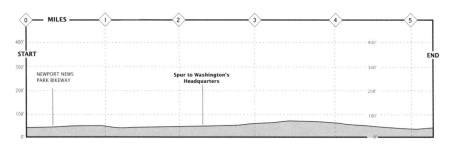

Yorktown Victory Monument.

Today, original Civil War fortifications covering over 10 miles still exist within the park, and most of these 130-year-old fortifications are in excellent condition. Some of the earthworks reach as high as 20 feet. The original Dam No.1 is now beneath the surface of the Lee Hall Reservoir, but can be seen from the footbridge, which crosses over the reservoir.

For cyclists interested in an incredible journey through American history, this easy, off-road ride in Newport News Park is the perfect way to get started. It begins from the second entrance to Newport News Park, at the Campsite Office entrance on the west side of the Lee Hall Reservoir. There is an information office with restrooms, parking, free literature, and bike rentals, should you leave yours behind. This loop is

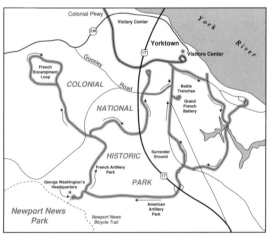

Bike through history at Yorktown's Colonial National Historical Park, accessible from Newport News Park's bicycle trail.

composed entirely of flat, gravel, and dirt roads that travel five miles through the park's northern section. "Bike way" signs will direct you along the way.

Halfway around this hard-packed dirt loop, you can take a short trail through the woods directly to George Washington's Headquarters, where Washington planned his battle on the eve of victory over the British at Yorktown.

Consider taking the time to travel the nearly 14 miles of paved tour roads through Yorktown's Colonial National Historical Park. These quiet tour roads roll gently through the famous park, allowing for a close-up view of the battlefield on which American forces defeated the great British Army in 1781 and ended British rule over the colonies. Interpretive signs and historical route markers guide the way. Return to George Washington's Headquarters to get back on the Newport News Park's mountain bike trail and head back to the ride's start.

Stop in at the Virginia Peninsula Visitor Information Center at the park's main entrance and find out more about the many different paved bike routes that the park service has to offer. Most of these routes are selected for their historic, scenic, and recreational interests and include loops from Yorktown to Jamestown to Williamsburg along gently rolling landscapes and lightly traveled roads.

Ride Information

🕐 Trail Contacts:
Newport News Park
(757) 888-3333

Yorktown Colonial National Historical Park
(757) 898-3400

🕐 Schedule:
Open daylight to dark, year-round

💲 Fees/Permits:
Yorktown Colonial National Historical Park, $8.00 per car, bike/foot: $2.00 per adult, 16 and under free, 9 a.m.–5 p.m.

❓ Local Information:
For local information, recreation, services, and more, go to the City of Newport News website at *www.newport-news.va.us*

🎗 Local Events/Attractions:
Yorktown Colonial National Historical Park
(757) 898-3400

🚲 Local Bike Shops:
Conte's Bikes & Fitness
Virginia Beach, VA
(757) 595-1333

The Open Road Bicycle Shop
Newport News, VA
(757) 930-0510

Colley Avenue Bike Shop
Norfolk, VA
(757) 622-0006

HDK Cycles
Hampton, VA
(757) 827-0606

Oceanfront Bicycles
Virginia Beach, VA
(757) 425-5120

Ⓝ Maps:
USGS maps: Yorktown, VA
ADC map: Virginia Peninsula road map
Newport News Park trail map

Beaverdam Reservoir Park

Ride Specs

Start: From the VA 606 entrance and the Ranger Station Trailhead

Length: 6-mile trail system with a long-term goal of about 25 miles of multi-use trails circumnavigating the lake.

Approximate Riding Time: 1–2 hours

Difficulty Rating: Easy to moderate, as most of the trail is flat singletrack. Lots of twists and turns with some exposed roots and a few sand traps will keep cyclists charged.

Trail Surface: Twisty, wooded singletrack with tight turns tempered by an occasional straightaway through dense eastern hardwoods and a few moderate hills. Trails can get pretty soggy after wet weather thanks to its low elevation and proximity to the marshy reservoir.

Land Status: County park

Nearest Town: Gloucester, VA

Other Trail Users: Hikers and equestrians

Canine Compatibility: Very good. There's plenty of water nearby for hydration. As with most local parks, though, dogs must be leashed.

Getting There

From Newport News/Hampton Roads Area: Follow U.S. 17 north over the Coleman Memorial Bridge at Yorktown. Take U.S. 17 to Gloucester. Pass downtown Gloucester and continue on U.S. 17 North to the crossroads at Ark. Turn right here onto Fary's Mill Road (VA 606). Travel 2.6 miles on Fary's Mill Road to the secondary park entrance on the right for Beaverdam Park. This isn't as clearly marked as the park's main entrance on Roaring Springs Road, so keep your eyes peeled. It shows up just after the bridge over the creek. Park in the gravel parking area (restrooms, snack, and drink machines are available here). The trailhead will be on the opposite side of the parking lot from the restrooms next to the trail sign-in book.

DeLorme: Virginia Atlas & Gazetteer. Page 50, A-2

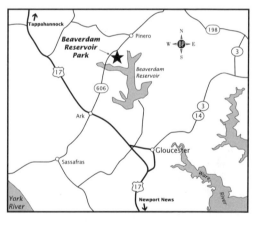

I t's always a bit odd to me when I stare across a beautiful lake surrounded by old hardwoods, teaming with wildlife, and home to such residents as the bald eagle, and I think, incredulously, that this didn't even exist more than a dozen years ago! Before 1990, this area was mostly wetlands, open fields, woods, and a few creeks. In 1990 an earthen dam was built through Beaverdam Swamp and the area was flooded, creating a 635-acre reservoir for the town of Gloucester's drinking water supply.

Today, rangers at Beaverdam Park claim this is one of the healthiest lakes in the state, and I'd have to agree. People come for miles to angle for the latest catch, which include largemouth bass, sunfish, perch, channel catfish, eel, and crappie. The policies are mostly catch and release, with a scale at the main office for weigh-

It's hard to imagine this beautiful lake didn't exist just a few years ago.

MilesDirections

START from the secondary entrance to Beaverdam Park just off VA 606. The trailhead is across the gravel parking area from the restrooms and covered picnic area. Where you're going and how to get back is pretty obvious along this well-marked trail system (wooden signposts at the beginning of each loop lead the way), so it would be pretty hard to get lost. Just be aware that the park boundary alongside the reservoir is fairly narrow (it extends maybe 200-300 feet from the reservoir) and everything bordering the park is private property.

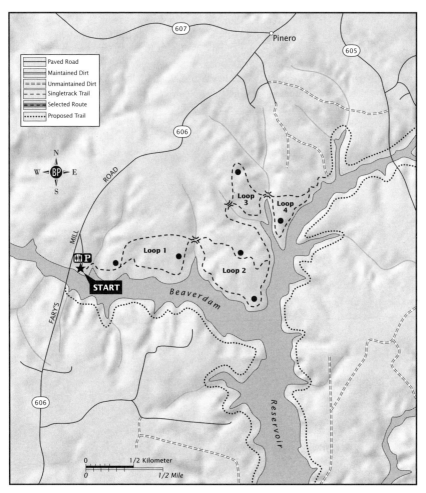

ins and ambitious record setters. And to the lake's credit, I watched an angler weigh in a largemouth bass at almost seven pounds before dropping it back in the water for another day. The main recreational uses at Beaverdam Park are unquestionably fishing and canoeing, although plenty of other activities are offered throughout the year (pick up a brochure from the park office before you leave for a list of all the activities available). But fishing was not the reason I came here and I was eager to head up to the park's secondary entrance and check out its network of mountain bike trails.

The multi-use trail located at the northern end of the park at the secondary entrance on Fary's Mill Road is designed for hiking, horseback riding, and mountain biking. So far the park, with the help of the Eastern Virginia Mountain Bike Association, has created four loops through a thick hardwood forest along the banks of the reservoir. Each of the loops, and the many more to come, is connected by the main Beaverdam Trail. The loops are a great way to break up the monotony of riding an out-an-back and offer trail users more room to explore the park's northern edges. Each year more trails are added, so depending on when you arrive, there may be more to explore than expected. When all is said and done, the park plans to extend this trail system around the entire reservoir, creating a multi-use trail nearly 25 miles long. The rangers readily admit, though, that this may not happen for some time, as they must clear more obstacles than simply cutting a trail through the forest. Because of the swampy, low-lying terrain, a series of bridges and other trail connectors will need to be constructed. And the weather can also sometimes stand in the way of progress as the park learned in 1999 when Hurricane Floyd blew through and caused extensive damage to the trails, closing "Loop 4" for months.

I'm all smiles because I know where I'm going, thanks to this well-marked trail system.

Ride Information

📞 Trail Contacts:
Beaverdam Park Manager
Ranger Station
(804) 693-2107
or *www.gohamptonroads.com/recreation/*
freshair/beverdam.html

Gloucester Parks & Recreation
Gloucester, VA
(804) 693-2355

⏰ Schedule:
Park hours vary throughout the year, but for the most part are from 8 a.m. to sunset, year-round.

📍 Local Events/Attractions:
Historic downtown Gloucester

🍴 Facilities:
The facilities at the trailhead, including well-kept restrooms, drink machines, and covered picnic tables, are excellent.

🅝 Maps:
USGS maps: Gloucester, VA
Beaverdam Park has a trail map and other literature available at the Main Park Entrance on Roaring Springs Road (VA 616).

Beaverdam Trail is currently maintained by both the park staff and the Eastern Virginia Mountain Bike Association and is considered to be a fairly well-kept secret among trail users, who will rarely find a crowd and can more often than not enjoy time alone in the hardwood forests around the lake. This well-marked trail system is mostly level with a few moderate hills and lots of twisty, fun singletrack to keep cyclists busy. Getting lost will be difficult as wooden signs clearly label "Loop 1" and "Loop 2" and so forth all along the way. Although it's not stated prior to entering the trailhead, my impression is that the trail is a bit too narrow to accommodate two-way traffic, so for caution's sake, it's probably best to travel in a clockwise direction to avoid running into oncoming trail traffic. Also, after rains and wet weather, the trails will get pretty soggy and are known to flood. Call first before heading out here if the weather hasn't been cooperating prior to your visit.

Hunting Season

Be very careful when riding out here during hunting season, which begins in the fall. Park boundaries are pretty narrow and all the adjacent land is private property. For opening and closing dates for the current hunting season, call the Virginia Department of Game and Inland Fisheries (540) 248-9360 or go to www.dgif.state.va.us.

For some, the best part of the trail system here at Beaverdam Park may be the facilities located right next to the trailhead. Excellent restrooms, covered picnic tables, and drink machines are open to the public during park hours and help to make your visit here more comfortable and refreshing. Don't forget to bring along bug spray if you come here. Most of the trails in this far eastern section of Virginia are near marshy lowlands and are mosquito breeding grounds. You'll be glad you did. Trust me.

8

Waller Mill Park

Ride Specs

Start: From the trailhead at park entrance
Length: 4.5-mile loop; 6 miles total
Approximate Riding Time: 1 hour
Difficulty Rating: Difficult due to hilly, twisty, singletrack through trees and over roots
Trail Surface: Hilly and wooded singletrack trails
Land Status: City park
Nearest Town: Williamsburg, VA
Other Trail Users: Hikers
Canine Compatibility: Dog friendly

Getting There

From Williamsburg: Take Richmond Road (U.S. 60) east approximately two miles to Airport Road. Turn right on Airport Road (VA 645). Go approximately 1.5 miles on Airport Road to Waller Mill Park entrance on the right. Dogwood Trail begins opposite the entrance to the park. **Seasonal Bus:** Take the Williamsburg Area Visitors Shuttle Green Route to stop #4 (U.S. 60 and Airport Road). Now on your bike, head east 1.5 miles on Airport Road to the Dogwood Trailhead on the left.

From Richmond or Newport News: Take I-64 to the Camp Peary exit. Make a hard right on Rochambeau Drive. Go approximately 1.5 miles past Bruton High School to Airport Road. Turn left on Airport Road (VA 645). Waller Mill Park entrance is on the left. Dogwood Trail begins opposite the entrance to the park. *DeLorme: Virginia Atlas & Gazetteer:* Page 50, B-1

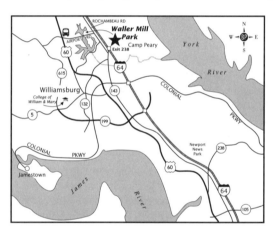

S ponsored by the Virginia Company of London, the colony of Jamestown was established in 1607. Hoping to make a profit on the land's untapped resources, the Virginia Company embarked on its mission from England in December 1606. Four months later, the first English colonists reached the shores of the "New World."

They landed along the Virginia coast, selecting a safe site with deep water to moor their ships. On May 14, 1607, the colonists began creating what would become the first permanent English settlement in the New World, marking the beginnings of our nation.

Tobacco, the largest cash crop of its time, took root around 1613, stimulating the rapid growth of Jamestown along the James River and other English colonies settling down in Eastern Virginia. By 1699 the seat of government in Virginia moved to Williamsburg. It remained there until 1780, when Virginians relocated it to Richmond to escape British troops. In 1694, a small college teaching arts and sciences, education, and law was granted its coat of arms—today the College of William and Mary is one of the nation's oldest public colleges.

Tearing it up on the Dogwood Trail's exciting singletrack. This and Yorktown's Marle Ravine Trail offer up some of the peninsula's finest riding.

MilesDirections

0.0 START from the parking lot at Waller Mill Park. Follow the entrance road back to the park entrance. Dogwood Trail begins across Airport Road (be careful crossing this road). Immediately across the road and in the woods, Dogwood Trail splits either left or right. Turn right, following Dogwood Trail in a counterclockwise direction. *[**Note**: Much like the Harwoods Mill Mountain Bike Trail in Newport News Park, Dogwood Trail must be traveled one way only—counterclockwise. While there are no signs dictating one direction over the other, counterclockwise appears to be understood as the preferred direction. The trails twist and turn frequently, the singletrack is very narrow, and passing anywhere on the trail would be difficult and dangerous. Ride with the flow to avoid any preventable accidents.]*

2.3 Pass a wooden bench overlooking the reservoir. This is a perfect spot for a nice break.

3.0 Dogwood Trail contours the hill around the tip of the alcove.

3.5 Head away from the reservoir toward the start of the ride.

4.5 Reach the end of the loop at the trailhead for the Dogwood Trail. Care to make another loop before heading home?

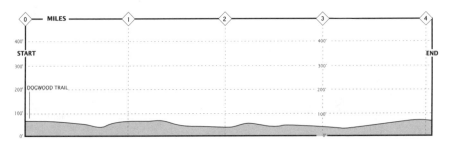

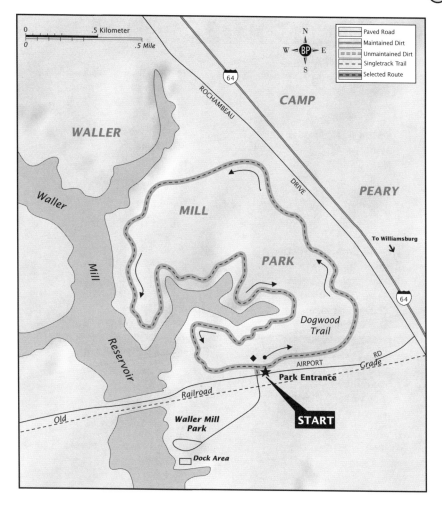

As towns and cities grew, Britain began imposing greater restrictions and higher taxes on colonists in this New World. This oppression ultimately lead to the call for independence. More than six years after the war against Britain began, America won its independence on the fields of Yorktown, only a few miles from the site of the original settlement. A nation was born and a revolution won on this small piece of historic land along the Virginia Peninsula.

Today, U.S. history is revisited at the Jamestown Settlement, Colonial Williamsburg, and Yorktown Victory Center's living history. Within minutes of each other along the Colonial Highway, these living museums bring to life the first chapters of America's history.

Moving forward through history to the present day, a new revolution is taking place on Virginia's historic peninsula—mountain biking, of course! In addition to Colonial Williamsburg, the Jamestown Settlement, Yorktown Victory Center,

Ride Information

Trail Contacts:

Williamsburg Parks Department
Waller Mill Park Office
(757) 220-6170

Eastern Virginia Mountain Bike Association
(757) 722-4609

Schedule:

Open 7:00 a.m.-7:00 p.m.
Closed for the winter (December-March)

Local Events/Attractions:

Historic Jamestown
Colonial Williamsburg
College of William and Mary
Yorktown Battlefield
Historic Yorktown
Colonial National Historic Park
Busch Gardens Theme Park

Local Bike Shops:

Conte's Bikes & Fitness
Virginia Beach, VA
(757) 595-1333

The Open Road Bicycle Shop
Newport News, VA
(757) 930-0510

Colley Avenue Bike Shop
Norfolk, VA
(757) 622-0006

HDK Cycles
Hampton, VA
(757) 827-0606

Oceanfront Bicycles
Virginia Beach, VA
(757) 425-5120

Maps:

USGS maps: Williamsburg, VA
ADC map: Virginia Peninsula road map
Waller Mill Park trail map

Busch Gardens Theme Park, and the College of William and Mary, the Virginia Peninsula has some superior singletrack to offer.

Only minutes from Colonial Williamsburg and a short bike ride from the College of William and Mary, the sensational Dogwood Trail awaits off-road riders eager to pedal supreme singletrack through hardwoods overlooking Waller Mill Reservoir. Loaded with hills, twisting trails, and inspiring scenery, this 4.5-mile loop contains the most exciting off-road riding in the Tidewater region.

Its home is Waller Mill Park, just off Interstate 64 and cycling distance from Williamsburg (actually, it's approximately four miles from downtown, so don't be fooled if you're not an avid cyclist). Dogwood Trail is maintained by the city of Williamsburg and is the park's only trail designated for bicycles, so it's particularly important to stay off the park's other trails.

The trail begins across from the park entrance on Airport Road. The first section of Dogwood Trail, traveled counterclockwise, is relatively new. Much of this portion of the trail was cut with the help of the Eastern Virginia Mountain Bike Association and is well marked. Negotiating many of the dips and turns of this wooded singletrack will get fairly tricky as you cut through the western half of Waller Mill Park. As the trail nears the reservoir, the terrain rolls more sharply, giving this already challenging trail an increased level of difficulty. At times the trail crests some of the park's small ridges to reveal scenic views of the reservoir below. Following the loop brings you back to the start of the ride, where you can decide to call it quits or continue for another loop around the Dogwood Trail.

York River State Park

Ride Specs

Start: From the Visitor Center
Length: 14.5 miles of off-road bicycling trails
Land Status: State park
Nearest Town: Williamsburg, VA
Other Trail Users: Hikers and equestrians
Canine Compatibility: Dogs are welcome in the park and would love the trails, but as always must be kept on a leash at all times.

Getting There

From Richmond or Newport News: Take I-64 to Exit 231B for Croaker on VA 607 North. At Croaker, turn right on Riverview Road (VA 606). Take this for 1.5 miles to York River Park Road (VA 696) and turn left. Follow York River Park Road to the Visitors Center. Parking available for a $2 fee. *DeLorme: Virginia Atlas & Gazetteer.* Page 50, A-1

There are five trails within York River State Park (nearly 15 miles worth) that are open to mountain biking, some of which share use with equestrians and hikers. Of these five trails, however, two were developed exclusively for mountain bikes and are maintained by local mountain bike volunteers through the Eastern Virginia Mountain Bike Association who have successfully created a partnership between the state park and the interests of local cyclists looking for great places to ride.

Partnerships like this didn't use to exist, however, and cyclists had to warily creep onto public lands in hopes riding some good trails without getting caught. Today, more and more parks are opening their arms and their land to cyclists, seeing mountain bikers as relevant and valuable trail users. York River State Park was one of the first and is certainly one of the best examples of parks that have embraced off-road cyclists. They have allowed local mountain bike volunteers to come in and, with park supervision, cut some of the best singletrack in Eastern Virginia—to be used exclusively by mountain bikers. The value to the park has meant greater park attendance, increased revenues, and a win-win situation for everyone.

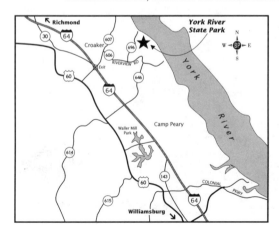

Currently the trails open to mountain bikers fall into two categories: multi-use trails, open for cyclists, hikers, and equestrians; and mountain bike specific trails, developed exclusively for off-road cyclists. Woodstock, Backbone, Riverview, and White-Tail are all multi-use trails within York River State Park and should be traveled with caution (bikes should always yield to everyone else on these trails). These trails are fairly easy to pedal along and can be enjoyed by anyone interested in

riding along unpaved trails and bridal paths through the hardwood forests of Eastern Virginia. The Laurel Glen Mountain Bike Trail and the Marle Ravine Mountain Bike Trail are the park's two mountain bike specific trails, built and maintained by local volunteer mountain bikers. While Laurel Glen is meant to accommodate beginners to the sport along its relatively modest single and doubletrack trails, the Marle Ravine Mountain Bike Trail packs lots of hills, switchbacks, bridges, and jumps into its six miles of advanced singletrack.

No matter what your skill level or riding interests are, it's clear that York River State Park is THE place to be in Eastern Virginia for a great off-road riding experience.

Before mountain bikes and advanced singletrack dominated the minds of park visitors, however, York River State Park was (and still is) well known for its unique coastal environment. This is where fresh water from the Pamunkey and Mattaponi (mat-a-pone-EYE) Rivers converge to form the York River (this actually happens approximately 10 miles upriver), which then mixes with the salt water from the Chesapeake. The result of this convergence of fresh and salt water creates a habitat rich in marine and plant life.

At some point long ago in history, the ocean covered nearly all of Tidewater Virginia up to Richmond. The Eastern Shore, Chesapeake Bay, Virginia Beach, and most of Eastern Virginia up to the city of Richmond were buried beneath hundreds of feet of ocean water. Today, fossil remains of prehistoric shellfish, sharks, and even whales can be found along the banks of the York River and its tributary streams near the park.

In the 17th and 18th centuries, when tobacco was the cash crop of the commonwealth, York River State Park was actually the site of a public tobacco warehouse called Taskinas Plantation. Local planters stored their crops in the warehouse before they were shipped across the Atlantic to England. The park was opened in its present form in 1980 to preserve a portion of this unique coastal environment and all its related marshes, while also providing a unique area for day-use outdoor recreation for all its visitors.

Laurel Glen Mountain Bike Trail

Start: From the Laurel Glen trailhead off of Backbone Trail near Woodstock Pond Trail
Length: 2-mile loop
Approximate Riding Time: 30 minutes
Difficulty Rating: Easy to moderate
Trail Surface: Hard-packed and sandy singletrack through woodlands, ridges, and swamps
Other Trail Users: Hikers

The Laurel Glen Mountain Bike Trail is made up of mostly gentle turns and hills with a few challenging climbs, drops, and log rolls. Cyclists new to the sport may want to consider pedaling along this trail first before trying to tackle the more challenging Marle Ravine singletrack.

Marle Ravine Mountain Bike Trail

Start: From the Marle Ravine trailhead off of Backbone Trail
Length: 6-mile loop
Approximate Riding Time: 1 hour
Difficulty Rating: Difficult due to twisting singletrack and short, steep ups and downs
Trail Surface: Hard-packed, narrow, twisty singletrack through woodlands and ravines
Other Trail Users: Hikers and equestrians

Considered by many to be one of the best rides in Eastern Virginia, the Marle Ravine Mountain Bike Trail was designed by and built for mountain bikers. Another success story for the Eastern Virginia Mountain Bike Association, the Marle Ravine Trail shows what cooperation and initiative can do for an interest group. Though the terrain is less difficult than the terrain at nearby Waller Mill Park or Harwoods Mill Mountain Bike Trail in Newport News, the more than six miles of bicycling trails in York River State Park offer plenty of enjoyable off-road adventures for nearly all cyclists.

Riverview Trail takes you out to this overlook on the York River.

Woodstock, Backbone, Riverview, White-Tail Trails

Start: From the Visitor Center
Length: 8.3-mile trail combination
Approximate Riding Time: 1-1½ hours
Difficulty Rating: Easy due to fairly flat terrain along carriage roads
Trail Surface: Hard-packed old road beds and singletrack through upper woodlands and old growth forest
Other Trail Users: Hikers and equestrians

This series of multi-use trails through the park offers mostly gentle turns and hills with a few challenging hills, dips, and log rolls through woodlands, ridges, and swamps.

The park's main trail, Backbone, begins at the visitors center, high on the banks of the York River. As the backbone to York River's trail system, Backbone Trail carries cyclists into the park's hardwood forests and links riders to each of the other trails open to bikes. Not all trails in the park are open to bicyclists, so be careful to stay only on designated

routes. The Woodstock Pond Trail, which is open to bicycles, follows a dirt road around the pond into the park before joining up with Backbone Trail—a flat dirt pathway that leads cyclists to each of the park's other trails. The other two multi-use trails open to bikes are the Riverview Trail and White-Tail Trail.

Riverview Trail is one of the park's more challenging multi-use trails. Narrow and sandy, this doubletrack winds its way through the park's forest toward the high banks of the river. Ivy and moss growing from the trees add to the thickness of the greenery, all the way to a spectacular view overlooking the river. Take a moment to climb down the steep cliffs, eroded and beaten by the river, and you may possibly find fossils of ancient fish and mammals.

White-Tail Trail leads you through the woods along the ridge on one of the park's many hillsides. This trail is more of a hard-packed, dirt forest road. It has a few quick descents, though it is mostly flat.

Cruising the singletrack on the Marle Ravine Trail.

MilesDirections

0.0 START at the York River Park Visitors Center. The Woodstock Pond Trail begins on the far east side of the visitors center. Follow this trail past the picnic area into the woods where it loops around Woodstock Pond.

0.3 Pass the beginning of the Mattaponi Trail. Continue traveling along the Woodstock Pond Trail.

0.8 Pass the other end of the Mattaponi Trail. Continue straight on the Woodstock Pond Trail.

0.9 Woodstock Trail loops around to the right and heads back to the visitors center at this point. Go straight on Backbone Trail.

2.2 Turn left on Riverview Trail.

2.3 Turn right at this gate to continue on Riverview Trail. At this point, the trail narrows.

2.8 This narrow singletrack turns into a sandy jeep trail the rest of the way to the river.

3.7 Reach the York River. After checking out the great view of the York River, turn around and head back along Riverview Trail to White Tail Trail.

5.3 Reach Backbone Trail. Immediately turn hard left on White Tail Trail.

5.9 Come to the end of White Tail Trail. This is a more wooded trail along the ridge of one of the park's many hillsides. It is mostly a hard-packed dirt trail with a few fun hills. Turn around and return to Backbone Trail.

6.5 Turn right on Backbone Trail.

7.8 Bear left on Woodstock Pond Trail, heading toward York River Park Road and the visitors center.

8.1 Turn right on York River Park Road.

8.3 Reach the Visitors Center.

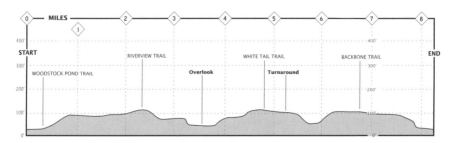

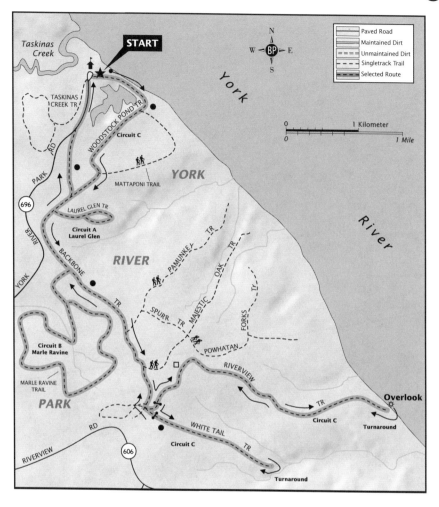

There are very few things mountain bikers will not love about the Marle Ravine Trail—except perhaps that there isn't more of it.

Ride Information

Trail Contacts:
York River State Park
(757) 566-3036
or *www.state.va.us/~dcr/parks*

**Eastern Virginia
Mountain Bike Association**
(757) 722-4609

Schedule:
Open 8:00 a.m. until dusk, year-round

Fees/Permits:
Parking: $1 per vehicle weekdays; $2 per vehicle weekends/holidays

Concessions:
Vending machines with snacks are available at the visitor center and Croaker Landing

Local Events/Attractions:
Annual Mountain Bike Duathalon (Bike/Run) in spring
May & June – Kayak Below the Cliffs, groups of 4 or more, 4 hour program, $50/person for group of 4, $40/person for 5 or more, pre-register (804) 214-9202
June – National Trails Day, great day to hike. Call for details.
Guided canoe trips on weekends
Colonial Williamsburg
Colonial Parkway
Jamestown Settlement
Yorktown Battlefield
Historic Yorktown
Colonial National Historic Park
Busch Gardens Theme Park

Local Bike Shops:
Bikes Unlimited
Williamsburg, VA
(757) 229-4620

Bikesmith of Williamsburg
Williamsburg, VA
(757) 229-9858

Conte's Bikes & Fitness
Virginia Beach, VA
(757) 595-1333

The Open Road Bicycle Shop
Newport News, VA
(757) 930-0510

Maps:
USGS maps: Gressitt, VA
ADC map: Virginia Peninsula road map
York River State Park trail map

Honorable Mentions

Coastal Virginia

Listed here is one of the great rides in the Coastal Virginia Area that didn't make the A-list this time around but deserves recognition. Check it out and let us know what you think. You may decide that this ride deserves higher status in future editions or, perhaps, you may have a ride of your own that merits some attention.

(A) Ipswitch: Chesapeake

Ipswitch has been around for years (once a Girl Scout park) and mountain bikers on the Chesapeake side of the bridge have made it their home for as long as mountain bikes have been around. There are trails everywhere, so making a loop may be difficult unless you're there with someone who knows the system. But honing your singletrack skills and gaining the "Ipswitch Advantage" is what most come here for. The trails are flat (you are near Virginia Beach after all), but the singletrack is tight, twisty, and sandy. So if you're finding it too easy here, you're not trying hard enough. Watch out for BMXers who frequent Ipswitch seeking air on a series of jumps and doubles. Also, be aware that the trails at Ipswitch are being tainted with the occasional "bad" element that may find expensive bikes, cars, and roof racks to be perfect prey. Bad things have happened here, so keep your radar on, and go only in groups.

To get there from Hampton and Norfolk, follow Interstate 64 east through Norfolk. Take the Indian River Road West exit. Once on Indian River Road heading west, make a left onto Level Green Boulevard (Level Green is a loop and has two entrances off Indian River, take either). This turn is right by a gas station. Drive down Level Green for about one mile, and then make a left onto Drew Drive. Take Drew about half a mile before coming to a three-way intersection and stop sign. Go through this stop sign and follow Drew Drive about a quarter-mile until the houses in this condo community disappear and there are trees on both side of the road. Park along the side of the road. You should see a trailhead on your right just before the "Ipswitch" sign (this is the name of the condo community). Call HDK Cycles at (757) 424-6151 if you have any questions on how to get here or want someone to ride with. **DeLorme: *Virginia Atlas & Gazetteer*:** Page 35, B-5

Central

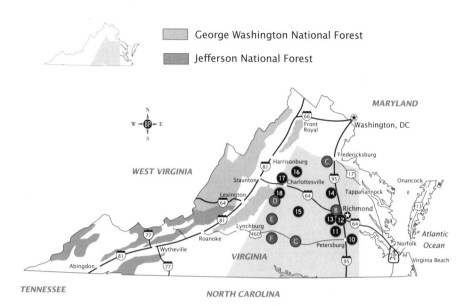

George Washington National Forest

Jefferson National Forest

MARYLAND

Washington, DC

Front Royal

Fredericksburg

WEST VIRGINIA

Harrisonburg

Staunton

Charlottesville

Tappahannock

Onancock

Lexington

Richmond

Atlantic Ocean

Lynchburg

Petersburg

Norfolk

Roanoke

Wytheville

VIRGINIA

Virginia Beach

Abingdon

TENNESSEE

NORTH CAROLINA

Virginia

10

Petersburg National Battlefield

Ride Specs

Start: From the Visitor Center

Length: 6 miles of trails

Approximate Riding Time: 1–2 hours of riding. Those interested in more than bicycling at the park, set aside at least two to four hours to visit the Main Unit. To visit all sites in the park, plan to spend at least a full day.

Difficulty Rating: Easy due to little elevation gains and smooth terrain.

Trail Surface: Dirt trails and singletrack

Land Status: National park

Nearest Town: Petersburg, VA

Other Trail Users: Hikers, motorists, and Civil War buffs

Canine Compatibility: Dogs are welcome but must be kept on a leash

Getting There

From I-95 at Petersburg: Take the Washington Street East (VA 36) exit into Petersburg. Go approximately 2.5 miles east on VA 36 to the Petersburg National Battlefield Park entrance on the right. Follow the entrance road through the tollgate to the parking lot at the visitor center. *DeLorme: Virginia Atlas & Gazetteer.* Page 48, C-3

Mountain biking at Petersburg National Battlefield Park used to conjure thoughts of well-maintained gravel or paved trails along an interpretive route of signs and exhibits—nothing very exciting. Upon further inspection, however, this proved not to be the case.

The park is a wonderfully preserved site of American history, maintaining and protecting the very ground on which the largest battle and the longest siege of the Civil War occurred.

Nearly 70,000 Americans died in the Petersburg area during its 9½-month siege. Reasons for such high casualties ranged from attacks, counterattacks, artillery and mortar shells, sharpshooting, disease, and the ultimate fate of becoming prisoners of war.

General Grant firmly believed the key to taking Richmond was first to take Petersburg. If Petersburg were captured, the Union army could cut off all of Richmond's railroad lines and roadways so vital to the Confederate Capitol's shipments of supplies and food. Many believed that if Richmond fell, the war would come to an end.

Grant's Union forces began arriving in mid June 1864 and would not fully smother the Confederate army for another 9½ miserable months. After outnumbering Lee's

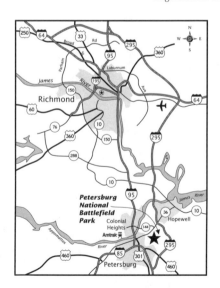

Cannons stand as monuments to the battles fought here in Petersburg.

cold, hungry, and exhausted soldiers, Grant ordered an all-out assault on April 2—Lee's army collapsed. One week later, at Appomattox Court House, Lee surrendered; the war was over.

Today, Petersburg National Battlefield Park offers enough wooded trails open to bicycling that one would have to make plans *not* to ride to study its historical exhibits. Backroads and trails with such names as Attack Road and Encampment Trail take you cycling past massive Civil War earthworks and through some of the dense forest that was once an open field of war. These trails are exciting and scenic and add a new dimension to off-road cycling. One day is not enough to hike all the trails in this park, though on a bike, you should have no worries about exploring each new off-road battlefield route.

Be sure, however, not to get too carried away on these great off-road trails; there is so much else worth seeing at this park. One such sight is the massive crater left by a federal attack (a 511-foot-long tunnel and four tons of gunpowder were used to blow up a Confederate battery). The resulting hole was nearly 170 feet long, 60 feet wide, and 30 feet deep. Unfortunately for the Union army, this attack, which took one month to prepare, turned out to be a horrible failure. After blasting the Confederate battery with the massive charge, Union troops dove right into the crater, rather than going around it, and were thereby trapped. Confederate troops then launched a counterattack and inflicted more than 4,000 casualties on the federal forces. There would be much more fighting before this siege would end.

The trails in this park are well maintained and don't represent a very high level of difficulty. They are open to the public, but are not meant for aggressive use. Ride gently on these historic paths and, by all means, stay on the designated trails. The Civil War earthworks are very fragile and can easily be scarred and damaged if ridden on. Take care of this National Historic Site and preserve it for future generations of cyclists and history buffs.

Cycling through the battlefield wilderness.

Ride Information

Trail Contacts:
Petersburg National Battlefield
(804) 732-3531

Schedule:
Visitor center/museum open daily, 8:00 a.m. to 5:00 p.m. with extended summer hours. The Park Tour Road closes at dusk. Closed: December 25, January 1.

Fees/Permits:
Costs vary from season to season. Be prepared to pay no less than $5 per person/$10 per vehicle during peak season (June through August) or as little as $3 per person/$5 per vehicle during off-season.

Local Events /Attractions:
A 17-minute relief map presentation is shown on the hour and half-hour at the visitor center.

Mid June through mid August, costumed interpreters demonstrate mortar and cannon firings and soldier life.

Accommodations:
There are no places to stay in the park, however variety of hotels, motels and RV camping sites are available in Petersburg and vicinity.

Local Bike Shops:
Pace Line Bicycles
Colonial Heights
(804) 526-1784

Maps:
USGS maps: Petersburg, VA; Prince George, VA
ADC map: Petersburg & Vicinity road map
National Park Service Battlefield trail map

MilesDirections

[**Note:** All of these trails connect, at some point or another, with the paved Park Tour Road. Leave your car at the visitor center and ride the bike lane along Park Tour Road to each of the different trails. Or, if you prefer, drive your car to the different parking areas along Park Tour Road and ride to the nearest off-road trail of your choice. Parking areas along Park Tour Road are shown on the map as small, black semi-circles.

Because there are so many individual trails weaving through this park, it would be unreasonable to create a directional route. Instead, each of these trails is described individually and it is left up to the reader to choose which trails to ride.]

Friend Trail

0.7 miles long. If you're riding into the park from the visitor center, this is the first trail you'll come across. Friend Trail starts on the right side of Park Tour Road, just across the bridge over VA 36. If you pass the traffic circle, you've gone too far. The trail dives down a set of steps into the battlefield wilderness and rambles along a picturesque, wooded trail past Battery 8. Black U.S. troops captured this battery and renamed it Fort Friend for a large Friend House nearby. After it was captured, Fort Friend served as an artillery position during the siege of Petersburg. Shortly after crossing Harrison Creek, this trail ends on a one-lane paved road. Turn left on this road to get back to Park Tour Road.

Encampment Trail

1.5 miles long. This trail begins from the maintenance area just off Park Tour Road. There is a sign here pointing into the woods for this trail. The trail is mostly a single-lane jeep trail that winds through the woods toward the site of the old Taylor Farm. The farm, located on a ridge overlooking the land west of the Taylor House, was quickly taken by troops at the start of the siege. During the battle of the Crater, Union troops lined up nearly 200 pieces of artillery on this ridge and fired down upon Confederate troops.

Harrison Creek Trail

1.0 mile long. There is a small parking area on Park Tour Road where you can get on this trail. Harrison Creek Trail crosses the road at this point and takes you through the woods along a National Historic Route. The short section of trail north of Park Tour Road is a fun, winding singletrack along the creek that will challenge anyone's skills. South of Park Tour Road the trail widens and allows for a more leisurely ramble through the forest.

During the siege, Confederate forces were driven back to Harrison Creek where they dug in and held their line for two days. Later, in the last month of battle, Lee launched one last offensive. This offensive was called the Battle of Fort Stedman and Lee's troops were stopped cold along this creek.

Attack Road

0.5 miles long. This old, dirt road connects VA 109 to Park Tour Road within the park. Harrison Creek Trail and the unnamed service road south of Park Tour Road intersect with Attack Road and lead to the Union Camp and Battery 9. Attack Road is lined on either side with heavy earthworks, built large and high to guard against a Confederate attack on the Union encampment.

Jordon Point Road

0.3 miles long. This dirt road and the other two roads, which together make a triangle, create what was an important supply route between Meade Station and the Union Camp. Meade Station provided a vital link along the City Point and Army Rail Line, which brought the Union Army supplies and medical equipment from City Point. This link ultimately secured the Union victory over Lee's troops as it brought in continuous supplies. Lee's army, meanwhile, grew cold and hungry over the 9½-month siege and fell to Grant's well-equipped troops.

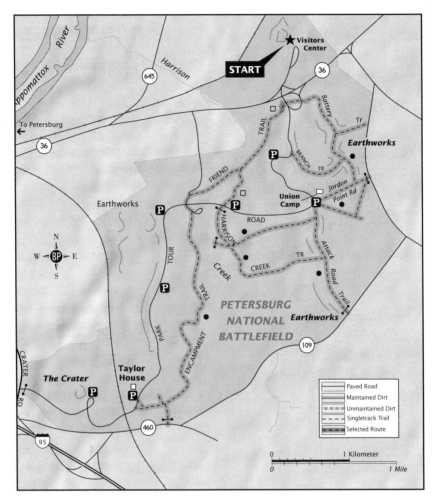

Branch Trail

0.3 miles long. Branch Trail and Battery Trail are very similar. Both trails wind through the thick Petersburg Battlefield forest, weaving around massive trenches and earthworks set up by the Union Army. Some of the earthworks are so high they cast shadows on the trail. Branch Trail takes you from Jordon Point Road to Park Tour Road where you can follow the bike trail back to the visitors center.

Battery Trail

0.7 miles long. Battery Trail, like Branch Trail, weaves around the massive earthworks constructed by Union troops during the 9½-month siege. This area is called Battery 9, where black U.S. troops captured this position on the first day of fighting and held it throughout the entire siege. From Jordon Point Road, Battery Trail takes you all the way back to the entrance road next to VA 36. The trailhead is opposite the trailhead for Friend Trail.

11

Pocahontas State Park

Ride Specs

Start: From the Park Office/Info Center
Length: There are over 20 miles of off-road bicycle trails in the state park, including a great singletrack loop, an easy-going double-track loop, and miles of forest roads.
Land Status: State park
Nearest Town: Chesterfield, VA
Other Trail Users: Hikers, equestrians, and dogs
Canine Compatibility: Dog friendly, however dogs must be kept on the leash.

Getting There

From Richmond: Take I-95 south to Exit 60. Follow VA 10 west approximately seven miles to Beach Road (VA 655). Turn left on VA 655, go approximately four miles, and follow the signs. Turn right into the park. The park office is just up the road. *DeLorme: Virginia Atlas & Gazetteer.* Page 48, A-B1

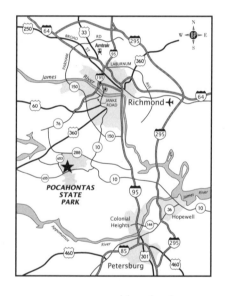

Pocahontas is a familiar name associated with early colonial America. According to legend, this younger daughter of Powhatan (chief of a federation of Algonquian Indian tribes living in the Tidewater region) saved Captain John Smith's life. As the story goes, Powhatan's warriors captured Smith, the self-appointed leader of the first Jamestown settlers, and sentenced him to death. Pocahontas, whose real name was Matoaka, pleaded with her father to spare him. A relenting Chief Powhatan allowed Smith to go free.

Legend holds that as a young girl, Pocahontas often visited Jamestown. As she grew older she would bring food to the settlers and warn the colonists of possible Indian attacks. Later, as a result of the settler's kindness toward her, she chose to convert to Christianity, and changed her name to Rebecca. While visiting Jamestown, she met John Rolfe, an early settler noted as the first commercial tobacco grower. They married on April 5, 1614, had a child named Thomas, then sailed to England for a visit. She was one of the first Native Americans to visit London. During her stay, however, Pocahontas contracted smallpox and died in March of 1617.

The name Pocahontas means "playful one," which might explain why the Commonwealth of Virginia chose the name for this state park. Unlike many other parks in Virginia, the forestland surrounding Pocahontas is deeded to the park, not the state, which gives recreational activities priority over other land uses such as tim-

The Old Mill Bicycle Trail crosses this bridge at the Beaver Lake dam.

ber production. This serves this populated region in Virginia well, as Pocahontas State Park is within just 20 minutes of both Richmond and Petersburg.

Because of its proximity to these growing metropolitan communities, Pocahontas has been one of the state's busiest parks since the Civilian Conservation Corps built the first recreation area in 1934. Today, hiking, swimming, horseback riding, and bicycling (both on and off-road) are all offered within the park's 7,604 acres. Along with the many trails that already exist for hiking and horseback riding, Pocahontas State Park has developed a number of outlets for eager cyclists in the region to enjoy. When you arrive, check them all out or combine them into a single ride. Central Virginia cyclists have struck gold here at Pocahontas and the recent popularity of mountain biking at the park will hopefully entice officials to consider opening up even more trails to bikes.

Singletrack Mountain Bike Trail

Start: From the Singletrack Mountain Bike Trail trailhead at the northern end of Old Mill Bicycle Trail.
Length: 10+ miles of challenging singletrack
Approximate Riding Time: 1 hour

Difficulty Rating: There are three marked trails, classified beginner, intermediate, or difficult.
Trail Surface: Hilly and technical singletrack

Bicycling has, for a long time, been a component of Pocahontas State Park's outdoor recreation plans. They opened the Old Mill Trail to bikes back in the early 1990s to accommodate the growing number of cyclists coming to the park before most other parks had even caught on. But the Old Mill Bicycle Trail, as nice as it is, wasn't quite enough for the growing masses of Central Virginia mountain bikers who were looking for more of a challenge and a place to test their skills. Dan Soper, the park's chief ranger, stepped in and, in cooperation with the Mountain Bike Virginia bike club, developed the park's latest all-singletrack addition, geared solely to the needs of singletrack hungry cyclists. Mountain bikers love it.

Within the Singletrack Mountain Bike Trail loop, located at the northern end of the Old Mill Bicycle Trail, there are three trails to follow: Green, Blue, and Red. Green is easiest, Blue is intermediate, and Red is for expert cyclists. The trailhead is clearly marked with a sign labeled "Singletrack Mountain Bike Trail" and all of the trails within the loop start from this point.

If you're new to the sport, stick to the Green Trail, which is classified as easy. This two-mile trail offers a good introduction to singletrack, but doesn't force the inexperienced cyclist to overdo it. If you want a challenge, head straight for the Blue or Red Trails. While the Red Trail is labeled expert, many consider the intermediate Blue Trail, which is also the longest trail at about four miles, to be the most fun. Cyclists on the Blue Trail will love the technical challenges combined with a few taxing uphill efforts to create a good hearty workout. But if difficult is what you came for, then difficult is what you'll get on the expert Red Trail. While this nearly four-mile stretch of expert riding may not require the same amount of stamina as the Blue Trail, it'll tax your concentration, challenge your confidence, and build bike handling skills you didn't even know existed. The Red Trail is full of chest-high log jumps, huge steeps, and what downhill racers will describe as monster g-outs (the "g" stands for gravity). A g-out is an abrupt dip with a sharp transition.

Cyclists are asked to register at the trailhead so the park staff can keep track of how much use the trails receive. Who knows? If there's enough use here (and the trail's popularity suggests there is) perhaps the park will consider opening even more new trails. Keep on biking!

Pocahontas State Park Forest Roads

Start: From the Visitor Center

Length: 10 miles of forest roads open to bikes

Approximate Riding Time: Varies

Difficulty Rating: Easy due to fairly flat terrain along carriage roads

Trail Surface: Hard-packed old forest roads and grassy doubletrack through what used to be classified as state forest land.

Other Trail Users: Hikers, equestrians, and dogs

In addition to Pocahontas' singletrack loops and the bike trail around Beaver Lake, there are more than 10 miles of old, grassy forest roads open to bikes. All of the forest roads are clearly marked and roll gently up and down through what was once designated state forestland. It's been a while since Pocahontas State Park has functioned also as a state forest and has been trying to shed the old State Forest moniker for some time. Today all the land surrounding the park is considered state parkland and is open to the public for recreational use. Pick up a brochure at the park office for trail maps of all the forest roads and head out into the woods to create a variety loops and out-and-back rides.

Old Mill Bicycle Trail

Start: From the Park Office/Info Center
Length: 6.1-mile loop around Old Mill Bicycle Trail
Approximate Riding Time: 1–1½ hours
Difficulty Rating: Easy

Trail Surface: Hard-packed dirt trails around Old Mill Bicycle Trail. Technical singletrack around the mountain bike loop.
Other Trail Users: Hikers, equestrians, and dogs

The Old Mill Bicycle Trail begins from the Information Center near the park entrance and follows Bottoms Forest Road into Pocahontas State Forest. The terrain is rolling and many of the trails are wide and inviting, allowing cyclists of all abilities to enjoy the wooded environment of this state park. Upon reaching the first split in the trail, turn right, following the white arrows painted on the ground. This will lead you counterclockwise around Beaver Lake, ensuring traffic travels in one direction. From here, the trail narrows and winds beneath a leafy canopy of a tall hardwood and pine forest. In less than one mile you will cross a small footbridge past the dam and climb a short, steep hill to the Nature Center. Bear left around the Nature Center on Crosstie Forest Road and continue along the rolling forest roads in the forest. Signs along the route point the way.

MilesDirections—Old Mill Bicycle Trail

0.0 START at the Park Office and Information Center. Bottoms Forest Road starts just across from the parking lot on the left side of the Park Road.

0.5 Bear right, continuing on Bottoms Forest Road. Signs along the trail will direct you.

1.2 Reach the main loop. Turn right on Old Mill Bicycle Trail. Follow the white arrows painted on the ground. These arrows point you in a counterclockwise direction around the loop.

2.1 Cross a little bridge over the creek on the other side of the Beaver Lake dam. This section is very scenic.

2.3 Reach the Nature Center. You must go in front of the nature center to stay on the trail. Turn left on Crosstie Forest Road.

3.1 Bear left, continuing on Crosstie Forest Road.

3.3 Follow along this forest road through a tunnel of tall loblolly pines.

3.4 Turn left on Horner Forest Road.

4.1 Turn left on Bottoms Forest Road.

4.7 Pass Beaver Lake Trail on the left. (Bikes are not allowed on this trail.)

5.0 Reach the beginning of the bicycle loop. Bear right, following Bottoms Forest Road through the woods back to the start of the ride.

6.1 Arrive back at the parking lot.

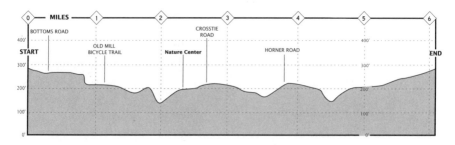

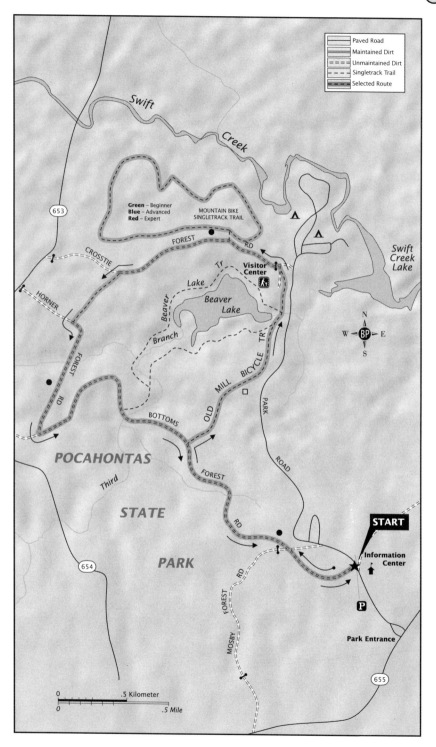

Paved Road
Maintained Dirt
Unmaintained Dirt
Singletrack Trail
Selected Route

Swift Creek

653

Green – Beginner
Blue – Advanced
Red – Expert

MOUNTAIN BIKE
SINGLETRACK TRAIL

FOREST

RD

CROSSTIE

Beaver Lake Tr

Visitor Center

HORNER

Beaver Lake

Lake

Swift Creek Lake

Branch

FOREST RD

BICYCLE TR

PARK

N
W BP E
S

OLD MILL

BOTTOMS

ROAD

POCAHONTAS

FOREST

Third

STATE

PARK

654

RD

START

Information Center

FOREST RD

P

MOSBY

Park Entrance

655

0   .5 Kilometer
0   .5 Mile

Chesterfield County

Getting ready to try out some of the singletrack at Pocahontas.

Ride Information

🌗 Trail Contacts:
Pocahontas State Park
(804) 796-4255

Mountain Bike Virginia bike club
(804) 782-7903

**Department of Conservation
& Recreation**
(804) 786-1712

🕐 Schedule:
Open 8:00 a.m. until dusk daily, year-round

💲 Fees/Permits:
Small parking, camping, and pool fee

🍴 Accommodations:
Camping and group cabins are available. Call for reservations at 1-800-933-PARK or (804) 225-3867.
Snack bar near the pool is open during the summer season.

💡 Local Events/Attractions:
Swimming pool at the park—*open Memorial Day to Labor Day*

Edgar Allan Poe Museum
Richmond, VA
(804) 648-5523

Museum and White House of the Confederacy
Richmond, VA
(804) 649-1861

Hollywood Cemetery
Albemarle and Cherry Sts.
Richmond, VA
Buried here among the many graves are two U.S. presidents (James Monroe and John Tyler), Jefferson Davis (President of the Confederacy), Confederate General J.E.B. Stuart, and 1800 Confederate soldiers.

🚲 Local Bike Shops:
Agee's Bicycles
Richmond, VA
(804) 672-3441
or *www.ageescycle.com; www.ageebike.com*

Conte's Bicycle and Fitness
Richmond, VA
(804) 935-0500
or *www.contebikes.com*

Rowlett's Bicycles
Richmond, VA
(804) 353-4489

Shipley's Bicycles
Richmond, VA
(804) 560-0646

Two Wheel Travel
Cary Street, Richmond, VA
(804) 359-2453

🅝 Maps:
USGS maps: Chesterfield, VA; Beach, VA
ADC map: Richmond & Vicinity Road Map: Page 23, E-8
Pocahontas State Park trail map

Belle Isle

Ride Specs

Start: From the Belle Isle parking lot

Length: Many miles of trails

Approximate Riding Time: Varies with distance

Difficulty Rating: Easy around the island's perimeter trail. Difficult on the inner island's hilly singletrack.

Trail Surface: Gravel path around the island's perimeter and rugged, hilly singletrack up in the island's higher ground.

Land Status: City park

Nearest City: Richmond, VA

Other Trail Users: Hikers and dogs

Canine Compatibility: Bring 'em if you've got 'em. Dogs love it here. Just be careful with the crowds.

Getting There

From I-95 through Downtown Richmond: Take Exit 74B to Franklin Street. Turn right on Franklin Street. At the first light, turn left on 14th Street. Go one block and turn right on Main Street (one way) at the light. Follow signs to Belle Isle and the Tredegar Iron Works. Turn left on 5th Street. Go two blocks, cross over the Downtown Expressway, and turn left on Byrd Street. Turn right at the Federal Reserve Building on 7th Street. At the fountain, bear right on Tredegar Street to the Belle Isle Parking Lot. **DeLorme: Virginia Atlas & Gazetteer.** Page 58, D-1

B elle Isle, part of the James River Park System and one of Richmond's most popular city parks, is located in the heart of Virginia's state capital, just across the river from the newly renovated Richmond Riverfront. This 54-acre island in the middle of the James River attracts thousands of visitors annually. Its high cliff walls, rushing rapids, stone ruins, and fascinating history together make this island one of the most unique mountain biking spots in the Richmond area.

But before I digress, let me warn you that we're talking about Richmond here, where a good cluster of trails often means a local park crowded with more bikes, walkers, and dogs than you can count on a calculator. But to the island's credit, cyclists interested in an afternoon ride can pedal across the river over the footbridge beneath the Robert E. Lee Bridge straight from downtown Richmond, where they will find huge drops, rocky, rooty singletrack, quick turns, and some great scenery. Views of Hollywood Cemetery, the Richmond skyline, sunsets over the James River, and the rushing Hollywood Rapids are always a good reason to pedal over to the island, whether or not you're looking for a workout.

Once a Native American fishing village, Belle Isle's shore provided great harvests of such foods as the American freshwater mussel, which still exist along the banks of the James. During America's colonial period, the island was called Broad Rock Island because of its large granite walls. It had a general store, crops growing on the east side, and a ferry that transported folks to and from the island.

The Civil War brought to the island a gruesome role. The northeastern section was used as a prisoner-of-war camp for captured Union soldiers. More than 20,000 prisoners were sent here, and at one time as many as 8,000 Union prisoners of war were detained in the island's notorious tent city. Thousands of captured soldiers sent to the island subsequently died of dysentery and disease.

During the Industrial Revolution, iron works came to Belle Isle. Ruins of the old Iron Rolling, Milling, and Slitting Manufactory still exist on the east side along the main trail. This plant ran on water power and slave labor in the early 19th Century and produced such products as horseshoes, nails, spikes, copper pots, and bowls.

105

Cyclists cross Belle Isle's footbridge.

Also during this time, a man named James Bell built a race track on the flat land of then Broad Rock Island's east side. Hundreds arrived nightly to "Bell's Island" to gamble and watch the races. It is reported that when James Bell left the island, ladies of Richmond attempted to restore the island's image by renaming it with a "more refined" French title of *Belle Isle*, which means in English, "the good island."

Today Belle Isle is used exclusively as an outdoor recreation area for Richmonders weary of the city's skyscrapers and pavement. The Belle Isle Footbridge transports visitors from Tredegar Street over the James River to Belle Isle's eastern flatland. The main trail around the island starts to the right of the bridge. This main trail makes a one-mile loop around the island, passing many of the historical artifacts left to ruin. For cyclists, this path is short and can be crowded on nice days, weekends, and holidays. Don't even try to ride here on Memorial Day or July 4. However, if you spin up the high hills of the inner island, you'll find a network of singletrack trails crisscrossing the island's high ground. While the trails up here may not be worth writing your friends in Colorado about, they do have a lot of great drops and climbs (about 20 in all), ranging in difficulty from not-so-steep to nearly vertical. Because of the island's size (very small) you could be doing these same drops and climbs all afternoon— enough at least for a quick sense of singletrack bliss in a city better known for its history than its hills.

These trails, though not technically closed to bikes, aren't recommended to cyclists by the park service because of their difficulty level and danger. Trails on the inner island are not maintained and should be approached with great caution and responsibility. In short, cyclists have to behave and stop crashing down cliff walls, breaking collar bones, and causing the park service unnecessary grief which might result in their banning bikes on the island altogether. Ride only on the inner trails and avoid the cliffs on the island's north side near the Hollywood Rapids. Remember to be careful, and you're guaranteed a great, but brief, ride on Belle Isle.

Ride Information

🕓 Trail Contacts:
Park Naturalist
James River Park
City of Richmond Parks & Rec.
(804) 780-8130

James River Park Visitors Center
(804) 780-5311

🕐 Schedule:
Open daylight to dusk, year-round

🍴 Restaurants:
Third Street Diner at the corner of 3ʳᵈ and Cary. Great diner food serving breakfast 24-7. Perfect for breakfast after a late afternoon bike ride.

⚲ Local Events/Attractions:
Richmond's Riverfront bordering Richmond's downtown along the James River, creates a one-mile corridor from the historic Tredegar Iron Works through Kanawha Canal and Haxall Canal. There are events here all year long. For more information, go to *www.richmondriverfront.com*

Local Bike Shops:
Agee's Bicycles
Richmond, VA

(804) 672-3441
or *www.ageescycle.com*;
www.ageebike.com

Conte's Bicycle and Fitness
Richmond, VA
(804) 935-0500
or *www.contebikes.com*

Rowlett's Bicycles
Richmond, VA
(804) 353-4489

Shipley's Bicycles
Richmond, VA
(804) 560-0646

Two Wheel Travel
Cary Street, Richmond, VA
(804) 359-2453

Ⓝ Maps:
USGS maps: Richmond, VA
ADC map: Richmond & Vicinity road map
Belle Isle Interpretive Guide and Trail Map

MilesDirections

0.0 START at the Belle Isle Parking Lot next to the Valentine Riverside Museum. Turn right, heading west, on Tredegar Street to the footbridge ramp. Cycle up the ramp and cross over the James River on the Footbride. Please be cautious and considerate of other footbridge traffic (people and dogs). It's a narrow bridge so you may think of simply walking the bike across.

0.25 Reach Belle Isle. The footbridge drops you onto the island. From here, pedal to the right along the dirt path. It's fairly obvious once you get here where to go to get on the main bike path around the island.

0.3 Reach the main bike route around the island. You may circle the island in either direction.

1.2 Reach the end of the loop. To return to the car, take the footbridge back over the James River to the parking lot.

1.5 Reach the parking lot.

*[**Note:** If you want to explore the hilly, single-track trails within the island, go straight at mile 0.3 and climb the dirt hill toward the center of the island. This hill is a short, steep climb.*

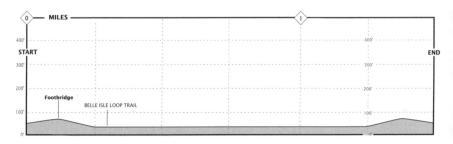

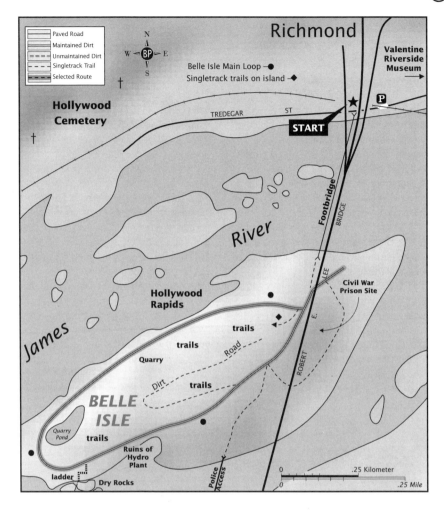

Paved Road
Maintained Dirt
Unmaintained Dirt
Singletrack Trail
Selected Route

N
W — BP — E
S

Belle Isle Main Loop → ●
Singletrack trails on island → ◆

Richmond

**Valentine
Riverside
Museum**
→

P

**Hollywood
Cemetery**

TREDEGAR   ST

START

Footbridge

BRIDGE

River

Civil War
Prison Site

**Hollywood
Rapids**

trails

trails

Quarry

Road

Dirt

trails

E. LEE

ROBERT

James

**BELLE
ISLE**

Quarry
Pond   trails

Ruins of
Hydro
Plant

Police Access

ladder   Dry Rocks

0   .25 Kilometer

0   .25 Mile

Once you're up this hill, there are trails everywhere that you may ride on. Many of these trails are quite difficult and some are downright hard. There are enough trails within this island to spend an afternoon exploring. The park service warns that many of the trails on Belle Isle are steep and rocky and should be treated with great caution.

As you pedal around the main loop of Belle Isle, you may notice there are a number of places to access the singletrack trails within the island. There are also a number of areas posted with signs that say, "No Bikes." Please don't ride in these areas.

When the weather's dry and the water is low, another fun spot for some cyclists is the dry rocks on the south side of the island. Walk across the metal walkway from the main trail, then climb down a ladder to the rocks. This is not the place to come expecting to ride with much speed, however. But with lots of technical bike-handling skills cyclists can maneuver from one rock to the next without falling into the river.

Keep in mind, on the weekends and holidays Belle Isle gets very crowded. Be extremely cautious when riding around here and, by all means, keep the speeds down.]

13

Powhite Park

Ride Specs

Start: The trailhead starts into the woods at the far end of the circular drive.

Length: There are approximately eight miles of singletrack on which you can ride

Approximate Riding Time: Varies depending on how long you want to have fun

Difficulty Rating: Moderate to difficult; the hilly, twisty nature of the singletrack here requires both stamina and skill to maneuver around. There are few flat sections and only a couple of resting spots.

Trail Surface: Wooded, narrow, twisty singletrack with some muddy sections

Land Status: Regional park

Nearest Town: Richmond, VA

Other Trail Users: Hikers and dogs

Canine Compatibility: Dog friendly

Getting There

From Downtown Richmond: Take the Powhite Parkway (VA 76) south toward Chesterfield. Take the Jahnke Road East Exit just after crossing over the Chippenham Parkway. As you head east on Jahnke Road, you will cross back under the Chippenham Parkway and will see almost immediately the Powhite Park entrance across the median on your left. Drive another 50 yards to the light at the Chippenham Medical Center and make a U-turn in order to get back to the park entrance. Make a right into the park entrance and proceed to the end of the entrance road to the circular drive (cul-de-sac). Park here. The trailhead starts into the woods at the far end of the circular drive. If the gate to the park entrance is closed, park at the post office across the street.

From the West End or the South Side of Richmond: Take the Chippenham Parkway to the Jahnke Road East Exit and follow the directions above. *DeLorme: Virginia Atlas & Gazetteer:* Page 58, D-1

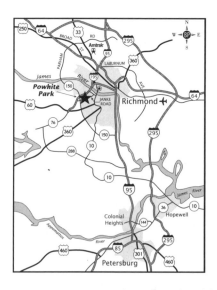

For a long while, years ago, Powhite Park (pronounced *po-white*) was a big question mark to local cyclists. Could we ride there or couldn't we? Well, of course, we all did for many years regardless, but always wondered whether—or rather *when*—we'd get kicked out for good. Well, that time never came and today mountain bikers have pretty much adopted the park as their own, even helping the park service to maintain the trails that exist.

Times sure have changed, and thankfully so in the case of Powhite Park, located right on the border of Richmond and Chesterfield County near the Chippenham Medical Center. So good are the trails here that once you've ridden the fast, rocky descents, the scenic side trails, and the must-ride half pipe, you'll be coming back again and again. Certainly one of the most attractive aspects of this park, aside from its sin-

The trails at Powhite Park are perfect for any singletrack lover in the Richmond area.

gletrack trail network, is its proximity to the Greater Richmond Area. Its convenient location allows die-hard cyclists and all of us working saps around the state capital a convenient place to zip on over to after a hard day's work. Powhite Park is located just off Chippenham Parkway across the street from the Chippenham Medical Center, making it a convenient drive from just about any direction. Of course, trying to get there right after work may pose a challenge as the parkway can back up pretty quickly with traffic. But while sitting in traffic, one might hardly notice the wooded hillsides between the Powhite and Jahnke Road exits to even know that this was a regional park and one of the city's finest off-road playgrounds.

111

You'll find the trailhead buried behind the trees right at the end of the park entrance road (at the head of the circular drive). Jump into the woods here and be ready to drop hard down a quick descent into the park. At the bottom of the descent you'll come to a swampy area that you must wade through in order to get to the main trail system. Future plans may someday include constructing a wooden bridge over this typically muddy mess, both to ease the slog factor on cyclists and to relieve the swampy ground from so much traffic. Once you're past this and into the main trail network, you've got lots of options from which to choose. The trails are fairly well marked and getting lost will be tough—major roads and neighborhoods surround the park on all sides.

MilesDirections

Due to the nature of this trail network, there's really no point in trying to create specific trail directions for cyclists to follow. Instead, enter the park at the main trailhead at the far end of the circular drive, head downhill and across the swampy area, then simply go where your bike will take you. The trails will dictate where you should go and shouldn't go and various signage throughout the park denotes private property. Please no trespassing. You can spend the better part of an afternoon at Powhite Park, so hit the trails and have fun!

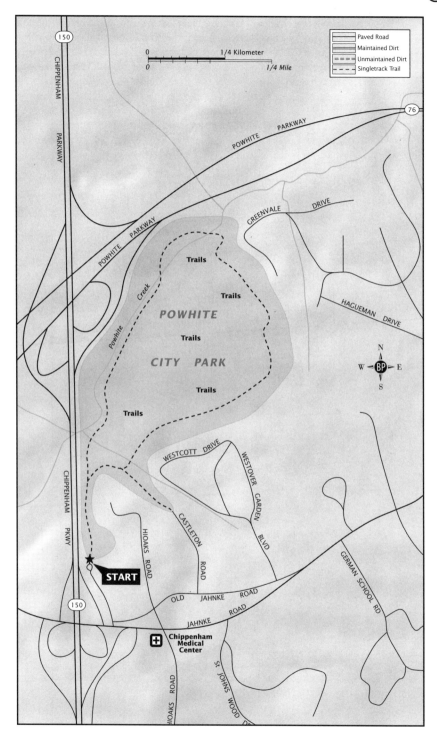

Paved Road
Maintained Dirt
Unmaintained Dirt
Singletrack Trail

1/4 Kilometer
0
0   1/4 Mile

150
CHIPPENHAM PARKWAY

POWHITE PARKWAY

76

GREENVALE DRIVE

Trails

Trails

POWHITE

Powhite Creek

HAGUEMAN DRIVE

Trails

CITY PARK

Trails

Trails

N
W BP E
S

WESTCOTT DRIVE

WESTOVER GARDEN BLVD

CHIPPENHAM PKWY

HIOAKS ROAD

CASTLETON ROAD

★
START

GERMAN SCHOOL RD

150

OLD   JAHNKE   ROAD

JAHNKE   ROAD

Chippenham
Medical
Center

HIOAKS ROAD

ST JOHNS WOOD

Be sure not to miss some of Powhite's finest features while you're here. While this maze of switchbacks, loops, log crossings and off-camber descents will keep you entertained, challenges like the great Doublerock Jump (a tricky descent) and the Buzz (a "half-pipe" with a series of quick dips through a dirt ravine) will keep you coming back again and again.

Get Connected:

If you were so inclined, it is possible to link Powhite Park to the James River Park by pedaling east on Jahnke Road to Westover Hills Boulevard (turn right on Forest Hill Avenue to get to Westover Hills Boulevard). Head down the hill next to the Nickel Bridge and you'll end up at the James River Park, which is full of trails. Crossing over the Nickel Bridge will take you into Maymont Park and Dogwood Dell, where more mountain bike trails exist. And if you followed the trails within the James River Park heading east, you will eventually reach a small pedestrian footbridge that crosses over the James River onto Belle Isle where even more singletrack awaits [see Ride 12]. Who says you need a car around here?

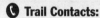

Ride Information

Trail Contacts:
Mountain Bike Virginia bike club
(804) 782-7903

Schedule:
Open daylight to dusk, year-round

Local Events/Attractions:
Edgar Allan Poe Museum
Richmond, VA
(804) 648-5523

Museum and White House of the Confederacy
Richmond, VA
(804) 649-1861

Hollywood Cemetery
Albemarle and Cherry Sts.
Richmond, VA
Buried here among the many graves are two U.S. presidents (James Monroe and John Tyler), Jefferson Davis (President of the Confederacy), Confederate General J.E.B. Stuart, and 1800 Confederate soldiers.

Local Bike Shops:
Agee's Bicycles
Richmond, VA
(804) 672-3441 or
www.ageescycle.com;www.ageebike.com

Conte's Bicycle and Fitness
Richmond, VA
(804) 935-0500 or
www.contebikes.com

Rowlett's Bicycles
Richmond, VA
(804) 353-4489

Shipley's Bicycles
Richmond, VA
(804) 560-0646

Two Wheel Travel
Cary Street, Richmond, VA
(804) 359-2453

Maps:
USGS maps: Richmond, VA; Bon Air, VA; Drewrys Bluff, VA; Chesterfield, VA

14

Poor Farm Park

Ride Specs

Start: From the Archery Range Trailhead

Length: Over 13 miles of trails

Approximate Riding Time: 2–3 hours

Difficulty Rating: Hilly, rugged singletrack makes this a moderate to difficult ride filled with roots, rocks, tight squeezes, big drops and, at times, high traffic.

Trail Surface: Roots, rocks, climbs, and twisty singletrack

Land Status: County park

Nearest Town: Ashland, VA

Other Trail Users: Hikers, dogs, nature tours, and the occasional archer

Canine Compatibility: Good. Lots of people and other dogs though. Dogs will love this place as much as mountain bikers will.

Getting There

From Richmond: Take I-95 north to Ashland. Take the VA 54 west at Ashland. Follow VA 54 west approximately five miles to Liberty Middle School. Turn left on VA 810, pass Liberty Middle School, and follow the signs for Poor Farm Park. VA 810 ends at the gravel parking lot for the park. Park here. **DeLorme: Virginia Atlas & Gazetteer.** Page 58, B-1

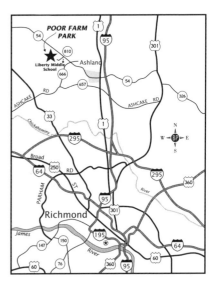

Richmond's mountain bikers know that finding good singletrack in the area is somewhat difficult. Like many of Virginia's urban areas, Richmond is far removed from the rugged hills of the Allegheny Mountains and vast public land of the state's national forests. Richmond's terrain, in fact, is typically flat to rolling (at best) and much of the surrounding land is privately owned. But like many other urban areas hard-pressed for singletrack, there are exceptions. While the Richmond area might, at first, appear to be a dry well for off-road riding, upon closer inspection, cyclists will find a spring of singletrack delight in a regional park called Poor Farm Park just west of nearby Ashland.

The park is located next to a middle school, and within its boundaries are playing fields, volleyball sandpits, soccer fields, picnic tables, and an amphitheater. But don't let these leisurely amenities fool you. Behind this regional-park facade, through the woods and down the hill from the playing fields lies a vast network of off-road cycling adventure, growing year by year into some of the best off-road riding in Central Virginia. Hills, steep trails, big drops, tough climbs, and fast descents abound in this woodland region and will keep cyclists of all interests and abilities content.

Maintained singletrack trails like this abound at Poor Farm.

Granted, this is a small regional park, so don't expect days of endless exploration. It is, however, possible to easily spend a few hours pedaling Poor Farm's wooded trails, honing that singletrack savvy and humbling face-plant steeps. And, if you manage to cross Stagg Creek (there's now a footbridge that takes you there), miles of singletrack await your tread beneath both the power lines and farther over in a whole series of newly cut trails.

Ride Information

● Trail Contacts:

Hanover County Parks and Recreation
(804) 798-8062

Hanover Visitor Information Center
(804) 752-6766

Mountain Bike Virginia bike club
(804) 782-7903

● Schedule:

Open daylight to dark, year-round. Trails are sometimes closed after heavy rains.

● Local Events /Attractions:

Poor Farm Park is home to a number of great mountain bike races each year, including the **Virginia Point Series**. Get in touch with your local bike shop for scheduled races or contact the Mountain Bike Virginia bike club at (804) 782-7903.

● Restaurants:

The town of Ashland has lots of restaurants for eating and hosts various festivals throughout the year.

● Local Bike Shops:

Agee's Bicycles
Richmond, VA
(804) 672-3441
or *www.ageescycle.com*;
www.ageebike.com

Conte's Bicycle and Fitness
Richmond, VA
(804) 935-0500
or *www.contebikes.com*

Rowlett's Bicycles
Richmond, VA
(804) 353-4489

Shipley's Bicycles
Richmond, VA
(804) 560-0646

Two Wheel Travel
Cary Street
Richmond, VA
(804) 359-2453

● Maps:

USGS maps: Hanover Academy, VA

One of the best ways to get onto the trail system at Poor Farm is to enter at the Archery Range trailhead. From the gravel parking lot at the end of the park entrance road, ride through the open gate, pedaling past the volleyball sand pits toward the soccer fields. Just beyond the sandpits, on the right side of the field, there is a large wooden sign hanging in front of a trail opening. This is the trailhead for the orange-blazed Archery Range Trail.

This trail will lead you downhill toward Stagg Creek, where you can go one of two ways. Turning right at the end of the descent allows you to continue following the loop around the archery course. A left turn will take you on a narrow trail marked with blue and white blazes along the creek. Both of these trails are challenging, with plenty of obstacles and steep hills guaranteed to keep you on your toes.

Besides these two main trails, you can branch off on one of the side trails to explore a little deeper into the park. Some of these trails are longer than others and have different degrees of difficulty.

The best way to approach cycling in this park, though, is to not worry about following specific routes. Rather, pedal your way into the woods on one of these many trails and just start riding, making up loops of your own.

Please be aware, of course, that this is a regional park open to all types of trail users. On most days there are certain to be other people enjoying the trails, particularly hikers and dog walkers. Richmond is lucky to have this place. But, remember to be courteous to the other trail users. They have a right to be here too.

You gotta keep up on this trail, or get left behind!

There's always another option to take, thanks to the vast network of trails here.

MilesDirections

As far as the trails go, each year a very enthusiastic Poor Farm Park loving mountain bike group adds more. It would be silly to try and create a loop that people should follow, so instead my best recommendation is to just go out and get lost for a few hours. When you are very lost, keep in mind these few major landmarks: the playing fields where you parked your car, the hills, the creek, and the power lines—in that order. So if you start wondering where you are and run out of playing fields, hills, creek, or power lines, then you're heading away from your car and you may want to start thinking of which way is back. If you're on the east side of Stagg Creek (where most of the trails are) simply head up hill, and in one place or another, you'll end up back at your car.

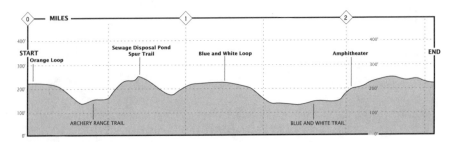

120

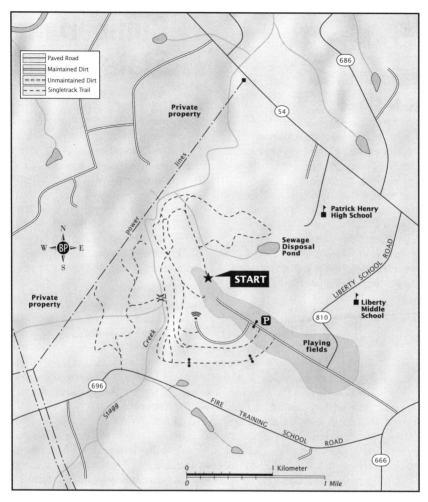

Start from the Archery Range Trailhead just off from the soccer fields. If you're into really hilly, sketchy, rocky singletrack trails, travel down toward the creek and head left. If you like flatter, but very rooty trails through dense woods, cross Stagg Creek (there's a wooden footbridge along the trail near the amphitheater). Over here, you'll find a whole new set of trails winding and zigzagging through the woods (my personal favorite area—just be careful to stay off private property). If you like tight, smooth sin-gletrack, stay on either side of the parking lot on the east side of the creek. There's an adrenaline-pumping downhill near the amphitheater and a couple more beneath the power lines.

Cyclists travel from as far as Fredericksburg to ride at Poor Farm, and so far as I know, no one has gone home disappointed. Whether you're looking for a good after-work ride, some after-dark riding (*shhh*), or some technical skill training that will knock your shorts off, Poor Farm Park will deliver.

15

Cumberland State Forest

Ride Specs

Start: From Bear Creek Lake State Park
Length: 40-50 miles of forest roads and trails
Approximate Riding Time: Varies with distance
Difficulty Rating: The trails and forest roads are rated easy to moderate
Trail Surface: Flat to rolling dirt roads, single-track around Bear Lake, and doubletrack trail segments.
Land Status: State forest
Nearest Town: Farmville, VA
Other Trail Users: Hikers and motorists (light)
Canine Compatibility: Dog friendly

Getting There

From Richmond: Take U.S. Route 60 west from Richmond approximately 40 miles to Cumberland State Forest. U.S. 60 travels through the forest. Turn right off U.S. 60 just east of Cumberland Courthouse on VA 622. Take VA 622 north 4.5 miles, then turn left on VA 629. VA 629 leads you into Bear Creek Lake State Park where you can park. Parking, information, camping, toilets, and showers are available. *DeLorme: Virginia Atlas & Gazetteer.* Page 56, D-2

B etween the Appalachian and Blue Ridge mountains to the west and the flat coastal plains to the east lies Virginia's Piedmont region, characterized by its gently rolling hills and quiet valleys. This is an area of few extremes, where the terrain is neither hilly nor flat and pines, cedars, and hardwoods grow side by side. Land from Manassas to Danville makes up Virginia's Piedmont, and just like Virginia's mountains and coast, off-road bicycling has found its way into this central region.

The majority of accessible mountain biking terrain in the Piedmont region is primarily within Virginia's state forests. The Virginia Division of Forestry administers four state forests in the Piedmont region: Cumberland, Appomattox-Buckingham, Prince Edward-Gallion, and Pocahontas State Forests, all of which comprise nearly 50,000 acres. This provides the largest publicly owned land open to mountain biking east of the Blue Ridge Mountains.

While mountain biking is popular in the state forests, Virginia's forests are primarily managed for such things as watershed protection, timber production, and research. For example, several natural areas in the different state forests are reserved exclusively for research. These natural areas are intended for use as outdoor laboratories for students of ecology, botany, and other natural sciences. In these areas, timber cutting and recreation (such as mountain biking) are strictly prohibited.

While the natural areas are safeguarded from overuse, there

The forest has many uses. Timber is one of its greatest resources.

are many areas in Virginia's state forests that are specifically designed for public use. Within each forest is a state park that provides a variety of outdoor activities, from camping and picnicking to swimming, boating, hiking, and cycling.

Cumberland State Forest is singled out in this guide as the representative state forest. It is also the headquarters for Virginia's Piedmont state forests. The other three state forests mentioned are similar in size and terrain, and all have many miles of unpaved forest roads and trails ideal for off-road bicycling.

Cumberland State Forest is situated in the heart of Virginia, just 35 miles west of Richmond and only a half-hour's drive from Farmville. Its nearly 17,000 acres of flat-to-rolling terrain are filled with forest roads, dead-end trails, and dirt paths. Many of the dirt roads lead you through scenic hardwood and pine forests and past the natural habitats of deer, turkey, quail, squirrels, rabbits, and raccoons. The areas that are absent of trees, which I'm sure you'll notice if you come for a visit, have been harvested by the state and sold as timber. The bare spots have been replanted, however, and will be closely monitored in the years to come. Cyclists are welcome on all the dirt forest roads to explore the forest's bounty.

One note of caution to anyone venturing into the forests: please be aware that the state forests make up a significant portion of land open to public hunting in Central Virginia. Be aware of hunting seasons and be careful not to get caught in the woods during a deer hunt.

Ride Information

🕐 Trail Contacts:
Cumberland State Forest
(804) 492-4121

Bear Creek Lake State Park
(804) 492-4410

🕐 Schedule:
Open dawn till dusk, year-round

💲 Fees/Permits:
There is a fee to enter Bear Creek Lake State Park. Bring up to $2 per person and $5 per car.

💡 Local Events /Attractions:
Lee's Retreat Driving Tour, Farmville. For information, go to *www.leesretreat.com*

⊟ Accommodations:
Bear Creek Lake State Park has a number of campgrounds available to the public. Call ahead for current information on prices and for reservations;
1-800-933-PARK

🚲 Bike Rentals:
Bikes are available at Bear Creek Lake State Park for $3/hour.

Ⓝ Maps:
USGS maps: Gold Hill, VA; Hillcrest, VA; Whiteville, VA

MilesDirections

START at Bear Creek Lake State Park. Bear Creek Lake State Park is a small state park with a 40-acre lake as its main attraction. Camping, picnicking, hiking, fishing, and swimming are some of the activities popular here. There is also a modern bathhouse and a full-service concession area. Leave your car at the lake and hit the forest roads and trails for a good day's bike ride, then return for a cool swim and hot shower.

Most of the roads are maintained forest service roads used by loggers for harvesting timber. There are countless dead-end trails and dry-weather roads that are gated, all of which branch off the main forest roads. Most of these trails are seeded to reduce erosion and improve game habitat. They travel into the woods sometimes up to half a mile before ending. At that point, just turn around and head back to the road. These trails provide a wonderful diversion from the main forest

roads and bring cyclists much closer to the forest's natural setting.

Folks interested in singletrack should head out on the Willis River Trail, which starts near Bear Creek Lake and travels north through Cumberland State Forest for nearly 16 miles point-to-point. The trail is fairly secluded, but never too far from a forest road, and rolls up and down over a variety of short climbs and descents. The trail is fairly well marked, so pick up a map and go for as long as you desire.

Note on the map the shaded area above VA 622. Cumberland State Forest continues well north of this road. In fact, only about half of the state forest is mapped in this guide. Be sure to get the Virginia Department of Forestry's *Guide to Virginia's Piedmont State Forests* if you wish to travel farther into the forest (Virginia Division of Parks and Recreation, 804-786-2132). In addition to

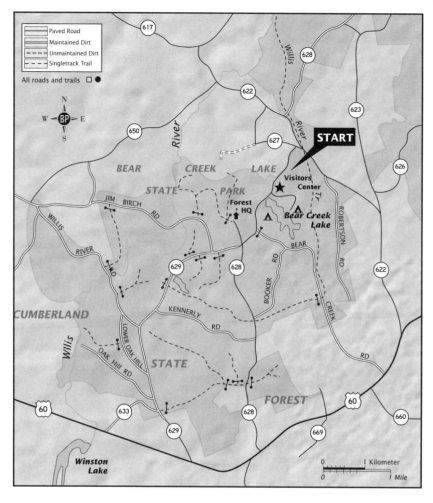

Cumberland State Forest, the Virginia Department of Forestry's guide also provides detailed maps of Appomattox-Buckingham State Forest, Prince Edward-Gallion State Forest, and Pocahontas State Forest. Each of these four different state forests have many miles of great forest roads and trails suitable for mountain biking.

*[**Note:** Because Cumberland State Forest has so many individual forest roads and trails suitable for cycling, it would be unreasonable to create a single loop. Instead, cyclists are encouraged to use the forest map provided*

and select your own routes through the state forest. For this reason, there is no profile map available.]

Hunting Season:

For opening and closing dates for the current hunting season, call the Virginia Department of Game and Inland Fisheries (540) 248-9360 or go to www.dgif.state.va.us.

Mountain Biking With Your Dog

Many people love to bring their canine companion along on mountain bike trails. Our furry friends make great trail partners because they're always good company and they never complain. If you take your dog mountain biking with you, or you're considering it, remember that there are a number of important items to keep in mind before hitting the trails.

Getting in Shape

It would be no better for your dog than it would you to tackle running a marathon without first getting into good physical condition. And if your pet has been a foot warmer much of his life, you will need to train him into reasonable shape before taking him along on those long weekend bike rides.

You can start your dog's training regimen by running or walking him around the neighborhood or, better yet, a local park. Frisbees and balls are also great tools to help get your dog physically fit for those upcoming mountain bike rides. Always remember that on a trail your dog probably runs twice as far as you ride. Build your dog's exercise regimen based on the mileage you plan to ride each time you head out. If you're going on a five-mile trail, assume your dog needs to be in shape for a 10-mile trail. Gradually build up your dog's stamina over a two to three month period before committing him to arduous afternoons of trying to keep up with you as you pedal along on your bike.

Training

Teaching your dog simple commands of obedience may help keep both you and your dog out of a heap of trouble while out there on public trails. The most important lesson is to train your dog to come when called. This will ensure he doesn't stray too far from the trail and possibly get lost. It may also protect him from troublesome situations, such as other trail users or perhaps coming in contact with local wildlife. Also teach your dog the "get behind" command. This comes in especially handy when you're on a singletrack trail and you run into other bikers. Teaching your dog to stay behind you and your bike and to follow your lead until the trail is clear can be a valuable and important lesson. Remember also to always carry a long leash with you in case, after all your prior training, you still have to tie your dog up to a tree at a campsite or succumb to local leash laws on crowded trails.

There are a number of good dog training books on the market that should help train you and your dog how to stay out of trouble with other trail users. Also, look to your local SPCA or kennel club for qualified dog trainers in the area.

Nutrition

Nutrition is important for all dogs. Never exercise a dog right after eating for the same reasons people shouldn't exercise right after eating. Feed your pet a high quality diet such as Hills Science Diet™ or Iams™. These products have higher quality ingredients and are more nutritionally balanced than generic grocery store dog foods. They may be more expensive than some generic brands, but your dog also doesn't need to eat as much of it to get the same nutrition and calories. If you insist on feeding your dog a grocery store diet, stick with the Purina™ brand, as it is still better for your dog than most others in this class.

Trail Tips

Try to pick your riding trails near lakes or streams. The biggest threat to your dog when biking is the heat, and water is essential to keep him cool. If the trail doesn't have water nearby then you need to bring as much liquid for him as you would drink yourself. A small lightweight plastic bowl can be used to give your dog water, or you can purchase a collapsible water bowl made from waterproof nylon (Call Ruff Wear™; (541) 388-1821). Also, you can use a waterbottle to squirt water into your dog's mouth.

- Try not to take your dog riding with you on a really hot day—hotter than 80 degrees. To avoid these temperatures, take your dog riding in the early morning or evening when the air is cooler and safer for your pet.
- Watch for signs of heat stroke. Dogs with heat stroke will: pant excessively, lie down and refuse to get up, become lethargic and disoriented. If your dog shows any of these signs, immediately hose him down with cool water and let him rest. If you're on the trail and nowhere near a hose, find a cool stream and lay your dog in the water to help bring his body temperature back to normal.
- Avoid the common foot pad injuries. Don't run your dog on hot pavement or along long stretches of gravel road. Always bring a first aid kit that includes disinfectant, cotton wrap, and stretchy foot bandage tape so you can treat and wrap your dog's paw if it becomes injured. You might also want to look into purchasing dog booties, useful for protecting your dog's pads and feet during long runs outdoors.
- Be sure to keep your dog's nails trimmed. If your dog's nails are too long, they might catch on an object along the trail and lead to soft tissue or joint injuries.
- Don't take your dog on crowded trails and always carry a leash with you. Remember, just because you love your dog doesn't mean other people will.

Charlottesville Dirt Ride

Ride Specs

Start: From the Stony Point Elementary School
Length: 20.3-mile loop
Approximate Riding Time: 2–2½ hours
Difficulty Rating: Moderate: Technically there are few challenges, as this ride follows well maintained gravel roads and pavement; physically, the ride is a bit longer than most and has a fairly steady climb near the start and middle of the route.
Trail Surface: Hilly dirt roads and paved roads
Land Status: Public roads
Nearest Town: Charlottesville, VA
Other Trail Users: Motorists
Canine Compatibility: Not good. Too many roads.

Getting There

From Charlottesville: Take VA 20 north for approximately eight miles to the Stony Point Elementary School. Park here. You can access VA 20 from I-64 and from U.S. 250 as well. *DeLorme: Virginia Atlas & Gazetteer.* Page 68, D-2

W hen I wrote the first edition of this book a number of years ago, I must have traveled thousands of miles throughout Virginia in search of good places to mountain bike. My bike, car, and I passed through countless towns, big and small, on our way to one trailhead, then another, and another. I got to see a lot of the state and learn a lot more about how rich, dynamic, and diverse Virginia really is. One town I passed through time and time again was Charlottesville, located right in the center of the state amidst the foothills of the Blue Ridge Mountains.

It didn't take long to grow fond of this beautiful little city of slightly more than 40,000 people and home to such well-known Americans as Thomas Jefferson, James Monroe, and even James Madison (if you consider Montpelier in the Charlottesville area). Don't let this number fool you though. The surrounding area has well over 100,000 residents and is growing strong. Thomas Jefferson's Monticello rests upon Carter Mountain overlooking the town, commanding a breathtaking view of the rolling countryside and his prestigious University of Virginia, founded in 1819. "The University" is now home to more than 11,000 students. And, to add one more name to the list, I moved here too.

Scenic, unpaved roads wind through the hilly countryside surrounding Charlottesville and Central Virginia.

The surrounding countryside is a great place to spend the day pedaling a bike past wineries, old plantations, fields of dogwood, and, of course, horses, horses, horses. Not every off-road ride, as you will see along these quiet backroads, need be a mountainous adventure with white-knuckled descents and bone-jarring trails. A change every now and then can be very enjoyable.

Change of pace is precisely why this scenic loop is included in the book. I designed this ride to showcase some of the treasures Central Virginia has to offer while, for the most part, staying off the pavement. The ride doesn't take you to every place that I'd like to show you, but it's great for the leisurely mountain biker with an appetite for the scenery and solitude of some peaceful backroads through the rolling foothills of Central Virginia.

129

Thoroughbreds grace Charlottesville's horse country.

The ride begins at the Stony Point Elementary School just off Virginia 20. Park your car in the school parking lot. You will travel up a quiet mountain road to the top of Charlottesville's Southwest Mountains before descending quickly toward the small town of Cismont. The Southwest Mountains have the highest peaks east of the Blue Ridge. Snacks and refreshments are available at the corner store along Virginia 231. Be careful along the next section of this ride on Virginia 22, as this is a bit more heavily traveled by cars.

Cruise through the equally small towns of Cobham and Cash Corner (food and drinks available) before heading back over the Southwest Mountains through Turkeysag Gap. Horse farms and colorful gardens provide the scenery all the way back

130

to the mountain. The rest of the ride is along more of the numerous backroads in this region, all of which are scenic, quiet, and peaceful-perfect for a leisurely ride through the countryside.

This may be the most off-road riding many could wish for. If you live in the Central Virginia region, especially near Charlottesville, you'll be pleased to know there are miles and miles of backroads like the roads presented on this ride. Many of these paths pass through old farmland, past exquisite horse stables, and near Central Virginia's famous wineries. Rides like this help to bring folks so much closer to the area's rural landscape than paved roads can deliver. So take some time to explore this off-road experience, and I'm sure you'll be pleased with your discoveries.

[**Note:** *Check out the Sugarloaf Mountain and The Waltons Ride in the Central Virginia Honorable Mentions section for another great ride along some of the peaceful backroads in the Charlottesville area.*]

Ride Information

◐ Trail Contacts:

Virginia Department of Transportation
HIGHWAY HELPLINE 1-800-367-ROAD
or *www.vdot.state.va.us/*

UVA Mountain Bike Club
http://scs.student.virginia.edu/~bikeclub/

Charlottesville Albemarle
Bicycling Association (CHABA)
www.chaba.homestead.com

◑ Schedule:
All roads open to the public year-round

❓ Local Information:
Charlottesville/Albemarle
Convention and Visitor's Bureau
www.charlottesvilletourism.org

♀ Local Events /Attractions:
Charlottesville/Albemarle
Convention and Visitor's Bureau
www.charlottesvilletourism.org

C-Ville Weekly
Charlottesville's News and Arts Weekly
www.c-ville.com

◑ Local Bike Shops:
Bike Factory of Charlottesville,
Charlottesville, VA (804) 975-2453

Blue Wheel Bikes, Charlottesville, VA
(804) 977-1870 or *www.bluewheel.com*

Extreme Sports, Charlottesville, VA
(804) 975-1900

Performance Bicycles, Charlottesville,
VA (804) 963-9161

Blue Ridge Mountain Sports,
Charlottesville, VA (804) 977-1397

Ⓝ Maps:
USGS maps: Barboursville, VA; Keswick,
VA; Charlottesville East, VA

MilesDirections

0.0 START at Stony Point Elementary School. Parking available. Turn right on VA 20 (paved).
0.3 Turn right on Stony Point Pass (VA 600) (hard-packed dirt and gravel). This road takes you through Charlottesville's Southwest Mountains.
3.4 Reach the summit. There's a small clearing here, but no real view except in the winter when the foliage is thin.

4.2 VA 600 changes to pavement.
4.4 VA 600 changes back to dirt.
4.7 End of the descent. Pass a very large horse stable on the left.
5.7 Cross Gordonsville Road (VA 231). Continue straight along the paved road through the small town of Cismont. Snacks, Coke machine, refreshments at the Chevron on this corner.

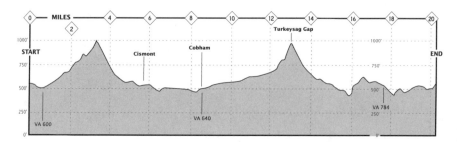

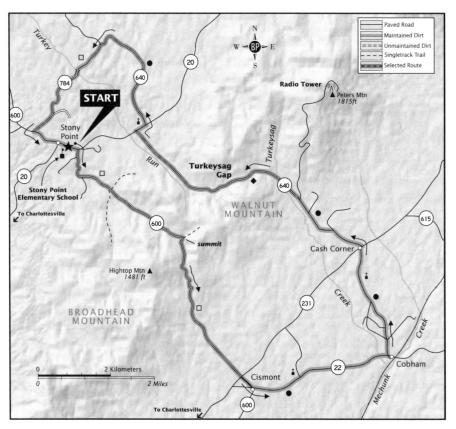

6.0 Turn left on Louisa Road (VA 22) (paved).

8.5 Arrive in the tiny town of Cobham. Turn left on VA 640 (paved). Heading back toward the mountain, this flat, paved road showcases the magnificent horse farms and stables that make this area famous.

10.5 Cross Gordonsville Road (VA 231). Get some snacks or drinks at the Cash Corner store. Stay on VA 640 (paved).

12.0 VA 640 changes to dirt and gravel and begins climbing back over the Southwest Mountains.

13.3 Reach the summit and cross through Turkeysag Gap.

15.4 Turn right on Stony Point Road (VA 20) (paved). Bobbi's grocery store at this intersection.

15.6 Turn left on Gilbert Station Road (VA 640) (paved).

15.7 Start climbing (dirt).

16.8 Reach the summit of this climb.

17.5 Bear left. Do *not* turn right on Brocks Mill Road (dirt).

17.7 Turn left at this intersection on VA 784 (dirt).

18.2 Paved descent.

18.4 Cross a small bridge at the bottom of this descent (dirt).

19.7 Turn left at the stop sign on VA 600 (paved).

20.2 Go straight through the intersection of VA 20 and VA 600.

20.3 Reach the Stony Point Elementary School. This ride would be fun on one of those horses!

Observatory Hill

Ride Specs

Start: McCormick Road near the University of Virginia's McCormick Observatory
Length: 7-mile combination of singletrack loops and trail segments
Approximate Riding Time: Varies depending on rider's discretion
Difficulty Rating: Moderate to difficult due to roots, rocks, hill climbs and other trail obstructions
Trail Surface: Narrow technical singletrack in a very hilly, wooded environment
Land Status: University of Virginia property
Nearest Town: Charlottesville, VA
Other Trail Users: Hikers, trail runners, and dogs
Canine Compatibility: Dog friendly

Getting There

From Downtown Charlottesville: Travel west on West Main Street, which then becomes University Avenue. Cross Emmett Street where University Avenue becomes Ivy Road. Continue for 0.5 miles and turn left on Alderman Avenue. Proceed on Alderman Road and turn right on McCormick Road at the Observatory Hill Dining Hall. Follow McCormick Road uphill. At the very top of the climb, bear a hard right at the water tanks. McCormick Road continues climbing sharply. Just up the road a bit more, you can park your vehicle on the side of the road, where you'll find the first of a number of marked trailheads. *DeLorme: Virginia Atlas & Gazetteer.* Page 67, D-7

From UVA: Follow McCormick Road west through the grounds toward Slaughterhouse Recreation Center. Reach Alderman Road. Turn left on Alderman Road and head uphill toward Observatory Hill Dining Hall. Turn right on McCormick Road at the Observatory Hill Dining Hall. Follow McCormick Road uphill. At the very top of the climb, bear a hard right at the water tanks. McCormick Road continues climbing sharply. Just up the road a bit more, you can park your vehicle on the side of the road, where you'll find the first of a number of marked trailheads.

Public Transportation: From the bus transfer point at 2nd and Water Street take Charlottesville Transit Service bus route number 4 (Fry's Spring) to the intersection of Jefferson Park and Fontaine Avenues. Now on your bike, pedal west on Fontaine Avenue for 0.5 miles to the southeast corner of the trail network on the right, just past the University of Virginia's Piedmont Apartments.

The McCormick Observatory, resting atop Mount Jefferson (O-Hill), is nearly 130 years old and still works like a charm.

W hat a bunch of lucky folks those UVA students are. They enjoy a beautiful campus with all the luxuries a fine university can offer: great instructors, a wonderful library, state-of-the-art facilities, and a dynamic downtown scene with all that a young crowd could want. But if that's not enough, students interested in burning off some post-class stress have an amazing network of mountain bike trails literally across the street from the main University grounds. And this is no ordinary terrain like you might expect from a downtown park, with a few zig-zag trails through generally flat terrain and soccer fields. O-Hill throws

the "mountain" in mountain biking and keeps it coming for a whole afternoon of power riding and technical skill work. Sharp climbs; long, fast descents; rocky mine fields; and some smooth runs all combine at O-Hill to create an atmosphere of real mountain bike adrenaline—and it's all right next to campus. Granted, after a few days spent here, cyclists will start to see the limitations this small plot of land presents. But nothing so close can beat the workout and the technical skills training O-Hill can offer.

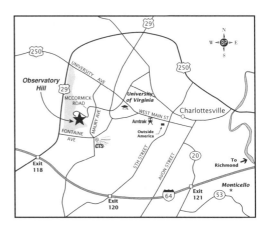

Now for those of us not lucky enough to have such backyard training grounds (actually I am one of the lucky ones because I live here) it may be difficult to appreciate its proximity. But there's no denying the challenges and great off-road riding this hill rewards whether you live five minutes away or have to travel an hour to get here. The fact is it's a great ride no matter where you're from. And with the university next door, countless restaurants and bars within walking distance, and more things to do in this small Blue Ridge city than you could shake a stick at, there's little reason not to come here in the first place. So while you're here, bring along your bike and go for a huge workout on O-Hill.

Okay, so I'm a bit excited about this place. I've lived in Virginia all my life and never have I had the opportunity or the luxury to go somewhere that didn't require time spent first in a car (growing up in Northern Virginia left me a bit jaded). But to find such a gem in the middle of town that isn't just another city park filled with baby buggies, little kids, and soccer fields is a real treasure.

MilesDirections

START—There are a handful of starting points for the trails at O-Hill, so take your pick. A lot of folks will drive up McCormick Road to the observatory, park their car, and start at the gated trailhead on the left. Others find it easier to pedal over to Fontaine Avenue and start riding at the gated forest road just before U.S. 29 (starting here helps to avoid finishing on top of the hill, which may help some riders avoid climbing to the top altogether). If you chose the Fontaine Avenue trailhead, you can still cruise the hilly and fun singletrack that contours the base of Mount Jefferson pretty much all afternoon without having to crank your way up to the top of the hill. But hey, where's the downhill fun in that? A third starting point is just off Ivy Road (U.S. 250 Business) past the UVA Police and Visitors Center and an Amoco gas station. There's a place to park under the trees, where the trailhead begins.

This view from atop O-hill reveals Pantops Mountain on the left and Carter Mountain on the right (Monticello sits in between those two trees).

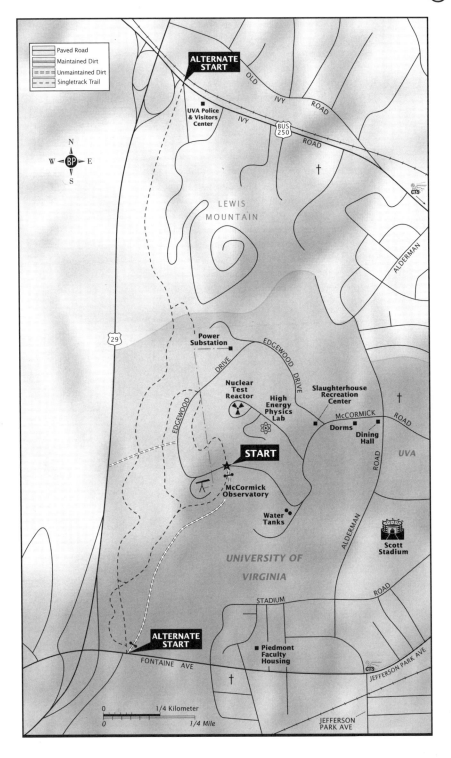

To know a little more about this place called Observatory Hill may help visitors appreciate these trails even more. The name of the hill on which the observatory rests is actually Mount Jefferson, named, of course, for this town's most famous resident. It was Mr. Jefferson's intent, when designing the University of Virginia, to include an observatory and a center for astronomical study. Unfortunately, he didn't live to see his plan to completion (he died in 1826), but the idea to build an observatory as part of the University didn't die with him. In 1877, Leander McCormick, a Rockbridge County native and founder of McCormick Harvesting Machine Company, donated a 26¼-inch telescope to the University. An observatory, which bears McCormick's name, was built atop Mount Jefferson to house the telescope and various other astrometric instruments. Construction on both the observatory and the director's house (the large house next to the observatory now named the Alden House after the observatory's third director) began in 1882 and was completed in 1884. It's interesting to note that, in the early 1800s, Leander McCormick's father, Robert, invented the mechanical reaper. Thanks to many improvements to the reaper by Leander, a successful patent application, and brisk sales to farmers across the Midwest the McCormick family became one of the nation's richest families.

Today, the observatory offers regular tours to interested visitors, so check out their schedule, get a time, and take the opportunity to see how an actual observation tower works.

UVA students come here to train... and sometimes just to walk.

Ride Information

🌀 Trail Contacts:
**Mountain Bike Club
at the University of Virginia**
(804) 293-9092
or *www.virginia.edu/~bikeclub*

**Charlottesville Albemarle
Bicycling Association (CHABA)**
www.chaba.homestead.com

⏱ Schedule:
Dawn to dusk, year-round

❓ Local Information:
University of Virginia
at *www.virginia.edu*

Charlottesville Transit Service
(804) 296-RIDE
www.transit.ci.charlottesville.us

**University of Virginia's
Department of Astronomy**—*learn more
about the observatory, upcoming
events, and much more*
www.astro.virginia.edu

**Charlottesville/Albemarle
Convention and Visitor's Bureau**
www.charlottesvilletourism.org

Hyperville (A C-ville web site)
www.hyperville.com

📍 Local Events /Attractions:
The O-Hill Meltdown Mountain Bike Race,
held annually toward the end of April.
Contact the Mountain Bike Club at the
University of Virginia for details.

**Charlottesville/Albemarle
Convention and Visitor's Bureau**
www.charlottesvilletourism.org

C-Ville Weekly
Charlottesville's News and Arts Weekly
www.c-ville.com

🚲 Local Bike Shops:
Bike Factory of Charlottesville,
Charlottesville, VA (804) 975-2453

Blue Wheel Bikes, Charlottesville, VA
(804) 977-1870 or *www.bluewheel.com*

Extreme Sports, Charlottesville, VA
(804) 975-1900

Performance Bicycles, Charlottesville, VA
(804) 963-9161

Blue Ridge Mountain Sports,
Charlottesville, VA (804) 977-1397

🅝 Maps:
USGS maps: Charlottesville West, VA
ADC map: Albemarle County: Page 35, G-10

Returning to more important matters, Observatory Hill offers a maze of technical and steep singletrack trails, rocky dirt roads, and some of the best mountain biking a downtown could offer. O-Hill is bounded on all sides by paved roads, apartments, and private homes, therefore specific trail directions are not needed for this ride because it'll be difficult to get lost. Be alert for other trail users especially on weekends and late afternoons and don't hesitate to call the Mountain Bike Club at the University of Virginia to get involved in trail maintenance and improvement.

18 Walnut Creek Park

Ride Specs

Start: From the Bicycle Parking Lot
Length: Approximately 15 miles of singletrack
Approximate Riding Time: 2–3 hours
Difficulty Rating: Moderate to difficult: Technically, the rocks, roots, and off-camber singletrack presents a challenge to most any level rider, while the length and hilly terrain will keep the heart working and the sweat pouring. Less ambitious riders may want to spend their time along the less strenuous lakeside trails.
Trail Surface: Rocky, rooty singletrack with occasional creek crossings through dense hardwood.
Land Status: County park
Nearest Town: Charlottesville, VA
Other Trail Users: Hikers, trail runners, and anglers

Getting There

From Charlottesville: From I-64 take U.S. 29 south for approximately 10 miles. Turn left onto VA 708 and follow VA 708 for approximately five miles. Turn right onto VA 631 (Old Lynchburg Road). The park is half a mile past the intersection of VA 708 and VA 631. Once in the park, follow signs for the bicycle parking into the first lot. A large trail map is posted on the bulletin board in the parking lot. Don't forget to pick up your trail map from the entrance gate. *DeLorme: Virginia Atlas & Gazetteer:* Page 55, A-7

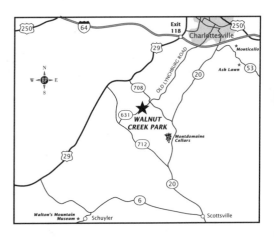

I f it isn't obvious right from the outset, this trail system was designed and is maintained by Charlottesville area mountain bikers. Trail names such as The Blue Wheel, Extreme Sports, Blazing Saddles Trail, and Bike Factory Trail all get their monikers from local C-ville bike shops. Wahoo Way throws in a sprinkle from The Mountain Bike Club at UVA. And Outward Bound Trail finds its roots in Orange County's Outward Bound. Let's not forget Wilkins Way, named after Doug Wilkins of the Mountain Bike Virginia bike club, who, along with so many others, has worked very hard in cooperation with the Albemarle County Parks Department to develop this amazing system of multi-use trails at Walnut Creek Park, just 10 miles south of Charlottesville.

Since its inception a few years back Central Virginia mountain bikers, trail runners, and hikers have all volunteered thousands of hours of their time to design, build,

This old farmhouse is one of the relics you'll see along the way.

and maintain these fantastic multi-use trails for our enjoyment. And their efforts have paid off big. Today there are over 13 miles of clearly marked singletrack trails on which to ride. These trails lead cyclists and other trail users over tight, twisting routes through a dense hardwood forest surrounding a 25-acre lake. There are countless log jumps, hairpin turns, quick descents, hills, ravines, and just about everything a well-planned trail system can throw at you.

The first thing to do when you arrive, aside from paying your park fee at the gate, is to pick up a trail map from the gate attendant. Clearly labeled and in color, the map will detail every trail in the park and what color blazes you'll need to follow in order to stay on track. Once you get into the woods, colored diamond blazes corresponding to the map help to guide the way. It'll be just plain difficult to get lost in this park.

Following the map, park in the trailhead parking lot next to the lake and follow the yellow blazes (Chimney Trail) across Walnut Branch and into the woods. After crossing the creek, you'll have a few options. The recommended loop to follow is the red trail (Wilkins Way). Follow this color all the way back to this point. The red loop (four miles around) is the park's original singletrack trail. You'll see from both the map and the additional trails within the park that things have come a long way. The red trail leads you around the eastern portion of the park and packs a real punch to any-one who takes on this moderate to difficult singletrack. Just about every obstacle these

Ride Information

Trail Contacts:
Albemarle County Parks
and Recreation Department
(804) 296-5844

Mountain Bike Club
at the University of Virginia
(804) 293-9092
or *www.virginia.edu/~bikeclub*

Schedule:
Open year-round

Fees/Permits:
$2 for Albemarle County residents. $3 for all non-residents. (City of Charlottesville residents should bring $3.)

Local Information:
University of Virginia at *www.virginia.edu*

Charlottesville/Albemarle
Convention and Visitor's Bureau
www.charlottesvilletourism.org

Local Events/Attractions:
A swimming beach and swim area is available at the second parking area.

Local Bike Shops:
Bike Factory of Charlottesville, Charlottesville, VA (804) 975-2453

Blue Wheel Bikes, Charlottesville, VA (804) 977-1870 or *www.bluewheel.com*

Extreme Sports, Charlottesville, VA (804) 975-1900

Performance Bicycles, Charlottesville, VA (804) 963-9161

Blue Ridge Mountain Sports, Charlottesville, VA (804) 977-1397

Maps:
USGS maps: Alberene, VA

MilesDirections

START—The trails are well blazed with colored plastic diamonds that correspond to the trail map handed out at the entrance gate. You won't have much trouble figuring out where you are and will find that it's difficult to get yourself lost. For a great starter loop, begin at the trailhead parking area and hook up with the red trail (Wilkins Way). This four-mile trail, the park's first, leads you through hairpin turns, steep hills, strategically-placed logs, streams, gullies, and more to give you a taste of what's in store for anyone heading off into the woods at Walnut Creek.

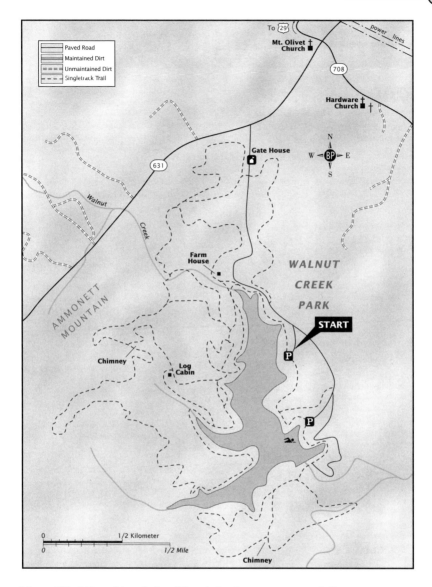

folks could build into this trail, they did; including hairpin turns, steep hills, strategically placed logs, streams, and gullies—you name it. This loop will give anyone a good workout. Along the way, you'll notice a number of other newer connector trails. Trail combinations are endless, so just go out there and have fun. Just keep in mind, it's recommended when on the red trail that you travel *clockwise* to avoid trail collisions.

Once you're done pedaling and it's time to cool off, swing on over to the beach house and go for a dip in the lake. Between Memorial Day and Labor Day, swimming and drinking water are available. There are plenty of other things to do at Walnut Creek Park as well, including canoeing, kayaking, hiking, and fishing. So come prepared to spend some time here and bring a good set of legs for the red trail.

Honorable Mentions

Central Virginia

Compiled here is an index of great rides in the Central Virginia region that didn't make the A-list this time around but deserve recognition. Check them out and let us know what you think. You may decide that one or more of these rides deserves higher status in future editions or, perhaps, you may have a ride of your own that merits some attention.

B) Dogwood Dell

In a most unlikely place, cyclists have discovered a series of singletrack trails just behind downtown Richmond's open-air amphitheater, Dogwood Dell. The amphitheater holds as many as 3,000 people who sit on grassy benches during the warm months of the year to watch everything from local musicians to Shakespeare. The trail network, thought to have as many as six miles worth of singletrack, could never hold as many folks as the amphitheater, but still affords intermediate to advanced cyclists plenty of playtime in the woods. The singletrack is tight but smooth, travelling up and down through dense hardwood, over creeks and gullies. Mountain bikers love this little pace in the city and follow the orange arrows through the woods with enthusiasm. Its proximity to the Fan and Virginia Commonwealth University (VCU) makes this a prime spot for singletrack-seeking cyclists stuck in the downtown.

To get there, head toward the James River down Boulevard to Maymont Park. The trail system at Dogwood Dell lies behind the Carillon (the large bell tower), accessible from a number of places just off the dirt access road left of the bell tower. Jump into the woods and have fun. You should be able to make as much or little as you'd like in this little area just off the James. *DeLorme: Virginia Atlas & Gazetteer*: Page 58, D1-2

Ⓒ Hollywood Farm

Considered by just about everyone who's ever been here to be some of the best riding south of DC, east of Richmond, north of Hampton Roads, and just about every place in between. Hollywood Farm is chock full of twisty, rooty, extremely tight singletrack (narrow your handlebars for this ride) that weaves in and out, creating a network of nearly nine miles of interlacing trails. The only problem is it's on private property. So far the property owners have been more than accommodating by allowing cyclists on their land but insist that visitors play by the rules (wear a helmet) and stay away during hunting season. To best understand your boundaries, keep the railroad tracks on one side and the open fields on the other. Everything in between is rideable.

The ride is just east of Fredericksburg near the Stafford/King George County line. From Fredericksburg, follow VA 3 east approximately five miles to Hollywood Farm Road (VA 601), just before the county line (if you've crossed into King George County, you've gone too far). Turn left on Hollywood Farm Road and go approximately two miles to a dirt road on the right just after the railroad tracks. Turn in here, park, and ride. For more information, call Bike Works at (540) 373-8900 or the Fredericksburg Cyclists (bike club) at (540) 373-1451 or visit *www.bikefred.com*. *DeLorme: Virginia Atlas & Gazetteer*: Page 70, B-C 3

Ⓓ Sugarloaf Mountain and The Waltons

This is a wonderful backroads ride through the foothills of the Blue Ridge Mountains, located approximately 20 miles south of Charlottesville just off U.S. 29. From Rockfish (VA 617), turn right on VA 623, then left on VA 640 (Wheeler Cove Road). VA 640, a scenic dirt road, winds through Thoroughfare Gap. Turn right on Dutch Creek Road (VA 641) toward Sugarloaf Mountain. A jeep road leads you from

Virginia 641 to the top of Sugarloaf Mountain. This three-mile ascent, however, is incredibly steep, but a breathtaking view of the Blue Ridge foothills and everything in its sight awaits at the top. And since you're in the area, make a quick drive over to Schuyler, just off VA 6 and Rockfish Road, where you can visit the Waltons Museum and the Hamner house. This is the town and the house from which the popular television show, *The Waltons*, was based. The house in which Earl Hamner grew up can be visited year-round. Check out the official Waltons web site at *www.the-waltons.com* for more. ***DeLorme: Virginia Atlas & Gazetteer:*** Page 55, B-5

Ⓔ James River State Park

James River State Park is the state's newest park, which officially opened June 20, 1999, and intends to meet the needs of a wind range of users, including mountain bikers. The park, which is still under development, currently offers cyclists access to 20 miles of multi-use trails, most of which are gravel forest roads and grassy doubletrack. And if things go well, park management hopes to build, with the help of local cyclists, some technical singletrack to meet the challenges of more hard-core Central Virginia mountain bikers. This scenic park along the James River offers a lot more than pleasant mountain bike trails, so when you come bring along a fishing pole, canoe, or tent and plan to spend a weekend. There are currently 15 primitive campsites, six picnic shelters, and three restrooms.

The park is fairly remote, so people will be coming from many directions. A good starting point is from a small crossroads called Bent Creek at the intersection of U.S 60, VA 26, and VA 605. From here, head north on VA 605 at the James River Bridge. Travel seven miles to VA 606. Turn left on VA 606 and follow the signs into the park. *DeLorme: Virginia Atlas & Gazetteer:* Page 55, C-D5

(F) Appomattox-Buckingham State Forest and Holliday Lake State Park

Appomattox-Buckingham State Forest is located 30 miles east of Lynchburg off Virginia 24. Part of Virginia's Piedmont Forest System, there are over 19,700 acres of rolling terrain here, making this Virginia's largest state forest. Miles of unpaved forest roads, trails, and dead-end paths wind through this pine and hardwood forest, most of which are ideal for off-road bikes. Holliday Lake State Park is situated within the forest with information, bathhouse, restrooms, camping, and showers. Park officials dedicated a multi-use trail named Carter Taylor Trail back in 1996 geared toward mountain bikers interested in pedaling from Holliday Lake. This generally easy 12-mile loop from the lake was designed to ease the traffic on Lakeshore Trail around Holliday Lake and give cyclists a little more room to have fun. For more information about Holliday Lake State Park, call (804) 786-1712 or visit *www.state.va.us/ ~dcr/parks/holliday.htm.*

Of course, don't overlook the nearby Appomattox Courthouse where Confederate General Robert E. Lee surrendered to Union General Ulysses S. Grant to end the Civil War. The Appomattox Courthouse National Historic Park is just down the road from Holliday Lake State Park on VA 24, north of Appomattox. For more information about the Appomattox Courthouse and the history that made it famous, visit *www.nps.gov/apco/index.htm.* **DeLorme:** *Virginia Atlas & Gazetteer:* Page 45, A-6

(G) Prince Edward-Gallion State Forest

Located off U.S. 360, 16 miles east of Farmville and 48 miles west of Petersburg, Prince Edward-Gallion State Forest is very similar to that of Appomattox-Buckingham State Forest, only smaller. As part of Virginia's Piedmont Forest System, there are nearly 7,000 acres of forested terrain with miles of unpaved forest roads on which to ride. Twin Lakes State Park, located within the state forest just off U.S. Route 360, is host to six miles of multi-use trails built for hiking, horseback riding and biking, taking visitors through the hardwood forest surrounding the lakes. The Prince Edward-Gallion Multi-use Trail is a 14-mile loop adjacent to the state forest and is open to hikers, bikers and equestrians.

Twin Lakes State Park has a multitude of accommodations, ranging from camp-sites with electric hook-ups to full-service cabins. All reservations must be made through the reservation center at 1-800-933-PARK. Bike rentals are also available, so call ahead and make plans to spend a weekend here. For more information call (804) 786-1712 or visit *www.state.va.us/~dcr/parks/twinlake.htm.* **DeLorme:** *Virginia Atlas & Gazetteer:* Page 46, C-2

Northern

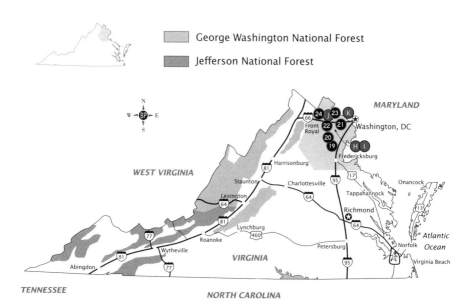

George Washington National Forest

Jefferson National Forest

Virginia

19

Prince William Forest Park

Ride Specs

Start: From the Prince William Forest Park Visitor Center
Length: Varies, depending on route chosen. (There are 8.2 miles of unpaved roads open to cyclists)
Approximate Riding Time: Varies, depending on route chosen
Difficulty Rating: Moderate
Trail Surface: Paved and unpaved park roads
Land Status: Administered by the National Park Service
Nearest Town: Dumfries, VA
Other Trail Users: Hikers, motorists, nature-lovers, and pyrite collectors
Canine Compatibility: Dog Friendly

Getting There

From the Capital Beltway (I-495): Take I-95 south toward Richmond for 20 miles to Exit 150, Joplin Road (VA 619 West). In one-tenth of a mile, turn right from Joplin Road to the Park Entrance Road. The Visitor Center is about one mile down this road where you'll find a telephone, restroom, park information, and trail maps. *DeLorme: Virginia Atlas & Gazetteer:* Page 76, D-3

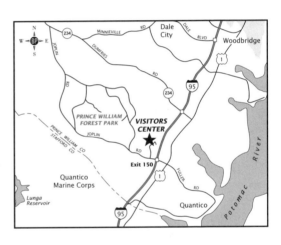

own here in Prince William County lies a relatively large park, preserved as one of the few remaining piedmont forest ecosystems in the National Park Service. Within its 18,000 acres are 35 miles of hiking trails, hundreds of acres open to primitive camping, a scenic paved road looping through the park (incidentally named Scenic Drive), and a plethora of wildlife and plant life for city folks to enjoy. Four miles of the Scenic Drive have a dedicated bike lane providing a paved, relatively flat surface ideal for beginning bicyclists. More experienced cyclists with mountain bikes have the option of off-road biking on any of the 10 fire roads in the park.

At one time Prince William Forest Park's thousands of acres of forestland were extensively farmed for tobacco. Then, when the hills eroded and the earth could no longer support their crops, farmers turned to dairy farming, already well established throughout the county. But for those living in the Quantico Creek area this too failed. The Civil War was equally taxing for those already struggling here. The

Confederates blockaded the Potomac, requiring large numbers of troops for support. Those living in the vicinity of the blockade were required to provide the troops with timber and food and found that what little they had before the war was no longer enough.

A mining operation near the confluence of the north and south branches of Conduce Creek provided a much-needed boost to the area's economy in 1889. But a strike over wages closed the high-grade pyrite ore mine in 1920, bringing down with it any hope for the area's recovery. It was soon thereafter that the United States Government bought the land, resettling nearly 150 families, and with the Civilian Conservation Corps began the effort to "return the depleted land to an ecological balance."

Originally established as the Chopawamsic Recreational Demonstration area by an Act of Congress in August 1933, Prince William Forest Park, a unit of the National Park Service, is mandated to "conserve the scenery and the natural and historic objects and the wildlife therein and to provide for the enjoyment of the same in such manner and by such means as will leave them unimpaired for the enjoyment of future generations." The park contains the largest example of an Eastern Piedmont forest ecosystem in the National Park System and is a sanctuary for native plants and animals in the midst of this rapidly developing metropolitan area.

All kinds of outdoor activities are available within the park for haggled Washingtonians to enjoy, one of which is bicycling. Riding on park trails, unfortunately, is prohibited. However, there are many unpaved, dirt roads throughout the park that can be used by cyclists. Many of these roads are separate out-and-back fire roads, in which case you may need to ride along the paved Scenic Drive Road to create loops. Scenic Drive Road is very well maintained and even has its own dedicated bike lane. Road cyclists from all around often come to Prince William Forest Park just to ride this paved loop through the forest, getting quite a workout from its hilly terrain.

Patomac Mills Shopping Center

Around here, in this metropolitan area, it's hard to really get away from it all no matter how hard you may try. And this point is never more evident than to drive a bit farther south of Prince William Forest Park on Interstate 95 to one of Virginia's greatest tourist attractions—Potomac Mills shopping center, a destination shopping attraction that brings in over 13,000 bus tours each year. Potomac Mills was reported in the Washington Post on September 8, 1991, as the top-rated tourist attraction in the state of Virginia ahead of both Colonial Williamsburg and Busch Gardens—and claims it continues to hold that rating even now!

With more than 52 acres of parking and 1.7 million square feet of fully enclosed shopping space, it's easy to understand how this super-regional specialty mall brings in the foot traffic. Their mixture of outlet stores and off-price retailers draw cost-conscious shoppers from around the globe to its market. It's really somewhat bewildering to wander Potomac Mills' crowded walkways past its hundreds of shops and thousands of people. The thought of getting back on the bike and pedaling to Prince William Forest Park becomes all the more enticing. But hey, if you're down in the area anyway, why not head to the largest, most crowded single-floor shopping mall on the planet? Buy some Power Bars and Lycra shorts then head back north and hit the trails.

Ride Information

Trail Contacts:
Prince William Forest Park
Visitors Center
(703) 221-7181

National Park Service
(703) 759-2915

Schedule:
Open daily from dawn to dusk. Registered campers and cabin campers have access 24 hours. The Visitor Center is open between 8:30 a.m. and 5:00 p.m.

Fees/Permits
A three-day Family Pass is $4.00 per vehicle within park, $2.00 for cyclists and walk-ins

Local Information:
Prince William County
Convention and Visitors Bureau
1-800-432-1792
or www.nps.gov/prwi/

Local Events/Attractions:
Lazy Susan Dinner Theater
(703) 550-7384

Waterworks Water Park
www.pwcces.com/waterworks

Historic town of Occoquan
www.occoquan.com

Harbor River Cruises in Occoquan
(703) 385-9433

Historic Occoquan Spring
Arts & Crafts Show
(703) 491-2168

Accommodations:
Oakridge Campground, $10 a night

Turkey Ridge Run Campground, $30 a night

Cabin Rental (703) 221-5843

Organizations:
Friends of Prince William Forest Park
www.bmsi.com/fpwfp

Maps:
USGS maps: Joplin, VA
ADC map: Prince William County road map

To witness the progress the forest has made in reclaiming what was once depleted and eroding farmland is a wonderful experience when you visit this 18,000-acre forest. And riding your mountain bike along the forest roads through the park gives you an up-close look at this process in action.

Folks looking to do more than just bike have as many as 35 miles of hiking trails along ridges, into valleys, and beside the two main creeks in the park on which to explore this wooded parkland. Scenic Drive provides access to all of the trails and features within the park. Bicycles are not allowed on any of the park's hiking trails.

MilesDirections

Liming Lane Fire Road 0.8 miles long. This forest road is, for the most part, moderately easy. It begins from the parking lot on Scenic Drive Road and takes you out of the park's boundaries to Joplin Road.

Taylor Farm Road 1.5 miles long. From the northern part of Scenic Drive Road, Taylor Farm Road is mostly level until it drops sharply to the South Branch Quantico Creek. The first nine-tenths of this road are part of the 9.7-mile South Valley Trail, which travels the circumference of this part of Prince William Forest Park.

Burma Road 1.5 miles long. Burma Road starts out as an easy forest road, then crosses over a series of hills, making this section moderately difficult. This forest road crosses Quantico Creek and takes you to Pleasant Road. From here, you have the possibility to create a loop back to Scenic Drive Road. Following Pleasant Road past Cabin Camp you can gather "fool's gold" at the site of the old pyrite mine. Cross Quantico Creek again and take Pyrite Mine Road back to Scenic Drive Road.

Pyrite Mine Road 1.0 miles long. This forest road takes you from Scenic Drive Road to Quantico Creek, the North Valley Trail, and the old pyrite mine. The trail is moderate in the beginning, then becomes steep at the end.

North Orenda Road 1.2 miles long. This is a moderate forest road that takes you down to the South Branch. Across the creek is South Orenda Fire Road that leads you back to the Visitors Center.

Lake One Road 0.6 miles long. Lake One Road starts from the parking lot along Scenic Drive Road and takes you down a moderately steep hill to Quantico Creek.

Old Black Top Road 1.6 miles long. Old Black Top Road starts from the Turkey Run Parking area and travels north, crossing Taylor Farm Road, then connects with Scenic Drive Road. The terrain is moderate and offers a good challenge through the middle of the park.

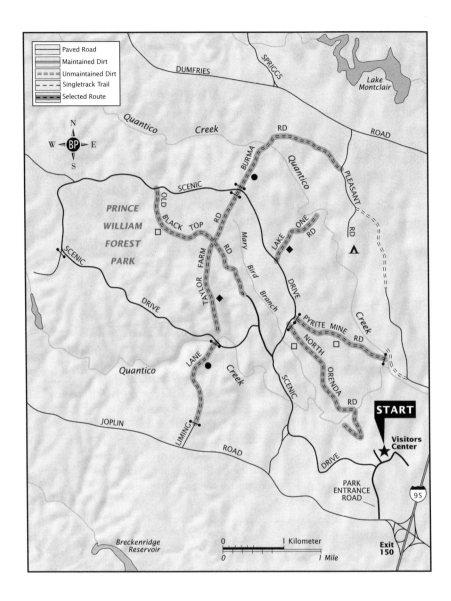

Fall Line

Prince William Forest Park lies along the border between two physiographic zones: the Piedmont and the Coastal Plain. Many of the faulted rocks represent the fall line, a unique geological feature where streams form falls or rapids as they leave the harder rocks of the Piedmont and enter the softer rocks of the Coastal Plain.

Fountainhead Regional Park

Ride Specs

Start: Fountainhead Park
Length: 4.5 miles
Approximate Riding Time: 1 hour
Difficulty Rating: Moderate to difficult
Trail Surface: Technical singletrack and doubletrack
Land Status: Northern Virginia regional park
Nearest Town: Springfield, VA
Other Trail Users: Hikers, boaters, swimmers, equestrians, campers, and anglers
Canine Compatibility: Dog Friendly

Getting There

From the Capital Beltway (I-495): Take Exit 5 west onto Braddock Road. Head south on VA 123. Continue past Burke Lake Park to the Fountainhead Regional Park sign on the right side of the road. Turn right at this sign on Hampton Road. Follow Hampton Road to the park entrance on the left. Park in the first parking lot on the right. The trailhead is to your left. *DeLorme: Virginia Atlas & Gazetteer.* Page 76, C-3

Here's your chance to ride a trail designed by mountain bikers for mountain bikers. As soon as your ride begins, you'll notice the thought that went into these trails. Curves and twists in the landscape will require your total concentration. Thanks to the efforts of the local mountain bike advocacy group MORE, riders in the Washington area can enjoy this great network of singletrack trails along the Occoquan Reservoir in southern Fairfax County.

The Doag Indians were the first to inhabit this area because of its abundance of natural resources, calling it "Occoquan"—at the end of the water—because of its proximity to the river. As with most Eastern American Indians, The Doags soon succumbed to English settlers, leaving the name Occoquan as one of the few legacies of their existence. During the Civil War this area served as a strategic line of defense between the North and South. Such famous Civil War battlegrounds as Bull Run are just a few miles upstream.

Today, the area serves as part of the larger Bull Run Recreation Area and is managed by the Northern Virginia Regional Park Authority (NVRPA). This off-road bicycling trail is the first of its kind for mountain bikers in Northern Virginia. The NVRPA envisions it as an example for the region—a pilot program of sorts.

If no user conflicts arise from this experiment, the NVRPA will consider opening more trails for off-road cyclists in the region. Let's set a good example here and help ensure the growth and acceptance of off-road bicycling trails throughout this area.

Your ride starts in the main parking lot as you head toward the marina. From the lot, pedal toward the trail entrance (staging area). This trail is one-way traffic only, so don't plan to travel it in any direction but clockwise. After a brief, fast, and technical downhill, you will bear left at the first trail intersection. Be sure to always avoid the right fork in this trail—equestrians/hikers only. A small technical stream crossing leads you to the first turn and the beginning of the loop. The trail takes you around

The Fountainhead Trail Project: A Ground-Breaking Event

The Fountainhead Regional Park Mountain Bike Trail was opened in the spring of 1997. Until then, bicycles were not permitted on any of the trails within the park. The trail is a single-direction trail (counterclockwise), clearly marked with trail signs and red blazes. If at any point the red blazes are on the back of the trees rather than on the front, then you are going in the wrong direction and should turn around.

As mentioned earlier, the Fountainhead Regional Park Mountain Bike Trail represents an important opportunity and major breakthrough for cyclists in the Washington metropolitan area. It was planned by the Northern Virginia Regional Park Authority (NVRPA) in close collaboration with the Mid-Atlantic Off-Road Enthusiasts (MORE), and initially funded, in large part, by REI (Recreation Equipment, Incorporated). This flagship mountain bike trail project was designed specifically by mountain bikers for mountain bikers and will serve as a real litmus test for other park officials watching closely who may be interested in constructing and maintaining mountain bike-specific trailways at their parks.

A paved trailhead and two-way access trail is lined with split-rail fence to resist erosion and discourage "trail braiding." The trail was designed to take advantage of the area's elevation and terrain, and water bars are widely employed on its steeper grades, including new rubber belt-style devices popular in California. Overall trail usage is expected to be very high, quite possibly exceeding 500 users per month. Please take extreme measures when riding here to ensure this trail's success and durability. The trail is built. Now it's our turn to make sure it stays open.

(703) 250-2473 is a dedicated trail line with daily updated messages about trail conditions, closings, and openings. Cyclists should always call this number before heading out to the trail. (703) 250-9124 is the Fountainhead Regional Park Number.

Ride Information

Trail Contacts:
Northern Virginia
Regional Park Authority
(703) 352-5900

Fountainhead Regional Park
(703) 250-9124

MORE (Mid-Atlantic Off-Road Enthusiasts)
(703) 502-0359

Schedule:
Open daily from dawn to dusk, March to November

Fees/Permits
$3.50 per car at Burke Lake Regional Park for nonresidents of Fairfax County

Local Information:
Occoquan's website for local information—*www.occoquan.com*

Fairfax County Convention and Visitors Bureau
1-800-7FAIRFAX
or *www.visitfairfax.org*

Local Events/Attractions:
Historic town of Occoquan
www.occoquan.com

Harbor River Cruises in Occoquan
(703) 385-9433

Historic Occoquan Spring Arts & Crafts Show
(703) 491-2168

Accommodations:
Bennett House Bed & Breakfast
Manassas, VA
(703) 368-6121

Sunrise Hill Farm B&B
Manassas, VA
(703) 754-8309

Local Bike Shops:
Bikes USA
Springfield Commons
Springfield, VA—near Springfield Mall
(703) 924-5100

Washington Bike Center
Fair Lakes Shopping Center
Fairfax, VA
(703) 968-2404

Maps:
USGS maps: Occoquan, VA
ADC map: Northern VA road map

and back on a series of small loops offering up to five miles of technical, challenging singletrack. If, after your first or second loop, you're still up for it, head out to the marina and rent a boat or even play a game of miniature golf.

While you're here, don't miss the quaint, historic downtown of Occoquan, rich with history, antique shops, arts and crafts, and great restaurants. You'll also find the nation's first automated gristmill. And don't forget to check out a host of historic homes and businesses, some of which have been in operation for over 200 years.

MilesDirections

0.0 START at the red trail trailhead, which is approximately 10 yards to the left of the "Nature Trail."

0.2 Turn left at this intersection and continue downhill toward the creek crossing. The trail, clearly marked as a "Bike Trail," briefly joins a hiking trail.

0.26 Take a left before a major creek crossing. Remember this is a one-directional trail. This is the only way to go. On your way back, you will have to negotiate Shockabilly Hill with its steep drop-offs. This is visible on the other side of the creek.

0.35 Cross the small creek and continue following the red blazes. Get ready to climb.

0.5 After a series of twists and one challenging ascent, turn left at the trail intersection, continuing down a gradual descent. Pay close attention to the exposed roots and stumps—unless you want to sample the soil! Turning right will take you to Shockabilly Hill.

0.84 There is a sharp sudden left switchback toward the bottom of the hill. Continue following the red blazes away from the reservoir. Do not go across the creek.

0.86 Turn right at this point and cross the small creek. Continue back toward the reservoir.

0.9 After a short steep hill you will be directly across from the previous switchback. Continue left, following the red blazes. The direction is clearly marked.

1.16 Continue following the trail signs and red blazes.

1.37 Turn right at this trail intersection. The trail to the right is an equestrian-only trail.

1.53 Turn left, following the trail toward the "Optional Dead End Loop." Prepare for a fun descent. This is a two-way section, so be careful.

1.61 Bear right onto the singletrack. After a twisty descent, the trail curves to the left, offering a great view of the reservoir.

2.1 You have completed the "Optional Dead End Loop." Turn right and continue up the two-way traffic section of trail.

2.2 Turn left at this intersection and continue down a fast descent. Keep alert, because you will have to turn left abruptly.

2.3 Follow the trail to the left.

2.4 Follow the switchback to the right. The trail continues to be blazed red.

2.66 Follow the trail to the left at another sign pointing to the parking lot. Go over the small wooden bridge and continue following the red blazes.

4.16 Reach Shockabilly Hill. Continue straight down this hill only if you are an expert. These directions lead you to the right, following the "easier" alternate route.

4.3 Turn right ove. the wooden bridge. At this point, if you choose, turn right immediately after the bridge and do the loop again. If not, continue straight toward the red/yellow blazes.

4.35 Turn right over the small wooden bridge.

4.5 Arrive back at the trailhead.

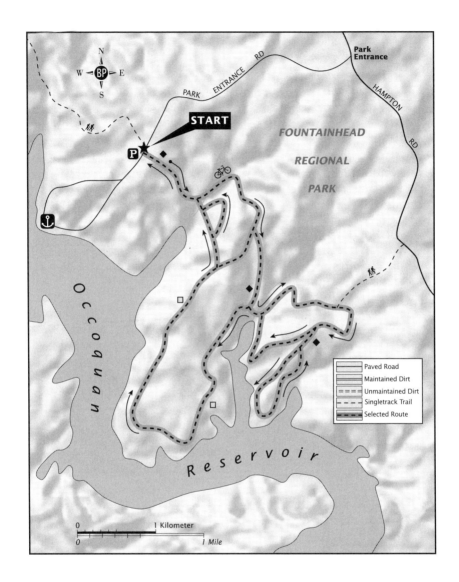

N
W ⬥BP⬥ E
S

Park
Entrance

PARK ENTRANCE RD

HAMPTON RD

START

P

⚓

FOUNTAINHEAD

REGIONAL

PARK

O
c
c
o
q
u
a
n

R e s e r v o i r

0   1 Kilometer
0   1 Mile

Paved Road
Maintained Dirt
Unmaintained Dirt
Singletrack Trail
Selected Route

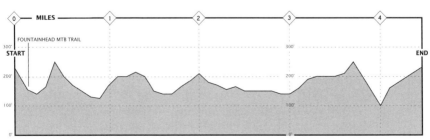

0 MILES 1 2 3 4

FOUNTAINHEAD MTB TRAIL
300'   300'
START
200'   200'
100'   100'
                                        END
0'   0'

Wakefield Park/ Accotink Trail

Ride Specs

Start: From the Wakefield Park Recreation Center
Length: 6.1 miles
Approximate Riding Time: 1 hour
Difficulty Rating: Main loop is rated easy. Off-shoot trails are more difficult.
Trail Surface: Singletrack and dirt trails
Land Status: County parks
Nearest Cities: Annandale and Alexandria, VA
Other Trail Users: Hikers
Canine Compatibility: This is a pretty crowded place, so unless your dog is well trained, it may be best to leave him behind.

Getting There

From the Capital Beltway (I-495): Exit west at Exit 5 onto Braddock Road. In less than 0.2 miles, turn right on Wakefield Park's Entrance Road. Go 0.6 miles to the parking and recreation center on the left. Phones, water, restrooms, food, etc. are available at Wakefield Recreation Center. *DeLorme: Virginia Atlas & Gazetteer.* Page 76, B-4

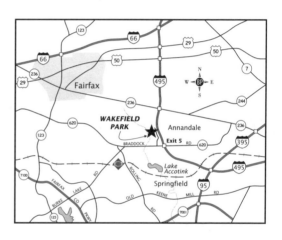

Host to countless mountain bike races and cross-country races throughout the season, Wakefield Park has become somewhat of a local stronghold for mountain bike excitement in Northern Virginia. With the nearby power lines behind Wakefield Park and trails that are perfect for a quick workout as you exit the Beltway from a long day's grind, this area is a sweet spot in the local off-road scene. And from here, cyclists less interested in mashing out their frustrations on technical track can instead leisurely pedal along a flat, dirt path, beneath Braddock Road and over to Lake Accotink Park. Here, a scenic, woodland preserve, as well as an abundance of short, steep hills, tree roots, quick dips, and fast turns await. Stop off after work and get out of traffic for this great mountain bike locale.

Sometimes it's interesting to see where you find singletrack. Typically, great mountain bike trails lie west or far north of the Washington suburbs. Out there—typ-

ically a "long drive" from where most of us live—singletrack and forest roads trace the landscape in all directions. The dirt's the limit. "If only we lived closer to the trails," goes the suburban cyclist's woeful anthem.

But a closer inspection reveals we *do* live near the trails—thanks to the Fairfax County Park Authority. Wakefield and Lake Accotink parks, less than half a mile from the Capital Beltway in Fairfax County, are filled with a network of fun, technical singletrack. Most of these singletrack trails are offshoots from the park's main loop, which is a scenic, wooded dirt trail around Accotink's scenic 70-acre lake.

Ride Information

🕩 Trail Contacts:

Fairfax County Park Authority
(703) 246-5700

Lake Accotink Park
(703) 569-3464

🕒 Schedule:
Open daylight to dark all year

❓ Local Information:
**Fairfax County Convention
and Visitors Bureau**
1-800-7FAIRFAX
or *www.visitfairfax.org*

🔾 Local Events/Attractions:
The Athenaeum in Alexandria
(703) 548-0035

Memorial Day Jazz Festival
Alexandria, VA
(703) 838-4844

Torpedo Factory Art Center
Alexandria, VA
(703) 838-4565

West End Dinner Theater
Alexandria, VA
1-800-368-3799
or *www.wedt.com*

🔵 Maps:
USGS maps: Annandale, VA
ADC map: Northern Virginia road map
Fairfax County Park Authority trail map

The Accotink Trail itself was once part of Orange and Alexandria Railroad's original roadbed built in the early 1850s. The rails and ties, of course, have since been removed, and a new rail was laid farther south along a straighter route.

Lake Accotink's history began in the 1930s when the U.S. Army Corps of Engineers dammed Accotink Creek to create a reservoir for Fort Belvoir, nearly five miles downstream. The lake and surrounding land was given to Fairfax County in 1965 by the federal government for park and recreational use. The park's great trails, open to bicycling, have been "maturing" ever since.

This ride begins from Wakefield Park and travels south along the Accotink Trail around the lake, then back to Wakefield. There are even some great trails that go north from Wakefield and cross challenging routes beneath the power lines.

For thrill seekers, there is an abundance of short, steep hills, tree roots, quick dips, and fast turns. For the off-road cyclist with a lighter touch, Accotink Trail takes you through a scenic woodland preserve, quiet and relaxing in the spring and summer, breathtaking in the fall. Who says you have to drive far to get out of the gridlock and into the woods? For Beltway commuters, Accotink is less than a stone's throw away.

MilesDirections

0.0 START at Wakefield Park Recreation Center near the big green recycling bins. The trail begins up near the park entrance road and heads south through Wakefield toward Braddock Road.

0.2 Cross the athletic fields parking lot. Accotink Trail continues on the other side of the parking lot.

0.6 Cross under Braddock Road.

0.7 Just across Braddock Road, bear left, continuing on the main trail.

1.0 Stay left at the fork in the trail and follow the wooden Accotink Trail post.

2.1 Trail comes to a "T." Turn right, following Accotink Trail. The creek should be on your right. This part of the trail winds up and down through the woods. A lot of fun.

2.9 Arrive at Lake Accotink's marina. Concessions, food, drinks, putt-putt golf, canoe and boat rental, etc. Stay right, crossing the parking lot toward the dam.

3.0 Cross Lake Accotink Dam. Following the bike path, which parallels the train trestle, head toward the woods opposite the dam.

3.3 Re-enter the woods, up a steep climb, on Accotink Trail.

4.5 Turn hard right off the dirt path on an asphalt trail, which takes you down on Danbury Forest Drive in the neighborhood of Danbury Forest. Kings Glen Elementary School on the right.

4.9 Re-enter Accotink Trail on the right just after Lonsdale Drive. This is a steep descent alongside the concrete steps into the woods.

5.0 Turn right off the asphalt path, following Accotink Trail across a wooden footbridge over Accotink creek.

5.1 Turn left on Accotink Trail.

5.5 Cross under Braddock Road.

6.1 Arrive back at the parking lot of Wakefield's Recreation Center.

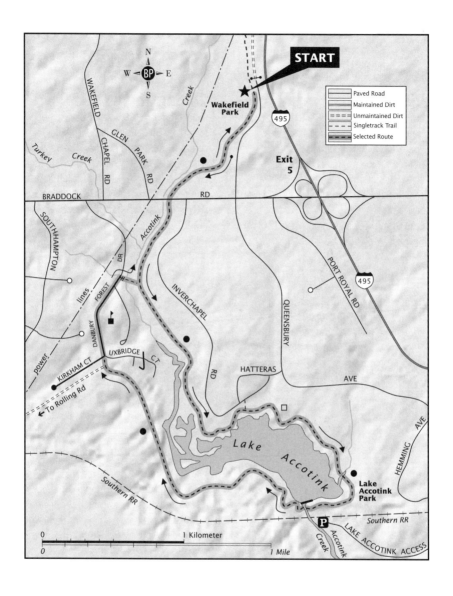

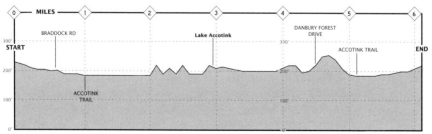

Centreville Power Lines

Ride Specs

Start: From Centreville Elementary School
Length: 7.8 miles
Approximate Riding Time: 1½–2 hours
Difficulty Rating: Difficult due to sections of very rugged terrain
Trail Surface: Rugged singletrack and paved bike paths
Land Status: Public and private right-of-ways
Nearest Towns: Centreville and Manassas, VA
Other Trail Users: Power line repairmen and 4WD motorists
Canine Compatibility: Leave the dog behind. This route follows some busy roads through busy suburban sprawl. No place for a dog,

Getting There

From Interstate 66: Take Exit 53, heading south on Sully Road (VA 28). Sully Road changes to Centreville Road across Lee Highway (U.S. 29). Follow Centreville Road for about two miles, then turn left into the Centreville Elementary School parking lot.
DeLorme: Virginia Atlas & Gazetteer: Page 76, B-2

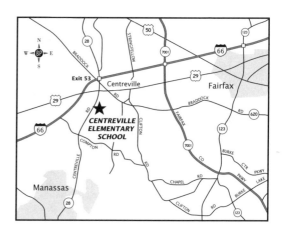

L ike so many communities in Northern Virginia, Centreville has seen its share of suburban sprawl. In fact, in the past few years, this once small town has been all but swallowed by the ever-expanding behemoth Northern Virginia. Surprisingly, though, this incredible growth was once not so easy to come by and Centreville struggled to get to where it is today.

Centreville had been trying to grow for some time, but for a while was having an altogether tough time of it. Since its establishment in 1792, this small trading center, located nearly equidistant from Leesburg, Warrenton, Middleburg, Washington, Georgetown, and Alexandria, tried diligently to become more than just a rest stop along Braddock Road.

When construction began on Little River Turnpike in the late 18th Century, for example, the town hoped this trade highway, stretching west from Alexandria, would be built to pass through their community. At the time, Alexandria was the Potomac's largest market town. Developers, however, routed Little River Turnpike north in favor of smoother, more even terrain, bypassing the town altogether. The town later

An endless source of off-road riding.

tried to house the District Court of Virginia, which served Fairfax, Fauquier, Loudoun, and Prince William Counties. This idea was also rejected in favor of Dumfries in Prince William County. Ever persistent, Centreville founded what it hoped would become a prestigious academy to attract outside scholars to take up residence in local homes. This also went without much success. At one time, Centreville was even known as a local center for slave rental and trade. But into the 20th Century, this small town remained nothing more than the unimposing rest stop it had always been.

Ride Information

Trail Contacts:
Virginia Power Company

Local Information:
Prince William County/Manassas
Conference and Visitors Bureau
1-800-432-1792
or www.visitpwc.com

Local Events/Attractions:
Civil War Weekends in Manassas, VA—
July, August 1-800-432-1792

Manassas National Battlefield Park
(703) 361-1339
or www.nps.gov/mana/online.htm

Splashdown Water Park
(703) 361-4451

Maps:
USGS maps: Manassas, VA
ADC map: Northern Virginia Road Map

As you pass through Centreville today, however, much of this history may seem very distant and unfamiliar, because the town has suddenly become a sprawling community of subdivisions, shopping centers, and beltway commuters. And it continues to expand at a phenomenal rate further and further west.

Centreville is not unlike many communities surrounding the Washington-Baltimore area that have, in the last 10 to 20 years, seen tremendous growth. This explosive growth has, in most cases, virtually wiped out the smalltown flavor that dominated the region west of the cities. Towns and villages, desperate for so long to attract more people and new businesses, could never have anticipated the recent boom in development, which has transformed these small hamlets into huge bedroom communities for the Washington/Baltimore megalopolis.

With this growth, precious back roads and trails were permanently lost, forcing local off-road cyclists to look even harder for places to ride. Thus, the discovery of the power lines! They may not be scenic mountain roads or offer endless backcountry exploration, but the rugged trails beneath these crackling wires make for the ultimate suburban offroad adventure. Power lines have it all—rocks, ditches, hills, dirt, and most important, open land on which to ride. You'll find yourself crashing down rocky descents, slogging through muddy streambeds, then up and over steep, rutted climbs that snake back and forth beneath the super-charged black cables that bring power to the surrounding homes and neighborhoods.

The most important thing to remember when riding the power lines is that there is *always* a way through the obstacles. Sometimes you just have to find it. Have fun!

MilesDirections

0.0 START at Centreville Elementary School. Travel south along the asphalt path parallel to Centreville Road. This leads you directly to the power lines.

0.2 Turn left off the asphalt path and hit the dirt trails beneath the power lines. Follow the trail on the left side.

0.75 Cross Bay Valley Lane.

0.8 Turn left at the small fenced-in substation, following the secondary power lines that run north along Little Rocky Run Creek to Braddock Road.

2.0 Pass a small park with tennis courts.

2.2 After passing the park, reenter the trail on the right side of the power lines.

2.4 Climb up the embankment at Braddock Road and turn right on the asphalt path. At this point, the trail beneath the power lines disappears as the power lines parallel Braddock Road.

2.8 Turn right on the asphalt bike path along Union Mill Road.

3.1 Centreville High School is on the left.

4.3 The bike path ends. Continue riding along the shoulder. Be careful of traffic.

4.8 At this intersection with Compton Road, go straight through the stop sign, continuing on Union Mill Road. Union Mill Road continues into a new housing development. Follow this to the power lines.

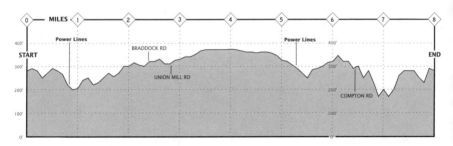

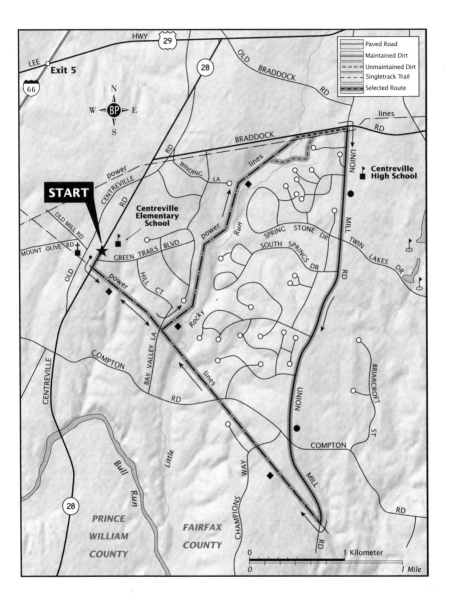

5.3 Turn right off Union Mill Road and ride to the power lines, heading west back to Centreville Road.

6.4 Cross Compton Road.

7.0 Pass the small fenced-in power station on the right. Continue straight. Cross Bay Valley Lane.

7.7 Reach Centreville Road. Turn right on the asphalt bike path back toward the school.

7.8 Arrive back at Centreville Elementary School. Tough ride, huh?

Great Falls National Park

Ride Specs

Start: From the Visitor Center
Length: 7.8 miles
Approximate Riding Time: 1–1½ hours
Difficulty Rating: Moderate due to occasional steep, rocky singletrack
Trail Surface: Rocky, dirt trails and carriage roads
Land Status: National park
Nearest Town: McLean, VA
Other Trail Users: Hikers, equestrians, climbers, kayakers, and tourists
Canine Compatibility: Dogs will love it here—except that they must be kept on a leash. It's a busy park.

Getting There

From the Capital Beltway (I-495): From Exit 13 northwest of McLean, take VA 193 (Georgetown Pike) west toward Great Falls. Go about four miles, then turn right on Old Dominion Road, which becomes the park entrance road. Go one mile to the end of this road and park at the Visitor Center. Telephones, water, food, restrooms, and information available inside the Visitor Center. *DeLorme: Virginia Atlas & Gazetteer: Page,* 76 A-4

G reat Falls is one of the United States' most popular national parks. How appropriate then for it to be located just 14 miles from our nation's capital. And what a thrill for cyclists to know that mountain biking is not only allowed at the park—it's welcome. Great Falls is a natural haven for thousands of Washingtonians seeking solitude from the daily grind of gridlock and government. Trails abound throughout this park on the river, offering cyclists, hikers, and equestrians alike terrain as rugged on land as it is in the water. Some portions of the park's trails are wide, dirt carriage roads dating back through history and meandering through the scenery, while others are steep, rocky, and narrow, keeping even agile cyclists on the tips of their seat.

There are over five miles of designated trails to enjoy in this park, all of which conveniently intersect to create hours of off-road adventure. The trails vary in inten-

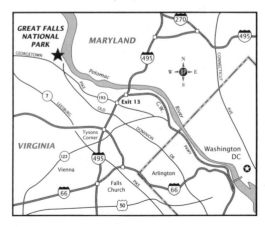

sity, ranging from rolling forest roads beneath tall oaks and maples to steep, rocky singletrack, overlooking the dramatic Mather Gorge. The park's unequaled beauty, proximity to Washington, and accessible trails combine to make Great Falls National Park Northern Virginia's most popular off-road cycling haven.

The ride begins at the visitor center parking lot and travels south along Old Carriage Road through the middle of the park.

Old Carriage was used in the 1700s to carry settlers to their dwellings at Matildaville, ruins of which still stand today. Henry Lee, a Revolutionary War hero and friend of George Washington's developed this small town. Named after Lee's first wife, Matildaville lasted only three decades before fading into history.

The route bends deep into the park and travels up and down the rocky pass along Ridge Trail. During the winter months, breathtaking views of the gorge show through deciduous trees. The trail then descends quickly to the Potomac (another great view) and follows along Difficult Run before heading north again back toward the start.

Great Falls has always been a popular place to visit for locals and world tourists alike. Some have come to survey the river's rapids, including George Washington, who formed the Patowmack Company in 1784 to build a series of canals around the falls. Theodore Roosevelt would come to Great Falls to hike and ride horses during his presidency. Today, thousands come to enjoy Great Falls as well. But they don't come to build canals, develop towns, make trade, or seek solitude from the presidential office. They come only to ride the park's great trails, kayak the rapids, climb the steep cliffs, and bear witness the magnificent scenery at Great Falls National Park.

Ride Information

📞 Trail Contacts:
National Park Service
(703) 759-2915

🕐 Schedule:
Park is open from 7 a.m. to sunset

💲 Fees/Permits
$2 entrance fee

❓ Local Information:
**Fairfax County Convention
and Visitors Bureau**
1-800-7FAIRFAX
or *www.visitfairfax.org*

📍 Local Events/Attractions:
Colvin Run Mill
(703) 759-2771

**Wolf Trap Farm Park
for the Performing Arts**
(703) 255-1800

🍽 Restaurants:
Evans Farm Inn & The Sitting Duck Pub
(703) 356-8000

🗺 Maps:
USGS maps: Vienna, VA Falls Church, VA
ADC map: Northern Virginia road map
**National Park Service Official Trail Map
and Guide**

MilesDirections

0.0 START at Great Falls Visitor Center. Follow the Horse/Biker Trail south along Entrance Road .

0.4 Bear right at the restrooms and go around the steel gate on Old Carriage Road (unpaved).

1.1 Bear left down the trail to Sandy Landing.

1.3 Arrive at Sandy Landing, a beautiful spot along the river, great for viewing Mather Gorge. Return to Old Carriage Road.

1.5 Turn left, continuing on Old Carriage Road. Begin a steady uphill.

1.9 Turn left near the top of this climb on Ridge Trail.

2.7 Turn left after the steep descent on Difficult Run Trail. Head toward the Potomac.

2.9 Arrive at the Potomac River. This is another great spot to view Sherwin Island where Mather Gorge and the Potomac River converge. Turn around and follow Difficult Run Trail west along Difficult Run Creek toward Georgetown Pike.

3.6 Turn right on Georgetown Pike. Be careful with traffic and ride on the dirt shoulder.

3.8 Turn right on Old Carriage Road. This is the first dirt road you come to along Georgetown Pike. Go around the gate and begin climbing.

4.0 Turn left on Ridge Trail. Follow this toward the entrance road.

4.7 Reach Great Falls' entrance road (Old Dominion Road). Turn around and continue back on Ridge Trail.

5.4 Turn left on Old Carriage Road.

6.4 Go through the gate at the beginning of Old Carriage Road and head back to the parking lot at the Visitor Center.

6.8 Arrive back at the Visitor Center and parking lot.

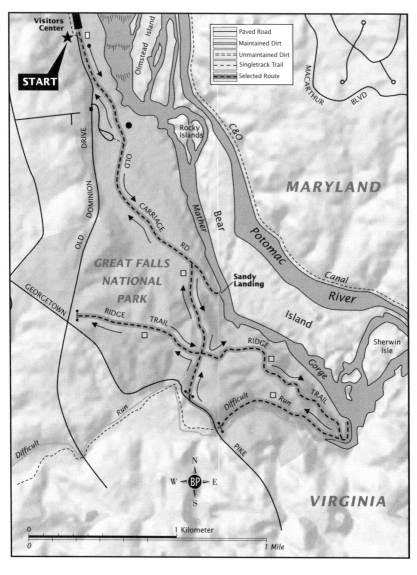

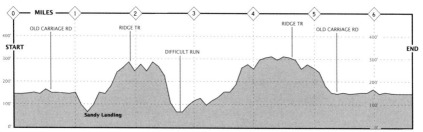

Middleburg Vineyard Tour

Ride Specs

Start: From the Middleburg Elementary School

Length: 23.1 miles

Approximate Riding Time: 2–3 hours (not counting stops at vineyards)

Difficulty Rating: Moderate to difficult (due to length)

Trail Surface: Unpaved dirt and gravel roads

Land Status: Public roads

Nearest Town: Middleburg, VA

Other Trail Users: Motorists and wine-tasters

Canine Compatibility: Your dog will hate you if you take him on this ride. So don't.

Getting There

From the Capital Beltway (I-495): Take I-66 west 8.5 miles to Exit 57, U.S. 50 west. Go 23 miles on U.S. 50 west into Middleburg. John Mosby Highway (U.S. 50) becomes Washington Street within the Middleburg town limits. From Washington Street, turn right on VA 626 (Madison Street). Go 0.1 miles and turn right into the Middleburg Elementary School parking lot. *DeLorme: Virginia Atlas & Gazetteer:* Page 75, A-7

A h, wine! To sip the fruit is lots of fun, but to ride and drink can't be outdone.

Yes, this ride travels through some of Virginia's finest wine country, where visits to the vineyards are always welcome and wine tasting is just part of the tour. Virginia is quickly becoming renown worldwide for its wine. And Loudoun County is home to a number of the Old Dominion's finest wineries. This mostly non-paved (gravel and dirt road) ride is set up to lead cyclists through the area's beautiful rolling horse country, connecting (or passing nearby) a number of Northern Virginia's most productive vineyards. Make plenty of time for this trip and stop often to taste the latest wine.

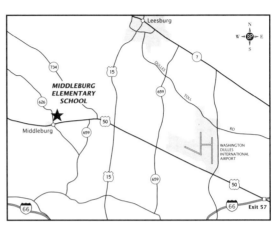

You start in the historic town of Middleburg, a small, touristy outpost in the middle of Hunt Country. Horses abound in this magnificent countryside. A town with a rich history, Middleburg has enjoyed its share of good fortune. Established in 1787, this centuries-old town was even graced by a U.S. president when the John F. Kennedy family attended the local Catholic church and built a home just outside town.

The ride starts on a route toward Piedmont Vineyard but breaks off from the main road onto backcountry dirt, perfect for an off-road tourist. This first section rolls comfortably past small estates and low-key horse farms. But when you turn east, the roads lift you into the hills. You'll pass some of the old and new—abandoned stone houses and state-of-the-art homes—then head toward Meredyth Vineyard to lavish in the land of the well-to-do. Gorgeous estates rest on acres of open land, where thoroughbreds graze in the warm sun. What a wonderful place to ride and dream. But don't forget to stop at the vineyard. (*Their hours are from 10–4 p.m.*) The rest of the ride rolls up and down below Bull Run Mountain, taking you past one more vineyard, the Swedenburg Estate, before leading you back into Middleburg.

If the wine doesn't get the best of you, then enjoy the endless dirt roads scattered throughout this region. This is excellent off-road riding for cyclists looking for a change of pace and scenery.

Mountain Biking and Wine:

If my assumption is correct, many of you are like myself and have never really refined your tastes in good wine. After all, we're mountain bikers for heaven's sake! If such is the case, then you may also find yourselves feeling about as silly and uneducated as I have when the proprietor of a winery serves samples of the vineyard's great variety of wines. You may understand little to none about what this person is talking about, and if you're like me, you politely sip the wine, nod your head at each flavor's description, and wonder how they can arrive at so many names for such similar tastes. Before subjecting yourself to this unnecessary display of embarrassing ignorance and vacant wine tasting, educate yourself a bit and enjoy tasting some of the vineyard's fine products. Hopefully, after reading some of the following information before cycling up to a winery's door, you may quite miraculously understand some of what the proprietor is telling you about his latest flavors and enjoy the samples that much more.

179

The process of making wine—in a nutshell.

White wine: Red and white grapes are stemmed and crushed before going into a horizontal press for more crushing (end plates in the horizontal press move toward each other and crush the grapes). The juice (sans the skin) then flows to a vat for fermenting. The juice has not had time to pick up color from the skins, leaving it white.

Red and rosé wines: The crushed grapes go directly into fermenting vats with their skins. After fermenting, the unpalatable red press wine is mixed with free-run wine.
The dry skins and pulp (called marc) can be distilled into cheap brandy.

Fermentation starts when wine yeast on the skins of ripe grapes come in contact with the grape juice. After running off into casks, the new wine then undergoes a series of chemical processes, including oxidation, precipitation of proteins, and fermentation of chemical compounds. Each of these processes creates the wine's characteristic bouquet (aroma). After periodic clarification and aging in casks, the wine is ready to be bottled.

Wine is the fermented juice of grapes. Nearly all the wine made throughout the world comes from one species of grape—Vitis vinifera. As many as 4,000 varieties of grape have been developed from this one species, each of which differs, sometimes only slightly, from each other in size, color, shape of the berry, juice composition, ripening time, and resistance to disease. Only about a dozen of the 4,000 or more varieties of grapes are commonly used for winemaking around the world. Chiefs among them are: Chardonnay, Riesling, Cabernet Sauvignon, Sauvignon Blanc, Pinot Noir, Gewurztraminer, and Muscat.

The main reason the varieties of Vitis vinifera are used throughout the world in wine production is for their high sugar content when ripe. Wine with an alcohol content of 10 percent or slightly higher is produced from the grapes' natural sugar content after fermentation. Wines with less alcohol are unstable and subject to bacterial spoilage.

Wine Colors

We're all familiar with colors of wine: white wine, rosé, and red wine. But why the different colors and what's the big deal anyway?

- White wine is produced when only the juice from the grape is used. The skin is removed before fermentation begins. The juice is normally colorless, though some varieties have a pink to reddish color. Because only the grape's juice is used, white wine tends to be much sweeter, thus much easier on the palate for most people unfamiliar with drinking wine.
- A rosé is produced when the skins of red or black grapes are removed after fermentation has begun.

- Red wine is produced when whole, crushed red or black grapes are used, including the skins. Red wine is often more bitter and has a stronger taste than white wine.

What are we supposed to eat with this stuff with anyway?

It's suggested that we drink white wines with light foods such as salads, chicken, and fish. Red wines are recommended for heavier flavored foods such as red meat. The reasons are strictly for the palate. A strong tasting red wine may overwhelm the light flavors of chicken or fish, while the sweeter, lighter flavor of white wine may get lost on a hearty, juicy steak. What should cyclists drink with their spaghetti? Either one is fine. Heck, who cares, It's wine!

Where does it come from?

Although Italy produces more wine, the world's leading wine producer in terms of quality is France, with outstanding products from Bordeaux and Burgundy, the Loire and Rhone valleys, and Alsace. Other major producers are Spain, the U.S., Germany, Chile, Argentina, South Africa, and Australia. In the U.S., California is the leading wine-producing region. Central Virginia is a close second.

Ride Information

Trail Contacts:
None

Schedule:
Meredith Vineyard 10 a.m.–5 p.m., 7 days a week

Piedmont Vineyard 10 a.m.–4 p.m., 7 days a week

Swedenburg Vineyard 10 a.m.–4 p.m., 7 days a week

Fees/Permits
$3–$5 per winery for wine tastings. Call in advance for current prices.

Local Information:
Loudoun Tourism Council
1-800-752-6118

Local Events/Attractions:
Meredyth Vineyard
(540) 687-6277

Piedmont Vineyard
(540) 687-5528
or www.piedmontwines.com

Swedenburg Estate Vineyard
540) 687-5219

Local Bike Shops:
Bicycle Outfitters
Leesburg, VA
(703) 777-6126

Maps:
USGS maps: Rectortown, VA; Middleburg, VA
ADC map: Loudoun County road map; **Fauquier County road map**

MilesDirections

0.0 START at the Middleburg Elementary School parking lot. Turn left on VA 626, Madison Street. (paved)

0.1 Turn right on Washington Street (U.S. 50). (paved)

0.3 Turn left on Plains Road (VA 626). Follow the purple vineyard sign. (paved)

1.1 Turn right on VA 705. (paved)

1.2 VA 705 changes to dirt. (unpaved)

3.2 Stay straight on VA 705 at this intersection. VA 706 turns right.

3.4 Stay right on VA 705 at this intersection. VA 706 turns left.

4.2 Turn left at the T, continuing on VA 705. VA 708 goes right. (unpaved)

5.3 Turn left at the stop sign on VA 702. (unpaved)

7.6 Turn left on VA 626. (paved)

7.9 Bear right on VA 679 at the bottom of the descent. This turns into VA 628.

9.1 Turn left on VA 628. This is slightly hidden. The turn comes after a long rock wall on the left, just past a large brick house with three chimneys. (unpaved)

9.4 Meredith Vineyards on the left. Stop in for a tour. Hours are from 10 a.m. to 4 p.m.

11.5 Turn right on Landmark School Road (VA 776). (paved)

For those who have had enough, you can turn left on Landmark School Road and take the shortcut back to Middleburg. 2.4 miles.

13.2 Turn left on Champe Ford Road (VA 629). (unpaved)

17.1 Turn left on John Mosby Highway (U.S. 50). Be careful of traffic. (paved)

17.5 Turn right on Cobb House Road (VA 629). (unpaved)

18.5 Turn left on Snickersville Road. (paved)

18.8 Turn left at the bottom of the hill on Carouters Farm Road (VA 627). (unpaved)

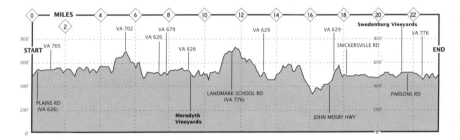

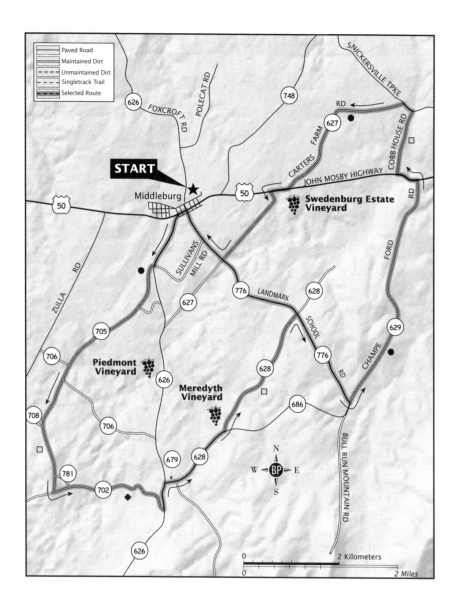

21.3 Turn right on John Mosby Highway (U.S. 50). (paved)
Pass Swedenburg Estate Vineyard. Stop for a sip of wine before continuing on.
21.5 Turn left on Parsons Road (VA 627). (unpaved)

22.6 Turn right on Landmark School Road (VA 776). (paved)
23.0 Arrive back in Middleburg. Cross Washington Street to Madison Street.
23.1 Turn right into the school parking lot. Drink too much wine?

Honorable Mentions

Northern Virginia

Compiled here is an index of great rides in Northern Virginia that didn't make the A-list this time around but deserve recognition. Check them out and let us know what you think. You may decide that one or more of these rides deserves higher status in future editions or, perhaps, you may have a ride of your own that merits some attention.

(H) Burke Lake Park Ride

It's called Burke Lake Park Ride, but this 7.3-mile route starts from South Run District Park and follows a scenic paved bike and hike path through the woods along South Run to get to Burke Lake. Obviously, cyclists don't have to go this route and can choose to start from Burke Lake Park directly, but the section from South Run Park adds a bit more dimension to the overall cycling experience.

This ride isn't designed for thrill seekers and singletrack lovers. Instead, it reveals the lighter side of off-road bicycle riding, leading cyclists on a pleasant off-road trip past flower gardens and lakeside vistas. The route is mostly flat and smooth, traveling along well maintained dirt paths around Burke Lake or meandering along South Run on a paved bicycle path. If you get eager to take on some rough stuff, simply cut out from the South Run bicycle path near South Run District Park and take on the rugged, hilly singletrack beneath the power lines. There's plenty for off-road cyclists to do along this easy route to and from Burke Lake, so bring the family and enjoy the ride.

To get there from the Capital Beltway, take I-95 south toward Richmond. Go only about 0.5 miles and take Springfield Exit 57, Old Keene Mill Road (VA 644 West). Follow Old Keene Mill Road west three miles, then turn left on Huntsman Boulevard. Follow Huntsman Boulevard 1.5 miles to the Fairfax County Parkway (VA 7100). Turn right on the Fairfax County Parkway, travel about 0.3 miles, and turn left into South Run District Park. Parking, water, phones, restrooms, and showers are available at the South Run Recreation Center. *DeLorme: Virginia Atlas & Gazetteer:* Page 76, B-3; *Mountain Bike America: Washington-Baltimore*, Ride 36.

ⓘ South Run Power Lines

A classic "power lines" ride if ever there was such a thing, this series of trails south of South Run District Park offers up some of the gnarliest singletrack in all of Northern Virginia. Steep climbs, deep-rutted singletrack, muddy bogs, and stream crossings provide the make-up for the section of trails beneath the power lines. As an added bonus, cyclists can continue from the power lines at Hampton Road (turn right on Hampton Road) and head down to Fountainhead Regional Park where more singletrack awaits the eager cyclists [See Fountainhead Regional Park, Ride 20]. Lately, the South Run Power Lines have been getting a bad rap thanks to all of the housing developments popping up on all sides. And the fact that Virginia Power has been posting "No Trespassing" signs throughout doesn't bode well for cyclists in the area. Nevertheless, the trails beneath the power lines are still a favorite among local cyclists and pose nothing short of a great ride.

To get there from the Capital Beltway, take Interstate 95 south toward Richmond. Go only about 0.5 miles and take Springfield Exit 57, Old Keene Mill Road (VA 644 West). Follow Old Keene Mill Road west three miles, then turn left on Huntsman Boulevard. Follow Huntsman Boulevard 1.5 miles to the Fairfax County Parkway (VA 7100). Turn right on the Fairfax County Parkway, travel about 0.3 miles, and turn left into South Run District Park. Parking, water, phones, restrooms, and showers are available at the South Run Recreation Center. **DeLorme: *Virginia Atlas & Gazetteer*:** Page 76, B-3; *Mountain Bike America: Washington-Baltimore*, Ride 34.

(J) Difficult Run Trail (Glade to Great Falls)

This 12-mile point-to-point route from the Twin Branches Trail in Reston, Virginia, to Great Falls National Park on the Potomac may define what could someday become a new breed of non-paved trail systems through the ever-growing and increasingly paved suburban landscape of Northern Virginia. Combining a mixture of clay-surfaced singletrack, bike paths, public parkland, and creek corridors, this ride follows what is perhaps the longest, most unique trail system in the Washington/Baltimore region. Mountain bikers will love it.

To get to the start of this ride from the Capital Beltway, take the Washington-Dulles Access Road (toll road) west for seven miles to Exit 5, Hunter Mill Road. Go south on Hunter Mill Road to Sunrise Valley Road and turn right. Go half a mile and turn left on South Lakes Drive. Turn left on Twin Branches Road. Follow Twin Branches Road to Glade Drive and park. Twin Branches Trail starts here. *DeLorme: Virginia Atlas & Gazetteer:* Page 76, A-3; *Mountain Bike America: Washington-Baltimore,* Ride 32.

(K) C&O Canal Towpath

Here's a ride for those slow-twitch muscle types who can ride on and on and on and on without so much as a need to stop and fill up the water bottle once or twice. With 185 miles of off-road riding in one fell-swoop (and this is just one way), the C&O canal towpath is one ride sure to challenge those who thrive on endurance activities. But few (in fact, almost none) of the cyclists who take to the canal each year attempt to ride the entire distance at once. However, anyone looking for a great trip along the Potomac River (leaving right from Georgetown) with virtually no elevation gain in sight should love this ride. Try it in sections, camp overnight, stay at some of the inns along the way to Cumberland, Maryland, or just ride up and down the canal near the city. Either way, it's a jewel for cyclists looking for an endless trip off the beaten path that leaves right from town.

To get there from downtown DC, start from the White House and head toward Georgetown. Take Pennsylvania Avenue NW toward Georgetown. Go 11 blocks to M Street, turn left into Georgetown, then go two blocks to Thomas Jefferson Street. Turn left on Thomas Jefferson Street. The Georgetown C&O Canal Visitor Center is here. This is the beginning of a great adventure. ***DeLorme: Maryland Atlas & Gazetteer:*** Page 46, C3; *Mountain Bike America: Washington-Baltimore*, Ride 40.

Western

George Washington National Forest

Jefferson National Forest

Virginia

25 Elizabeth Furnace

Ride Specs

Start: From the opposite campground
Length: 13.3-mile loop
Approximate Riding Time: 3–5 hours
Difficulty Rating: Difficult. Bring full-suspension, extra tubes, and a lot of fitness. This is a ride your girlfriend won't appreciate.
Trail Surface: Mountainous, rocky singletrack and forest roads
Land Status: National forest
Nearest Town: Front Royal, VA
Other Trail Users: Hikers and equestrians
Canine Compatibility: Dog friendly

Getting There

From Front Royal: Take VA 55 approximately five miles west to Waterlick. From Waterlick take Fort Valley Road (VA 678) southwest for 4.5 miles to the overnight camping area on the left and gravel parking area on the right. Turn right into the gravel parking area. Park here. *DeLorme: Virginia Atlas & Gazetteer.* Page 74, A-2

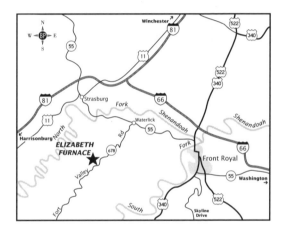

I won't lie to anyone out there. This is a tough ride. Folks new to the sport will hate it unless they turn around at Strasburg Reservoir and stay away from Signal Knob and the Green Mountain climb. People come here all the time to tame the steeps and conquer the rocky descents on their high-end full suspension bikes. They usually fail.

So why do so many cyclists keep coming back year-round, winter, spring, summer, and fall? Simply put, Elizabeth Furnace is home to some of the best all-around mountain bike trails in all of Northern Virginia. Bar none. It's steep. It's dangerous. It's long. It's fast. It's a blast.

Located about one hour west of Washington, DC, just outside Front Royal, Virginia, the tall, northern ridge of Massanutten Mountain stands alone, high above the Shenandoah Valley. Mountain bikers come in droves to this northeastern piece of the George Washington National Forest to test their skills, endurance, and patience on its tricky ridgelines, rocky singletrack, and brutal climbs. It's easy to understand why this piece of mountain is Northern Virginia's Marilyn Monroe of mountain bike destinations. Cyclists just love it.

Just grin and bear it!

Its proximity to Washington makes it the closest bikeable mountain for peak-starved Northern Virginia off-roaders. Elizabeth Furnace's many trails travel along and through small creeks, up and down mountain ridges, and to paths where even the most hard-core rock huggers have difficulty keeping the rubber side down. But let's not overlook the softer side of Elizabeth Furnace. This off-road cycling sanc-

Even if you have to push, the climb is worth the effort.

tuary is not all difficult. There are a bunch of forest roads that travel through Fort Valley, the scenic hollow cradled between the east and west ridges of Massanutten Mountain (had he been defeated at the Battle of Yorktown, George Washington would have used this valley as a retreat). And most of the steep sections can be avoided by turning back at Strasburg Reservoir before committing yourself to the tortuous climbs to Signal Knob or to the top of Green Mountain. Most of the ride up to Strasburg Reservoir is only moderately difficult, and if you're not feeling particularly adventurous, just turn around and follow the trails back to the start.

The ride starts from the gravel parking lot off Fort Valley Road and progresses rather easily along Forest Service Road 1350. Past the gates, the forest road becomes overgrown, rolling up and down the ridgeline as it makes its way over Green Mountain. There are some wonderful views of Fort Valley and Massanutten Mountain from this road. Approximately three miles later, Forest Service Road 1350 ends in what resembles a large, dirt cul-de-sac overrun by with small pine trees and tall grass.

You'll notice a worn trail descending into the woods at the end of this cul-de-sac. This trail takes you to Little Passage Creek. Turn right and follow the creek to Massanutten Mountain Road. You'll cross through the creek five times, so be prepared to get wet. This road leads to Strasburg Reservoir, a good place to turn around if you'd prefer to avoid the steep, rocky ascents and blistering downhills that follow. For those with a conquering spirit, though, I heartily recommend making the push to reach Signal Knob. You may end up hiking it most of the way, but it's worth it.

Signal Knob's 2,106-foot peak reveals a sweeping panoramic view of the Shenandoah Valley. During the Civil War, Confederate soldiers used the peak to spot Union troops moving south from Winchester. Soldiers hiked what is now the orange-blazed Massanutten Mountain West Trail and searched the valleys below for troop movement. Any information was subsequently flagged from Signal Knob to points farther south. This information would eventually reach the Confederate capitol of Richmond. This didn't, however, stop Union troops from making Fort Valley and its iron-producing furnaces a regular target, wreaking havoc on its mines, furnaces, and farmland.

The reward! Views of the Shenandoah Valley from atop Signal Knob.

Ride Information

📞 Trail Contacts:
Lee Ranger District
George Washington National Forest
(540) 984-4101 or 984-4102

George Washington National Forest Headquarters
(703) 564-8300

Potomac Appalachian Trail Club (PATC)
(703) 242-0693
or *www.patc.net*

🕐 Schedule:
Public land, accessible year-round.

🛏 Accommodations:
Camping is available at the Elizabeth Furnace Recreation Area. Primitive camping is available in the surrounding George Washington National Forest.

🚲 Local Bike Shops:
Sarah Zane Bicycle Co.
Winchester
(540) 662-7654

Element Sports
Winchester
(540) 662-5744

🅝 Maps:
USGS maps: Strasburg, VA; Toms Brook, VA
George Washington National Forest topo map: Lee Ranger District
National Forest Service trail map

Hunting Season

Be very careful when riding out here during hunting season, which begins in the fall. For opening and closing dates for the current hunting season, call the Virginia Department of Game and Inland Fisheries (540) 248-9360 or go to www.dgif.state.va.us.

Most of the Massanutten Mountain West Trail is challenging but still very rideable. It isn't until the climb's final 500 feet does pedaling a bike become something more akin to hallucination than reality. Walking, for some, becomes the only alternative. BUT KEEP GOING! The view from the top, and the subsequent descent, is worth the effort.

On the return trip, grip your brakes and hang low over your rear wheel in order to conquer this double-black-diamond descent. It's quite possible to ride back down the Orange Trail. But be fairly warned of possible misfortune. Watch for trail signs on the way down from Signal Knob that direct you to the blue-blazed Bear Wallow Trail. The rewards for cycling Bear Wallow Trail over Green Mountain are enormous once on top of Meneka Peak, but these rewards must be earned. After crossing over a small creek, Bear Wallow heads straight toward the sky over rocks, roots, and ridges. Over the top, the woods become dense and dark where larger trees grow thick and swallow up the light. Despite its foreboding appearance, the trail repays your strident efforts with an exhilarating, downhill run all the way back to the car.

Be prepared to spend anywhere from two to five hours on these trails, so bring plenty of food and water. Tools and extra tubes may also be necessary baggage, considering the nature of some of these trails. Ride hard and have fun!

MilesDirections

0.0 START from the gravel parking lot opposite the Elizabeth Furnace Recreation Area and overnight campground. Ride west through the first gate out of the parking lot and follow FS (Forest Service Road) 1350 to the right.

0.1 Go through the second gate, continuing up FS 1350.

0.2 Pass the Bear Wallow Trail trailhead on the right. This takes you up to Signal Knob. Continue on FS 1350.

1.4 Reach the end of the first steady climb. FS 1350 starts to roll more. From this old wagon trail, once used in the 1840s to transport pig iron to Elizabeth Furnace, you can see across Fort Valley to the eastern ridge of Massanutten Mountain. Fall colors are brilliant along this route.

2.6 Begin the fun descent toward Mudhole Gap and Little Passage Creek.

3.3 FS 1350 ends in what resembles a large, dirt cul-de-sac overgrown with small pine and scrub. At the opposite end of this open area is a trail leading straight into the woods. Take this short, rocky trail downhill to Little Passage Creek.

3.35 Bear right along the creek, traveling upstream through Mudhole Gap. Stay on the trail that runs parallel with Little Passage Creek. There are five stream crossings along this trail between here and FS 66.

3.6 First stream crossing.

3.65 Second stream crossing.

3.8 Third stream crossing.

3.9 Fourth stream crossing.

4.1 Fifth stream crossing. Go around the gate after this last stream crossing, then turn

right on FS 66 (orange blaze). This dirt road heads north toward Strasburg Reservoir and Signal Knob.

6.1 Pass a trailhead for a trail traveling to Signal Knob on the left. Both FS 66 and this wet, slightly overgrown trail lead to Strasburg Reservoir and meet again on the west bank of the lake.

6.3 Following FS 66 — Reach the Strasburg Reservoir. Turn left and cross the dam.

6.4 Once on the other side of the dam, bear right with the shoreline. Go another 20 yards along the western shoreline until the trail next to the reservoir appears to end at an embankment. Hop over a large rock, push the bike up the embankment, and discover yourself on the Massanutten Mountain West Trail (orange blaze).

7.0 Pass Bear Wallow Trail (blue blaze) on the right. From this point up to Signal Knob things get pretty steep and difficult.

8.1 Trail goes vertical! The trail becomes little more than a rockslide, scaling up to the top of the mountain toward Signal Knob. If you can, push yourself to get to the top. Signal Knob is well worth this extra effort.

8.3 Reach Signal Knob (2,106 feet). Whew! Catch a sweeping view of the Shenandoah Valley. The town of Strasburg is on the left. Return back down Massanutten Mountain West toward Bear Wallow Trail. *[Alternate route down from Signal Knob: Follow Signal Knob Trail (yellow) from the radio tower to Meneka Peak Trail (white), which then cuts back over to Bear Wallow Trail (blue) and heads back to the start. Beware the Yellow*

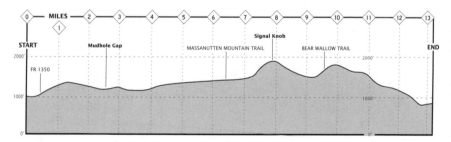

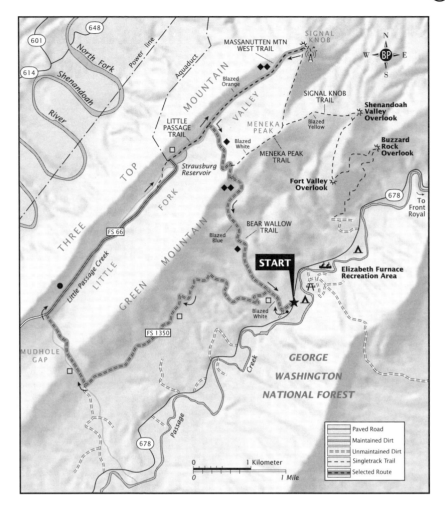

Trail from top to bottom. This trail become mostly unrideable and shouldering your bike will get really old after all the riding you've already done.]

8.5 Steep, rocky section ends. Trail becomes a more negotiable singletrack.

9.6 Turn left on Bear Wallow Trail (blue blaze). Begin a grueling, switchback climb to the top of Green Mountain.

10.3 Reach the top of Green Mountain. To the left is Meneka Peak Trail (white blaze). Start the descent back down to Elizabeth Furnace, continuing on Bear Wallow Trail (blue blaze).

10.7 Overlook to Fort Valley.

12.1 Pass the Glass House Trail on the right. Continue straight on Bear Wallow Trail (blue blaze).

12.9 Reach the bottom of a wild descent at the intersection with the blue and white-blazed trails. Turn right, following the White-Blazed Trail back to FS 1350. The blue-blazed trail travels left across a small creek to Elizabeth Furnace picnic grounds.

13.1 Turn left on FS 1350, heading back to the car.

13.2 Go around the gate.

13.3 Arrive at the parking lot. Hope you survived the climb over Green Mountain.

Massanutten Mountain

Ride Specs

Start: From the steel gate on VA 636 at Runkles Gap
Length: 30-mile out-and-back
Approximate Riding Time: 2–3 hours
Difficulty Rating: Physically moderate due to length and extended climbing. Technically easy as most of the route is on well-maintained gravel and dirt roads.
Trail Surface: Rolling gravel forest roads
Land Status: National forest
Nearest Town: Harrisonburg, VA
Other Trail Users: Motorists (very few if any)
Canine Compatibility: Not good. This long gravel road ride may tear up his pads.

Getting There

From Harrisonburg: Take U.S. 33 east for 11 miles toward Massanutten Mountain. Just past the entrance for the resort area, turn left on VA 602 and go about five miles to Greenwood. At Greenwood, turn left on Cub Run Road (VA 636) and follow this two miles up Massanutten Mountain into George Washington National Forest. Start at the National Forest boundary where the road changes to gravel. *DeLorme: Virginia Atlas & Gazetteer:* Page 67, A-6

M assanutten is probably best known for its four-seasons resort, 18-hole PGA golf course, and 68 acres of downhill skiing. Nonetheless, this private resort area, located 15 minutes east of Harrisonburg, encompasses only the southern tip of this unique mountain which stretches along the Shenandoah Valley from Harrisonburg all the way north to Front Royal. The remaining land on Massanutten Mountain is contained within the boundaries of the George Washington National Forest and is full of great public land on which to explore. More than 90 percent of the mountain is open to mountain bikers, although much of the rideable terrain is along old forest roads and wide doubletrack. While it may not be the downhiller's mountain of choice or the extreme singletrack destination (very little extreme terrain is available unless you go north to Elizabeth Furnace or can somehow pedal along the sin-

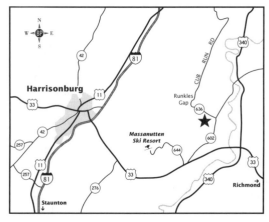

gletrack at Massanutten Resort), it is nonetheless a great place for extended overnight trips and long, leisurely off-road rambles.

Massanutten Mountain is part of the 182,000-acre Lee Ranger District of the George Washington National Forest. The mountain covers roughly one-third of that land and stands apart from the rest of the national forest in the center of the Shenandoah Valley. Bordering Massanutten on the east are Shenandoah National

There are lots of trails on Massanutten Mountain, including a whole network at Massanutten Four-Seasons Resort.

Park and the Blue Ridge Mountains; to the west lie the Allegheny Mountains. Massanutten's lonely place within the Shenandoah Valley, its proximity to Harrisonburg, and its unique plow-headed shape make it a landmark for all who travel through Virginia's heartland.

Much of your ride will be along Cub Run and Pitt Spring Run.

In the late 1800s and early 1900s much of Massanutten Mountain was being mined for iron ore. During that time most of the mountain's southern half was stripped bare of its trees. Later, during the mountain's recovery, a forestry official declared he could not find a single tree more than six inches in diameter.

Since that time, the mountain has managed to recover quite handsomely, with thick forests now covering its craggy slopes. The legacy left by those mining operations is a myriad of old dirt roads and trails used to transport iron ore and other supplies to the many different iron furnaces, including Catherine Furnace and Elizabeth Furnace. These roads and trails are now owned and maintained by the National Forest Service for public use.

This relatively non-technical ride starts from the southern end of Massanutten Mountain near Harrisonburg and travels north through its core, revealing the mountain's scenic beauty from a well-maintained gravel road. The route starts from the national forest boundary on Virginia 636. The road then becomes gravel and hard-packed dirt.

198

You begin with a moderate climb up the mountain through Runkles Gap. The route rolls up and down along Cub Run Road for approximately one mile before descending into the mountain's inner valley along the cascading Cub Run. Just before mile 9.0, Cub Run intersects with Pitt Spring Run and Roaring Run, both of which turn east and rush downhill before running into the Shenandoah River's south fork. Turn left at this intersection and follow Forest Service Road 375 uphill along the beautiful Pitt Spring Run (toward the radio towers).

The climb is a workout, but the scenic waterfalls and mountain cliffs provide a wonderful distraction along this route. Don't expect much of an overlook once you reach the radio towers. The trees are pretty thick and you'll have to hike around to find the best view. However, if you do get a good glimpse through the trees you can see to the west over the great Shenandoah Valley and the town of Timberville. To the east, Page Valley and the South Fork Shenandoah River are also visible.

The technical difficulty of this ride is fairly minimal. For cyclists wanting a peaceful ride far-removed from the motorized world, though, this is just the place for a quiet and scenic afternoon. To further augment this leisurely ride, bring a lunch and relax along the cascades of Cub Run at one of the many small picnic areas and parking areas along the way.

Ride Information

Trail Contacts:
Lee Ranger District
George Washington National Forest
(540) 984-4101

George Washington National Forest Headquarters
(703) 564-8300

Schedule:
Public Land, accessible year-round

Local Events /Attractions:
Massanutten Four-Seasons Resort
1-800-207-MASS
or www.massresort.com

Bill's Barbecue on U.S. 33 just before turning up VA 602 toward Massanutten Resort. Great barbecue!

Local Bike Shops:
Blue Ridge Cycle Works
Harrisonburg
(540) 433-0323

Wilderness Voyagers
Harrisonburg
(540) 434-7234

Maps:
USGS maps: Elkton West, VA; Tenth Legion, VA
George Washington National Forest topo map: Lee Ranger District

The familiar plow-headed peak of Massanutten Mountain rises above the Shenandoah Valley.

MilesDirections

0.0 START along VA 636 at the George Washington National Forest boundary. Park your car on the side of the road and head up the east side of Massanutten Mountain on Cub Run Road (VA 636).

0.1 Go through the gate. Cub Run Road turns to gravel and become FS 65.

0.8 Pass through Runkles Gap.

2.3 Reach the top of the first climb (2,152 feet).

7.7 Pass a campground on the right.

9.2 Reach the intersection of Cub Run Road and FS 375. Turn left on FS 375. *[**Note:** Go straight for 0.25 miles to reach Catherine Furnace. This is one of the old iron furnaces used in the late 1800s to convert iron ore*

mined on Massanutten Mountain into usable plate iron.]

14.5 Reach the gate just before the radio towers. Go around this gate and continue up the mountain to the summit.

15.0 Reach the summit of Big Mountain (one of the peaks of Massanutten Mountain) at 2,962 feet. From this high point you can peak through the trees and see parts of the Shenandoah Valley to the west and Page Valley to the east. The radio tower is owned and operated by WSVA–TV. From the summit, turn around, enjoy the descent to Catherine Furnace, and return to the start of the ride the same way you came.

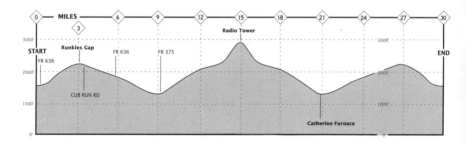

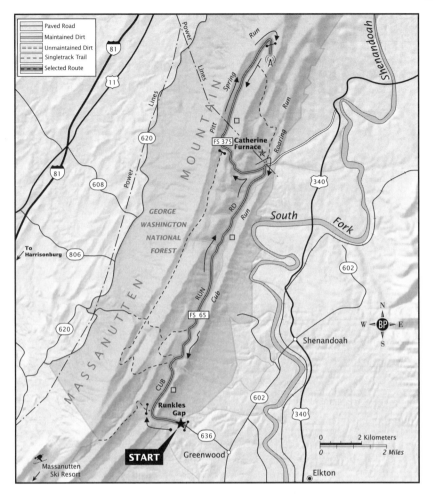

Massanutten Four-Seasons Resort

Cyclists on the southern edge of Massanutten Mountain looking for more of a challenge should consider Massanutten Mountain Resort, which opens the property on their western slope during certain times of the year for off-road cyclists. Guests and residents of the resort are welcome to ride here year-round. Call the resort for more information about mountain biking on their property and ask for a schedule of events. They also have a detailed map of their western slope trail system. Massanutten has recently held such prestigious events as the Grundig/World Cup Downhill Race and various amateur cross-country mountain bike races. 1-800-207-MASS or www.massresort.com

Virginia's National Forests

The Commonwealth of Virginia is blessed with an abundance of national forest land. Nearly 1.7 million acres of public land was set aside in Virginia in the early 1900s; today forests, lakes, mountain meadows, wildlife, vistas, and scenic wonders await all who wish to explore its endless beauty.

The real treasure of the national forests, however, is that every acre is open to the public. This means that you don't need the landowner's permission to travel on any of the thousands of miles of trails and dirt roads.

In Virginia, there are two national forests that make up the state's huge parcel of public land: the George Washington National Forest and the Jefferson National Forest.

The George Washington National Forest has over one million acres, 945,000 of which are in Virginia. It extends over 140 miles along the Appalachian Mountains in Northwestern Virginia and attracts nearly four million visitors per year. Within this forest are more than 800 miles of trails open to mountain biking. Endless miles of dirt forest roads connect these trails, which wind up and down the mountain slopes and through the many valleys. In addition, camping is allowed at undeveloped sites almost anywhere within forest boundaries.

The Jefferson National Forest has 690,000 acres of wooded mountains and valleys. It covers much of the state's southwestern portion, from the James River south to Mount Rogers. There are over 900 miles of trails and dirt forest roads open to mountain biking.

Located within the Jefferson National Forest is Mount Rogers National Recreation Area. More than 115,000 acres make up this mountainous wonderland, home to Virginia's two highest peaks—Mount Rogers (5729 feet) and Whitetop Mountain (5520 feet). There are over 400 miles of trails open to bike travel, all of which wind through the valleys and atop the highest peaks. Mountain biking is welcome throughout the Mount Rogers National Recreation Area, and because it is within national forest land, camping is allowed at undeveloped sites almost anywhere.

It's important to note that there are some restricted areas and trails within Virginia's national forests that allow only foot and horseback travel. Mountain bikers cannot ride on the Appalachian Trail under any circumstances and are also restricted from riding in any of the national forest's Wilderness Areas. None of the rides in this guide use either the Appalachian Trail or Wilderness Areas.

The rides included in this book are considered by many cyclists and forest rangers to be some of the more popular places and trails on which to ride in the national forests. While virtually all the trails and forest roads in both the George Washington and Jefferson National Forests are open to everyone, the rides in this guide attempt to avoid routes that might be sensitive to overuse or yield user conflicts. Like all places, however, bicyclists must always yield the right-of-way and tread lightly.

Second Mountain

Ride Specs

Start: From the intersection of trails on FS 72, 6-miles uphill from VA 612

Length: 4.3-mile out-and-back

Approximate Riding Time: 1½ hours, depending on your level of adventure for the day

Difficulty Rating: Moderate. The trails are wide due to the use of 4WD vehicles and are very rocky.

Trail Surface: There are several roller coaster sections with terrific downhills.

Land Status: National forest

Nearest Town: Rawley Springs, VA

Other Trail Users: ORVs

Canine Compatibility: Dog friendly

Getting There

From Harrisonburg: Drive U.S. 33 West toward Rawley Springs. Before Rawley Springs turn right onto VA 612. Continue on VA 612 until you see a national park sign on the left for ORV access. Turn left onto FS 72. Make sure your vehicle has adequate ground clearance to make this six-mile climb to the trail intersection. *DeLorme: Virginia Atlas & Gazetteer:* Page 72, D-3

Second Mountain is a mecca for local riders from the Harrisonburg area. Even though the grounds are shared with many motorcyclists and 4WD enthusiasts, there is an ample amount of acreage to go around. Many of the trails are not as popular with motorized traffic so these trails can be explored with great vigor. The roller coaster theme weighs heavy and the extent of damage is fairly minimal. These trails were transformed from their original function as fire roads into recreational access roads. This gives ATV enthusiasts a chance to get on the trail but also limits their trail usage.

Make sure you have a vehicle with good ground clearance if you choose to drive to the top. Also, make sure you pack plenty of water because you'll be in a really remote area. Camping at the top can be rewarding if you've got a clear night and can take in the stars. The elevation affords spectacular views of the surrounding George Washington National Park.

These ORV trails make mountain biking here on Second Mountain a real challenge. But it's a blast!

When you arrive at the base of Forest Service Road 72, which takes you to the top, there will be a large brown sign with Smokey the Bear on it. From there it's six miles to the top. Along the way you can experiment with any of the side roads. Most likely smaller motorized vehicles will occupy them. Forest Service Road 72 is surprisingly smooth, but runoff has caused a few deep ruts that may not be cleared by low profile vehicles. But if you can make it, it's a spectacular ride to the top. There's a mixture of exposed rock that consists of loose shale, limestone, and granite. Most of the switchbacks have steep inclines of worn rock that have obviously been scaled by trucks. Be careful while making your way around each bend because you could unexpectedly meet one of these trucks.

The intersection of trails at the top are marked clearly with small, vertical, brown signs that identify the trail name. As you venture onto the Second Mountain Trail you'll notice a maintained gravel parking area for vehicles with trailers. This area has a directional sign and points of reference. This is where Forest Service Road 442 (Dictum Ridge) joins with U.S. Route 33.

MilesDirections

0.0 START by riding south on Second Mountain Trail (FS 502). Go past the gate and climb an immediate but slight uphill section.

0.4 This area is full of technical sections of rolling up hills and down hills.

0.8 Come to a gravel parking lot for trucks with ORV trailers and a trail intersection called Clines Hacking. Continue straight on Second Mountain Trail. The spur on the right is Dictum Ridge Trail (FS 442).

1.5 Continue straight past the spur on the left.

2.1 Cross under power lines.

2.2 Continue straight past the spur on the right.

2.3 Continue straight past the spur on the right.

3.2 Continue straight past the spur on the left.

3.3 Cross under power lines again.

6.0 Reach the trail's end at U.S. 33. Take a right onto U.S. 33 to reach your shuttle vehicle. Be cautious of traffic.

6.6 Reach the parking lot and your vehicle.

Loop Option: *Instead of ending the ride at the Riven Rock picnic area, follow the signs and take a right off of U.S. 33 onto Dictum Ridge Trail. Dictum Ridge Trail is a rutted, rocky, and reasonably steep forest road which leads back up to Clines Hacking. From Clines Hacking it is less than a mile to the start of the ride.*

Alternate Start: *For those of you who don't have 4WD, here is a loop option. Park and start your ride from the Riven Rock picnic area off of U.S. 33. You then have a choice of how to do the loop. You may either start up the Dictum Ridge Trail and then fly down the Second Mountain Trail, or vice versa.*

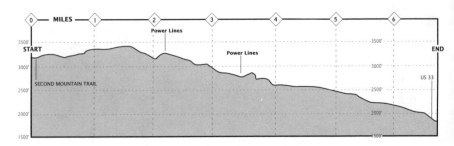

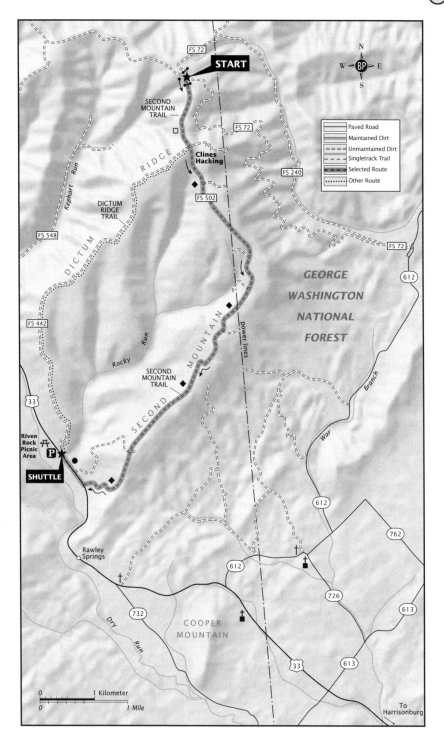

Paved Road
Maintained Dirt
Unmaintained Dirt
Singletrack Trail
Selected Route
Other Route

START

FS 72

SECOND
MOUNTAIN
TRAIL

Clines
Hacking

FS 72

FS 240

FS 72

FS 502

612

GEORGE

WASHINGTON

DICTUM
RIDGE
TRAIL

NATIONAL

FS 548

FOREST

DICTUM

Kephart Run

RIDGE

FS 442

Rocky Run

power lines

SECOND

MOUNTAIN

War Branch

SECOND
MOUNTAIN
TRAIL

33

Riven
Rock
Picnic
Area

P

SHUTTLE

612

762

Rawley
Springs

612

726

613

732

COOPER

MOUNTAIN

33

613

0   1 Kilometer

0   1 Mile

To
Harrisonburg

Large granite boulders challenge your technical ability as you pass the power lines. The fine, sandy powder that coats most of the flat-rock sections can be very slippery. This rock exposure supplies an element of smoothness that keeps you on your toes. When passing through the roller coaster-like sections, be observant of your speed. The excitement may tempt you to jump, but you can be sure that the other side hides a dangerous boulder or two. If you cling to either side of the trail, the passage should be much smoother.

Ride Information

🛈 Trail Contacts:
George Washington National Forest
Roanoke, VA
(540) 564-8300

🕐 Schedule:
Open year-round, weather permitting, but best from April through November.

❓ Local Information:
Harrisonburg-Rockingham
Convention & Visitors Bureau
Harrisonburg, VA
(540) 433-2293

📍 Local Events/Attractions:
Court Square Theater
Harrisonburg, VA
(540) 433-9188

James Madison University
Harrisonburg, VA
(540) 568-6211
or *www.jmu.edu*

Eastern Mennonite University
Harrisonburg, VA
(540) 432-4159
or *www.emu.edu*

🛏 Accommodations:
Boxwood Bed and Breakfast
Hinton, VA
(540) 867-5772

🚲 Local Bike Shops:
Cradle Mountain Ski, Skate & Golf
Harrisonburg, VA
(540) 433-7201

Blue Ridge Cycle Works
Harrisonburg, VA
(540) 432-0280

🅽 Maps:
USGS maps: Rawley Springs, VA

Returning to the trailhead, you have the option of going into the Gauley Ridge Valley or riding out the Forest Service Road 72 until you reach Feedstone Mountain. Even tooling around the parking area is enough to keep anyone occupied until the cows come home.

Harrisonburg is part of the Shenandoah Driving Tour and should be considered for those who are a long distance from home. Named after Thomas Harrison and established in 1780, Harrisonburg is home to James Madison University and Eastern Mennonite College and Seminary. There are many choices for nightly entertainment in the area, and many of the hotspots host live bands and a wide range of frothy refreshments.

28

Blueberry Trail

Ride Specs

Start: From the signed trailhead on VA 742, west of Harrisonburg
Length: 4.1-mile loop
Approximate Riding Time: 1 hour
Difficulty Rating: Moderate. The few technical uphill sections are overshadowed by the superior downhill to the finish.
Trail Surface: Relatively smooth with technical uphill and fast water bars
Land Status: National forest
Nearest Town: Ottobine, VA
Other Trail Users: Hikers
Canine Compatibility: Dog friendly

Getting There

From Harrisonburg: Follow VA 257 / VA 42 west toward Ottobine. At the intersection of VA 257 and VA 613 continue straight onto VA 742. This eventually turns into VA 933. Follow VA 933, a gravel road, past the dam on the left until you reach the sign on the left that reads "Blueberry Trail." Once you are inside the George Washington National Forest, VA 933 becomes FS 225. *DeLorme: Virginia Atlas & Gazetteer.* Page 66, A-2

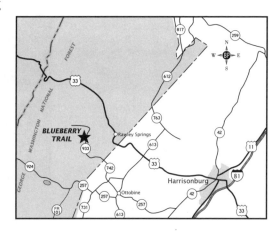

E xpect to encounter wildlife at some point along this ride. The porous soil and rock foundation provide ideal conditions for blueberry growth. And where there are berries, you'll find wildlife. Many black bears are tagged and monitored in this region, so springtime riders should use extra caution when traversing past the blueberries. If you *think* you saw a bear, you probably did. Even though bear sightings are rare, you can never be too careful.

This is also a popular trek for Harrisonburg locals. Visitors are attracted to its accessibility and relatively short track. Make sure to take a rest at the plateau above Mud Gap because the 1.6-mile downhill will toss you if you're sleeping. There are many houses along the road so make sure you are within legal limits. Multiple trails do exist and will provide ample entertainment.

The light sand color of the rocks is due to wear by vehicles and the exposure to rain and altitude. The average rainfall in this area is above average so erosion can be extreme in some places. Most of the sloped sections have water bars that stand about three feet high by three feet wide. They provide speed control for larger vehicles and mountain bikes as well. The temptation to jump the bumps is high, however the terrain on the backside can be treacherous and requires prior assessment.

Ride Information

☏ Trail Contacts:
George Washington National Forest
Roanoke, VA
(540) 564-8300

⏱ Schedule:
Open year round, weather permitting, but
best from April through November.

❓ Local Information:
Harrisonburg-Rockingham
County Visitors Center
Harrisonburg, VA
(540) 434-2319

🛏 Accommodations:
The Village Inn
Harrisonburg, VA
1-800-736-7355

🚲 Local Bike Shops:
Cradle Mt. Ski, Skate, & Golf
Harrisonburg, VA
(540) 433-7201

Blue Ridge Cycle Works
Harrisonburg, VA
(540) 432-0280

N Maps:
USGS maps: Briery Branch, VA

Starting at the trailhead, the gradual climb takes you through groves of wild blueberries that grow in shrub form about two feet off the ground. In the spring, Mud Pond provides a delightful spot to eat some berries and take a break. Make sure to bring some "bug juice" because the pond hosts many insects during warmer seasons. Rattlesnakes especially like this area. The unique combination of small brush, granite terrain, and a water source creates the natural habitat for the rattler.

When you reach the plateau and trail intersection at mile 2.4, you have the option of continuing uphill or taking the dramatic downhill adventure. Venturing uphill will transport you to Oak Knob. There is another intersecting trail that can take you back downhill and will spit you out on Virginia 933, closer to hardtop than where you parked. This only makes for a slightly longer trip back to the car.

Most of the ride will cover terrain that requires middle gears. Clipless pedals are a bonus because the upward crank allows you to get through some of the technical and rockier uphill sections. Don't be discouraged by the uphill sections. The flatter sections will allow for your recovery. The trail began as a fire road and is still used for that purpose, but it seconds as a training ground for local cycling enthusiasts.

Try your hand at the numerous joining trails to Mud Pond and Blueberry Trail. When you visit the area, make sure to join some of the group rides that are offered through the local bike shops. They are sure to add some local history to your adventure and technical advice about your riding.

MilesDirections

0.0 START at the Blueberry Trail gate and sign, located across the road from a limited parking area. A smooth section just before a gradual uphill will start off your ride.

0.2 The first switchback is left.

0.4 A switchback right points you toward a steeper uphill.

1.1 The gradual incline continues through sections of blueberry bushes.

1.6 This is where you reach Mud Pond Gap.

2.4 The trail makes a "Y." Ride directly left on Mud Pond Gap Trail to start the downhill back to FS 225.

3.4 A flat traverse allows you to peddle for speed.

3.5 An extremely short and steep section of trail hides a slick rock face that should be taken with caution.

3.9 A large, wide creek crossing is sure to get your feet wet.

4.0 A white gate with candy cane reflectors marks the road intersection. At the "Y" intersection, ride left and uphill onto FS 225.

4.2 Arrive back at your car.

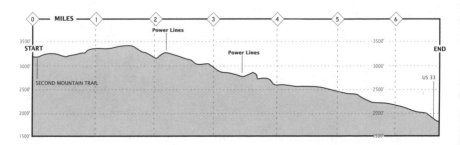

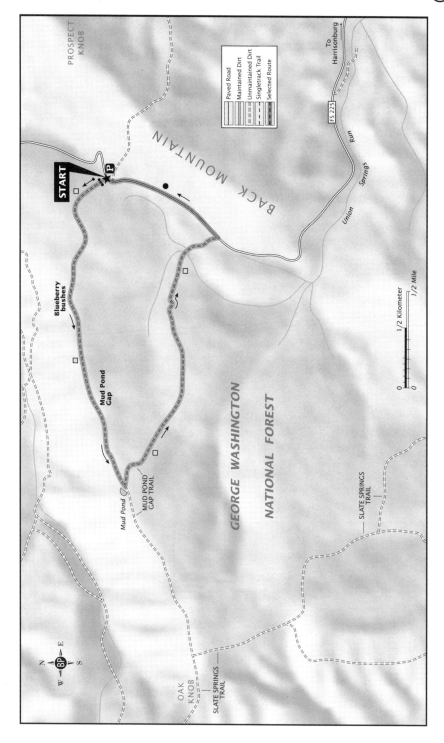

PROSPECT KNOB

BACK MOUNTAIN

To Harrisonburg

FS 225

Union Springs Run

START

P

Blueberry bushes

Mud Pond Gap

Mud Pond

MUD POND GAP TRAIL

GEORGE WASHINGTON

NATIONAL FOREST

SLATE SPRINGS TRAIL

OAK KNOB

SLATE SPRINGS TRAIL

Paved Road
Maintained Dirt
Unmaintained Dirt
Singletrack Trail
Selected Route

1/2 Kilometer
1/2 Mile

0
0

N
W — E
S

Reddish Knob

Ride Specs

Start: From Briery Branch Dam
Length: 20.5-mile loop. This would be a very good shuttle ride as well.
Approximate Riding Time: 2½–3 hours
Dificulty Rating: Most difficult if ridden to the top. Timber Ridge is a both technically difficult and physically draining.
Trail Surface: Mountainous singletrack, gravel forest roads, and pavement
Land Status: National forest
Nearest Town: Harrisonburg, VA
Other Trail Users: Hikers and hang gliders
Canine Compatibility: Bring a dog only if you're doing a shuttle.

Getting There

From Harrisonburg: Take VA 42 south for 4.5 miles to Dayton. From Dayton turn right on VA 257 heading west. Go about six miles and reach the small town of Ottobine. Bear left, continuing on VA 257. Go about three miles to Briery Branch and turn left on VA 731. In less than a quarter mile, turn right on VA 924 toward the mountains. Follow VA 924 about five miles into the George Washington National Forest to Briery Branch Dam on the left. Park here. *DeLorme: Virginia Atlas & Gazetteer.* Page 66, A-2

M any years ago, when I first came through here looking for good rides in the Harrisonburg area, one of the guys at a now defunct bike shop called Cool Breeze Cyclery & Fitness raved on and on about a backwoods mountain bike adventure he took with some fellow cyclists into the George Washington National Forest just west of town. After more than eight hours of cycling virtually endless unexplored trails, he explained, they chose to end their epic adventure. The sheer magnitude of rideable terrain in the mountains and national forest land just west of Harrisonburg area was just too much for one day. That was all I needed to hear. I pulled my bike from the roof rack, eyed the tall Alleghany Mountains to the west, and set out to explore this land of mystic mountain bike terrain. I was not disappointed.

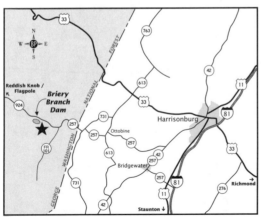

Augusta County was founded in 1736 and at its greatest size embraced land as far west as the Mississippi River. What is now West Virginia, Kentucky, Ohio, Indiana, Illinois, Michigan, Wisconsin, and much of Western Pennsylvania was once part of Augusta County. So that frontier residents could more easily access America's court of law and system of justice, Virginia's Augusta County Court was placed in what is known today as Pittsburgh, Pennsylvania.

Do I sense some apprehension here? Timber Ridge can be pretty tough.

Although Augusta County no longer contains the land it once held more than two centuries ago, it remains Virginia's second-largest county and includes land from the Blue Ridge to the Allegheny Mountains and much of the Shenandoah Valley. With its thousands of acres of national forest land, it is no wonder such singletrack bounty exits within its boundaries.

My first mountain bike ride into Augusta County's backwoods took me skyward through the George Washington National Forest into the Allegheny Mountains of Western Virginia. The ride began up an unforgiving paved climb to the famed Reddish Knob. As the second-highest peak in Augusta County, Reddish Knob measures in at nearly 4,400 feet above sea level, and the climb to the summit (albeit along a paved road to the top) is relentless. But the views this peak offers are nothing short of spectacular. Locals claim that on the clearest days it's possible to see into five states. So far, in all the times I've been back to this ride (one of my all-time favorites) I've been hard-pressed to see that far through summer haze or winter gray. But this 360-degree view from the top of Reddish Knob is certainly one of Virginia's greatest treasures.

The ride begins at the Briery Branch Dam along Virginia 924, west of Harrisonburg. The climb to Briery Branch Gap, a very long, four-mile stretch of pavement, never eases up. Plan a shuttle if you'd rather spend time tearing it up on endless descents rather than climbing the endless road up Virginia 924. For a shuttle, park one vehicle at the Briery Branch Dam, then hop in the next vehicle for a drive to the top of Reddish Knob (a paved parking lot area is on top). The descent down Timber Ridge may take well over an hour. Going down California Ridge will take less time but is a smoother descent through mountain laurel and soft singletrack.

Mountain Laurel lines the smooth singletrack down California Ridge.

Ride Information

🕓 Trail Contacts:
Lee Ranger District
GW National Forest
(540) 984-4101

George Washington National Forest
Roanoke, VA
(540) 564-8300

🕐 Schedule:
Open year-round, weather permitting, but best from April through November.

❓ Local Information:
Harrisonburg-Rockingham Convention & Visitors Bureau
Harrisonburg, VA
(540) 433-2293

📍 Local Events/Attractions:
Court Square Theater
Harrisonburg, VA
(540) 433-9188

James Madison University
Harrisonburg, VA
(540) 568-6211
or www.jmu.edu

Eastern Mennonite University
Harrisonburg, VA
(540) 432-4159
or www.emu.edu

🛏 Accommodations:
Boxwood Bed and Breakfast
Hinton, VA
(540) 867-5772

The Village Inn
Harrisonburg, VA
1-800-736-7355

🚲 Local Bike Shops:
Cradle Mountain Ski, Skate & Golf
Harrisonburg, VA
(540) 433-7201

Blue Ridge Cycle Works
Harrisonburg, VA
(540) 432-0280

🅝 Maps:
USGS maps: Briery Branch, VA; Reddish Knob, VA, WVA
George Washington National Forest topo map: Lee Ranger District

If you ride your bike to the top, though, be sure to notice the tombstone less than one half-mile from the summit of Virginia 924 marking the death of Samual Curry. His body was found December 23, 1922, on this very spot, and no explanation has ever been given. My guess, though, is he was trying to ride a bike up this climb and keeled over two thirds of the way up.

Just beyond Curry's grave marker, the sight of which may deal a demoralizing blow to those of you brave enough to make this climb on a bike, you'll reach Briery Branch Gap. The roads split here. You'll need to bear a hard left, continuing up the paved road toward Reddish Knob. Forest Service Road 85 gives you the first break on this relentless mountain and reveals the height at which you've climbed. Views of the Shenandoah Valley to the east are breathtaking. At one point along Forest Service Road 85 you will literally be riding along the Virginia/West Virginia state line. Pedaling on the left side of the road has you in Virginia; the right side of the road, West Virginia. A few more pedal strokes and you reach Reddish Knob (4397 feet).

sh Knob (29)

Views atop Reddish Knob are stunning. Getting there is another story.

MilesDirections

0.0 START from the parking area next to Briery Branch Dam on VA 924 (paved).

0.1 Outdoor toilet on the left.

4.2 Pass Samual Curry's tombstone up the embankment on the left.

4.4 Reach the intersection at Briery Branch Gap. Turn hard left, continuing up the mountain on FS 85 (paved) toward Reddish Knob.

4.6 Cross over the county line into Augusta County.

5.5 Overlook on the left.

6.3 The road divides Virginia and West Virginia along this ridge. The ridge is only as wide as the road itself.

6.5 Bear left at the split in the road. Continue uphill toward Reddish Knob.

6.9 Reach the summit of Reddish Knob, clearly the top of the world in these parts.

*[**Alternate Start:** From the Reddish Knob parking area, head downhill to locate the trailhead on the right side of the road.]*

7.1 Returning downhill from Reddish Knob, turn right on Timber Ridge Trail (yellow blaze).

*[**Note:** This trailhead is slightly hidden. Look for a yellow-diamond marker on a wooden trail post. This trail starts out a bit sketchy, then crosses a small rock slide. Once past the rock slide, follow the power lines downhill to the trail split.]*

7.4 Cross the rock slide. Vista overlooking Middle Ridge and Buck Mountain on the right.

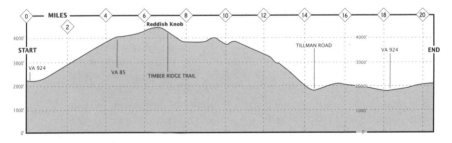

MILES

Reddish Knob

4000'

START

VA 924

VA 85

TIMBER RIDGE TRAIL

3000'

2000'

1000'

0'

4000'

TILLMAN ROAD

VA 924

END

3000'

2000'

1000'

0'

220

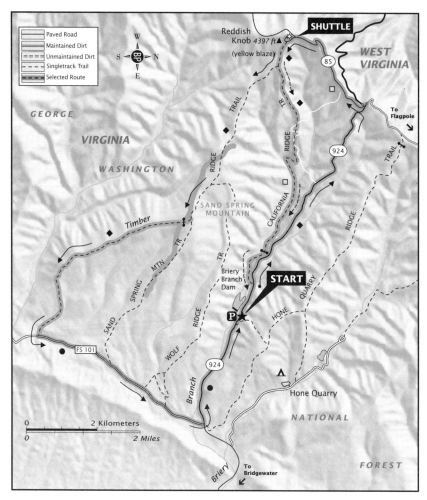

7.6 Reach the trail split. There is a wooden trail sign pointing left to California Ridge Trail or right to Timber Ridge Trail. Turn right on Timber Ridge Trail (yellow blaze) and continue to follow the yellow diamonds toward Tillman Road (FS 101).

*[**Alternate Route:** If you're not interested in the long, rugged descent down Timber Ridge, turn left here and follow California Ridge Trail directly back to Briery Branch Dam. California Ridge Trail has a smoother surface and easier terrain.]*

10.0 Pass Wolf Ridge Trail on the left. Stay right, continuing on Timber Ridge Trail (yellow blaze) to Sandspring Mountain. Wolf Ridge

Trail is five miles to Tillman Road (FS 101).

10.7 Reach Sandspring Mountain. Bear right at this split, continuing to follow Timber Ridge Trail (yellow blaze) to the bottom. Watch out for the steel bar across Timber Ridge Trail less than 20 yards from this split!

14.7 Reach the bottom of one of the best downhills on the planet! Turn left on Tillman Road (FS 101). This is a well-maintained gravel road, which is nearly all downhill to VA 924.

18.3 Turn left on VA 924 (paved). Head back to Briery Branch Dam. This uphill section is fairly moderate.

20.5 Reach Briery Branch Dam and the car.

Flagpole

Ride Specs

Start: From Briery Branch Dam

Length: 17.6-mile loop or shuttle

Approximate Riding Time: 2½–3 hours

Difficulty Rating: Most difficult if ridden to the top. Slate Springs Jeep Trail is an extremely fast and challenging descent that can last as long as an hour.

Trail Surface: Mountainous singletrack, gravel forest roads, and pavement

Land Status: National forest

Nearest Town: Harrisonburg, VA

Other Trail Users: Hikers and equestrians

Canine Compatibility: Bring a dog only if you're doing a shuttle.

Getting There

From Harrisonburg: Take VA 42 south for 4.5 miles to Dayton. From Dayton turn right on VA 257 heading west. Go about six miles and reach the small town of Ottobine. Bear left, continuing on VA 257. Go about three miles to Briery Branch and turn left on VA 731. In less than a quarter mile, turn right on VA 924 toward the mountains. Follow VA 924 about five miles into the George Washington National Forest to Briery Branch Dam on the left. Park here. ***DeLorme: Virginia Atlas & Gazetteer:*** Page 66, A-2

T his ride is one of the state's all-time greats. Its only drawback, perhaps, is the daunting 7.5-mile climb in the first 7.5miles of the ride—not much of a warm-up. Of course, this can be avoided if you make it into a shuttle ride, leaving one car at Briery Branch Dam and taking another car up to the intersection at Briery Branch Gap. You can then start your ride much closer to the top and avoid the bulk of the brutal ascent up Virginia 924.

Otherwise, like the ride up to Reddish Knob, start from the parking area at Briery Branch Dam before climbing the relentless ascent up Virginia 924 to Briery Branch Gap. Once you reach the Gap, rather than turning left toward Reddish Knob, continue straight, following the hard, rocky dirt road. This road quickly switches north along the top of the Shenandoah Mountain's ridgeline and travels parallel to the Virginia/West Virginia border. There is another 3.5 miles of climbing before reaching Flagpole.

It hardly seems reasonable to spend the first 7.5 miles climbing. But like those long chair lift rides to the top of the nation's greatest downhill ski runs, you will reach the summit, take a deep breath, and launch yourself on an incredible journey to the bottom.

And what a journey this ride becomes! At mile 7.8, you'll need to bear right, off the main road, through a hollow of trees to reach the grassy, mountaintop meadow called Flagpole. You may notice a pine tree on the edge of this meadow that is much taller than its neighbors. This wind-blown tree distinguishes itself because it can be seen from the roads below, resembling a flag on a flagpole blowing in the strong mountain gusts.

Ride Information

🌜 Trail Contacts:
Lee Ranger District
GW National Forest
(540) 984-4101

George Washington National Forest
Roanoke, VA
(540) 564-8300

🕑 Schedule:
Open year-round, weather permitting, but best from April through November.

❓ Local Information:
Harrisonburg-Rockingham Convention & Visitors Bureau
Harrisonburg, VA
(540) 433-2293

💡 Local Events/Attractions:
Court Square Theater
Harrisonburg, VA
(540) 433-9188

James Madison University
Harrisonburg, VA
(540) 568-6211
or www.jmu.edu

Eastern Mennonite University
Harrisonburg, VA
(540) 432-4159
or www.emu.edu

🛏 Accommodations:
Boxwood Bed and Breakfast
Hinton, VA
(540) 867-5772

The Village Inn
Harrisonburg, VA
1-800-736-7355

🚲 Local Bike Shops:
Cradle Mountain Ski, Skate & Golf
Harrisonburg, VA
(540) 433-7201

Blue Ridge Cycle Works
Harrisonburg, VA
(540) 432-0280

🅽 Maps:
USGS maps: Briery Branch, VA; Brandywine, WVA, VA
GW National Forest topo map: Lee Ranger District

The view from Flagpole is spectacular, and on a clear day you can see east over the mountaintops into the Shenandoah Valley. Though the view is less dramatic than that from the summit of Reddish Knob, you will see the popular mountain peak not far to the south.

While enjoying the view from Flagpole, gather your wits and replenish your system. You'll need every ounce of courage and strength to negotiate what lay ahead. Just down the road is the orange-blazed Slate Springs trailhead and Slate Springs Trail, the path that will take you on a crazy downhill adventure to Hone Quarry Dam.

From Flagpole, get back on the dirt road and ride only one tenth of a mile. Keep a sharp eye on the right side of the road for the bright, orange-diamond trail marker tacked to a tree. This marker is partially hidden, so if you pass a small camping area on the left and go sharply downhill on this main road, then you've gone too far.

For nearly seven long miles after turning onto Slate Springs AA Jeep Trail, you will descend, first along a twisting, narrow off-camber goat trail of a singletrack that contours the mountain. Then you will descend, descend, and descend some more before being afforded a quick break as you pass a rocky little overlook. After this, the trail just drops, and down you go along a grassy path littered with out-of-control waterbars that are more like moguls than trail maintenance. At this point, of course, your forearms are toast and if you're not careful, these larger-than-life waterbars will throw you so skyward you'll wonder whether you're riding a bike or a sled. At last, just when your forearms are registering red and your two-fingered break levers now require both hands, the descent finally tapers off and follows the orange blazes across Hone Quarry Run. You then get a nice cruise along a fast, dirt road back toward Virginia 924. Pass the Hone Quarry Reservoir, glide through a tunnel of tall pines, then coast up to the paved road (Virginia 924). Turn right on Virginia 924 and pedal back up to Briery Branch Gap and the start of the ride.

If you shuttled this one, get back in the car, grab your shuttle on top, and do it all over again.

It may look tame, but the ride down Slate Springs Jeep Trail is brutal.

Cruising atop Flagpole.

MilesDirections

0.0 START from the parking area next to Briery Branch Dam on VA 924 (paved).
0.1 Outdoor toilet on the left.
4.2 Pass Samual Curry's tombstone up the embankment on the left. Might this be a fore-shadowing to the day's ride?
4.4 Reach the intersection at Briery Branch Gap. Continue straight on the Forest Road, continuing to climb northeast toward Flagpole.
5.4 Pass Hone Quarry Ridge Jeep Trail on the right.

5.5 Overlook on the right. A little trail on the right takes you to this overlook, then brings you back to the Forest Road.
7.7 Reach Flagpole! Bear right to get to the meadow. To continue this ride, get back on the Forest Road, heading northeast.
7.8 Just past Flagpole, from the Forest Road, turn right on Slate Springs AA Jeep Trail. This narrow singletrack clings to the edge of the ridge. Your brake pads will be smoking by the end of this descent.

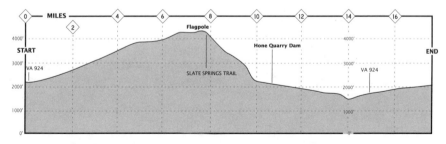

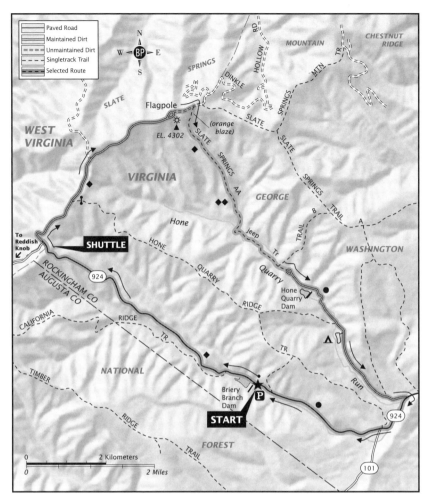

[**Note:** The trailhead for Slate Springs AA Jeep Trail is very hidden. Just before this trail on the left is a small clearing used for primitive camping. There is a stone campfire ring in the clearing. Past this campground, the dirt road drops downhill very dramatically. If you pass this primitive campground and begin a dramatic, rocky descent, you've gone too far. Look for a bright, orange, diamond trail marker stapled to a tree on the right just below the forest road.]

8.7 Rock outcrop overlooking Hone Quarry Ridge. Stop and let your brakes cool. Prepare for a grassy, vertical descent.

10.4 Reach the bottom of the descent and bear to the right, continuing on the orange-blazed trail. Follow along Hone Quarry Creek downhill toward Hone Quarry Reservoir.

10.7 Slate Springs AA Jeep Trail ends at a dirt road. Turn left on this Forest Service Road. Note the metal multi-use trail post marking the trail you were just on.

11.1 Pass Hone Quarry Reservoir on the right.

14.9 Turn right on VA 924 (paved).

17.6 Reach Briery Branch Dam.

227

North Mountain Trail
to Elliot Knob

Ride Specs

Start: From the trailhead on VA 688, west of Staunton
Length: 9.8-mile out-and-back
Approximate Riding Time: 2½ hours
Difficulty Rating: Most Difficult. Many sections contain areas of loose rock.
Trail Surface: The incline and flat sections are smooth and challenging. The sections toward the top become extremely rocky.
Land Status: National forest
Nearest Town: Staunton, VA
Other Trail Users: Hikers
Canine Compatibility: Dog friendly

Getting There

From Staunton: Follow VA 254 West. Bear left onto VA 42 South for 0.7 miles and then turn right onto VA 688 West in Buffalo Gap. Travel four miles until you reach the trailhead/intersection of North Mountain Trail and Crawford Mountain Trail. There is ample parking to the left in front of the white steel pole gate. *DeLorme: Virginia Atlas & Gazetteer.* Page 66, C-1

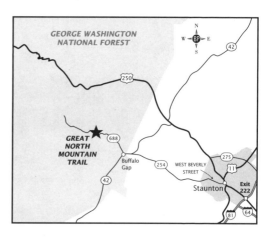

I n the 1730s Scotch-Irish, Welsh, and Germans began migrating down the Great Valley into Western Virginia from Pennsylvania. The Augusta County area became a point of settlement for Scotch-Irish Presbyterians. In 1738 Augusta was formed from Orange County and named after the wife of Frederick Louis, the Prince of Wales. Due to the county's small number of inhabitants, the local government did not convene until 1745. Today, a large portion of the county is protected within the George Washington Forest and a small portion of the Shenandoah National Park, not to mention a few other state and national preserves.

The county saw a fair amount of action during the Civil War's Valley campaigns. The ridges that frame the central valley provided cover and vantage for troops and ended up playing a key role in the war. On the way to North Mountain Trail you'll see signs for Civil War attractions such as Fort Johnson, McDowell Battlefield, and Camp Allegheny. The hardwoods, pines, and rhododendrons along the trail create a scenic background by which to imagine the Civil War campaigns. Take the time to enjoy and engulf yourself in the history of this area.

At 4463 feet, Elliot Knob is the highest point in the George Washington National Forest.

Visitors can stop at the Deerfield Ranger District office on Virginia 254 West, outside of Staunton, for advice and local maps of the Great North Mountain. The Deerfield Office contains many animal specimens that have been recovered or donated to the Forest Service. The first one you see as you walk in is a barn owl with its wings reaching straight up. Some of the other animals are a baby deer, a screech owl, a hornet's nest, a falcon, and a big beaver.

The intersection of Crawford Mountain Trail and North Mountain Trail is the center of many mountain biking options. The trails that intersect this section of the North Mountain Trail are numerous and include Cold Springs Trail, Archer Run Road, Hite Hollow Road, and Ferris Hollow Trail. All of these trails extend southward as you ride past Elliot Knob. Consult a map and plan accordingly if you choose to go farther south or north on the North Mountain Trail. Riding north will eventually take you to the Ramsey's Draft Wilderness Area. Though off-limits to bikes, hikers will enjoy the virgin stands of hemlock trees—a rarity in Virginia. The distance from the start point of this chapter ride to Ramsey's Draft is about 14 miles.

When you venture onto the Great North Mountain make sure to pack some essential biking tools. An extra tube and pump are a good idea. This trail is not for beginners, so don't be fooled. Physically, it can be downright exhausting. The trail starts on an old logging road and follows the Great North Mountain ridgeline to Elliot Knob. Plan to scramble over narrow paths and rugged terrain, attain high speeds on hair-raising descents, and climb stiff ascents to panoramic views. Riders not interested in taking this challenging ride can opt for another route that can be reached by staying on Virginia 42 *[see Alternate Starts].*

Elliot Knob has many variations of flora and fauna. Hardwoods and spruce shade the hearty undergrowth of rhododendrons and young saplings. At 4463 feet, the Knob is one of the highest point in George Washington National Forest, and the views, especially of the Shenandoah Valley, are as glorious as you'd expect.

While in the Staunton area, plan on driving either the Blue Ridge Parkway (no charge) or Skyline Drive (currently $10 for entry, but you can buy a $20 pass for the year). This is near where the two roads meet and extend south and north, respectively. Staunton was an important Confederate supply depot and railroad link. Make a stop at the Historic Train Station, which was dubbed the "Breadbasket of the Confederacy." Thornrose Cemetery is another landmark that contains the graves of Confederate soldiers who defended Richmond from Union advances over the Shenandoah.

Ride Information

◐ Trail Contacts:
Deerfield Ranger District
Staunton, VA
(540) 885-8028

George Washington National Forest
Roanoke, VA
(540) 564-8300

◑ Schedule:
Open year round, weather permitting, but best from April through November.

❓ Local Information:
Augusta County Visitors Center
Staunton, VA
1-800-332-5219

Rockfish Gap Regional Visitors Center
Waynesboro, VA
1-800-471-3109

◑ Local Events/Attractions:
McDowell Battlefield
Monterey, VA
(540) 468-2550

◎ Accommodations:
Inn at Keezletown Road
Bed & Breakfast
Weyers Cave, VA
1-800-465-0100 or (540) 234-0644
or *www.bbhsv.org/keezlinn*

◑ Local Bike Shops:
Cycle-Recycle Co.
Waynesboro, VA
(540) 949-8973
or *www.cyclerecycle.com*

Rockfish Gap Outfitters
Waynesboro, VA
(540) 229-4584

◑ Maps:
USGS maps: Elliot Knob, VA

MilesDirections

0.0 START at the parking area next to the gates, limited parking only. Facing west, take the trailhead to the left that goes uphill.

0.4 Reach the end of the first of many uphill climbs.

0.5 Commence the beginning of the first downhill section, which contains many switchbacks.

0.6 A technical rock section of singletrack and steep trail sloping to the right will take you uphill.

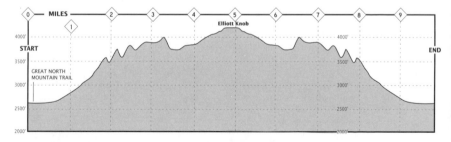

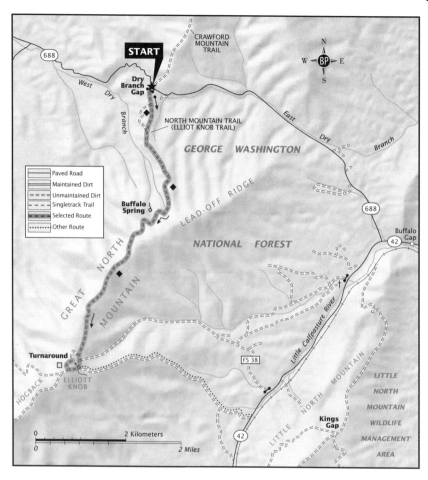

1.1 There is a gradual switchback left.

1.7 Please use caution here. This is a very rocky and technical section.

1.8 The trail heading west leads to Buffalo Spring.

1.9 Come to a large section that contains a series of switchbacks and inclines.

2.1 Reach the third section of technical rock singletrack. Keep in mind that this is mainly a hiking trail so most of the terrain is not meant for fast bike traffic.

4.0 Reach the intersection of a closed forest road (FS 38) and Elliot Knob.

4.4 Veer left. A side road on the right leads to Elliot Knob, 730 feet away.

4.9 Turn right onto the road that leads to Elliot Knob. From here there are spectacular views of the Shenandoah Valley and beyond. Turn around and return by the same route.

9.8 Reach the parking area and your vehicle.

Alternate Starts: *Continue driving past Buffalo Gap toward Chapin on VA 42 West. The right after FS 38 will be a direct uphill to Elliot Knob (4463 feet). It is a direct ascent to the peak, but the journey back down is a little sweeter.*

Williamsville Loop

Ride Specs

Start: From the Bullpasture Gorge suspension bridge parking area
Length: 7.3-mile loop
Approximate Riding Time: 2 hours
Difficulty Rating: Moderate. The first mile is a technical uphill and the rest is downhill.
Trail Surface: Rocky uphill and a smooth singletrack downhill
Land Status: National forest
Nearest Town: Flood, VA
Other Trail Users: Hunters, anglers, and spelunkers
Canine Compatibility: Dog friendly

Getting There

From Staunton: Drive west on U.S. 250 toward McDowell for 30 miles. Turn left onto VA 678. There is a parking area on the left as the road begins to incline on Bullpasture Mountain. This parking area is land marked by the Bullpasture Gorge suspension bridge. Park here for the start of your ride. *DeLorme: Virginia Atlas & Gazetteer.* Page 65, C-6

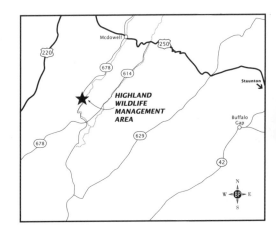

The Hupman Valley Trail provides a challenging loop that ends at a beautiful bend in the Bullpasture Gorge. You'll likely find anglers catching trout here. Since hunters also enjoy the area, it's highly recommended that you not ride here during hunting season.

The ride starts from the parking lot and allows you a nice warm-up along the hardtop before you reach the Hupman Valley trailhead. From the Bullpasture Gorge suspension bridge ride uphill on Virginia 678 until you pass through Williamsville. The spectacular view of the river will no doubt inspire you to continue on. Follow Virginia 614 east until the road turns to gravel. A green gate on the left marks the Hupman Valley trailhead. The trail begins with several switchbacks and rocky terrain. Keep a good line and you can make it to the flatter sections, which allow you time to catch your breath and suck down some water. Try not to look west too much because the view westward of the Shenandoah Mountains could take your breath away. When you reach 2,420 feet the ride becomes a roller coaster through hardwoods and high grasses. The singletrack is overgrown with

marsh grasses and briars. Always use caution in this section because a hidden surface rock could do some damage to your tires—make sure you have a spare tube and pump.

The ride itself does not take that long and the scenery is spectacular. This spot is very remote though, so make sure you have plenty of gas because Williamsville doesn't have a gas station. The nearest stations are in McDowell and Flood.

The Bullpasture Gorge suspension bridge parking area is central to a number of recreational options. Camping is permitted free-of-charge in the parking area. The suspension bridge allows access to the trail, fishing, and a small cave. The bridge entrance can be found by walking up the rockslide, left of the trail as you leave the parking lot. Crossing the hardtop road from the parking lot will take you to the underground origin of the joining river. There's a beach inside the cave, if you can stand the chilly temperature of the water and hold your breath long enough. This area is quite popular with locals, so weekends can be crowded during the warmer months. Bullpasture Gorge is a very private and wonderful escape from the greater world.

The Bullpasture River is located in the heart of the Appalachian Mountains and runs for approximately five miles. The highest elevation on Bullpasture Mountain is 3,240 feet. The mountain provides many opportunities for caving. One of these cave openings is located uphill, to the right, as you reach the river. It's advised by local officials to seek professional guidance when caving if you've never been before. So contact the George Washington National Forest office if you're interested and they should be able to help find you a professional guide.

West of McDowell, you'll find wonderful accommodations at the Ginseng Mountain Lodge. The Ginseng Country Store is sure to please you with local arts and crafts such as woodworking, sheepskins, maple syrup, and regional folklore. While you're in the area, make sure to check out all the events in the Staunton region. If you have the time to drive then indulging in the Shenandoah Driving Tour along U.S. Route 11 is definitely the way to go. The tour starts as far north as Winchester. Picking up the tour in Staunton allows you to visit historic places such as the Woodrow Wilson Birthplace and Museum, the Statler Brothers Mini-Museum, and the Museum of American Frontier Culture. Of particular interest to cyclists is the annual Shenandoah Fall Foliage Bike Festival.

Ride Information

Trail Contacts:
George Washington National Forest
Roanoke, VA
(540) 564-8300

Schedule:
Open year round, weather permitting, but best from April through November.

Local Information:
Highland County Chamber of Commerce
Monterey, VA
(540) 468-2550

Shenandoah Valley Visitor Center
New Market, VA
(540) 740-3132
or www.svta.org

Local Events/Attractions:
Shenandoah Fall Foliage Bike Festival
20-22 October 2000
Williamsville, VA
(757) 229-0507
www.bikevirginia.org

Museum of American Frontier Culture
Staunton, VA
(540) 332-7850
or www.frontiermuseum.org

Statler Brothers Mini-Museum
Staunton, VA
(540) 885-7297

Woodrow Wilson Birthplace
and Museum
Staunton, VA
(540) 885-0897
or www.woodrowwilson.org

Accommodations:
Mill Gap Ruritan Camp Ground
Monterey, VA
(540) 499-2435

Ginseng Mountain Lodging
Highland County, VA
(540) 474-5137

Local Bike Shops:
Cycle–Recycle Co.
Waynesboro, VA
(540) 949-8973
or www.cyclerecycle.com

Maps:
USGS maps: Williamsville, VA

MilesDirections

0.0 START from the Bullpasture Gorge sus-pension bridge parking area. Ride the hardtop road VA 678 through Williamsville.

2.0 After passing through Williamsville turn left and cross the gorge onto VA 614. The road will turn from pavement to gravel.

3.0 Turn left through the first green gate, lead-ing to Hupman Valley Trail. There is an old

stone foundation in the woods to the left of the gate.

3.1 The first switchback left will be on a grad-ual slope.

3.4 The first switchback right swings you around to face the Shenandoah Mountains.

3.5 Your second switchback left heads back in an eastern direction.

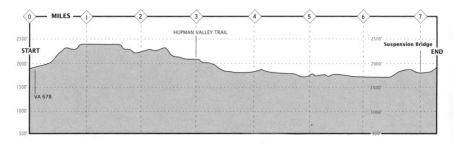

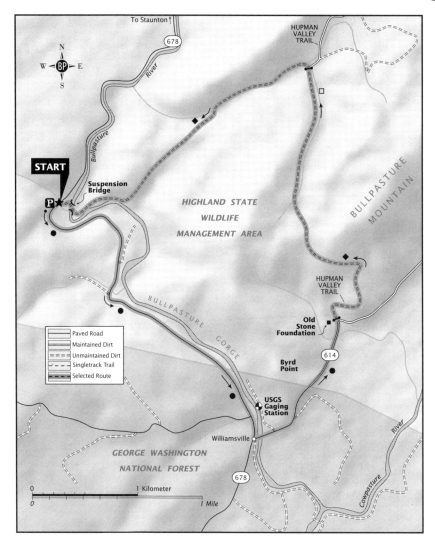

3.9 This level section is rocky and places you within visible distance of the top.

4.1 The plateau of the trail is not the highest part. Either side of the trail can take you to a higher elevation by foot.

4.2 There is a large area of fallen hardwoods on the left.

5.1 A green gate marks the "Y" intersection of Hupman Valley Road. Continue straight ahead and not down the maintained gravel jeep road.

5.2 Begin downhill toward Bullpasture Gorge.

5.8 This switchback right brings you within audible distance of the Bullpasture Gorge.

5.9 The last switchback right leads you along the gorge and back to the parking area.

7.1 A large and very flexible suspension bridge takes you across the gorge to the parking area.

7.3 You will arrive at the parking lot, which provides a wonderful place to cool your feet or jump off the rope swing.

33

Ellis Loop Trail

Ride Specs

Start: From the Dun's Gap Road parking area
Length: 5.6-mile loop
Approximate Riding Time: 1 hour
Difficulty Rating: Moderate. You'll need a moderate degree of technical bike handling skills to bump your way through the sections of rocky, rolling singletrack and ATV ruts. The ride isn't very long, but there are a couple of steep rollers that will keep you huffing.
Trail Surface: Dirt roads and singletrack
Land Status: National forest
Nearest Town: Hot Springs, VA
Other Trail Users: Hikers, equestrians, and ATVs
Canine Compatibility: Dog friendly

Getting There

From Hot Springs: Take U.S. 220 north for approximately 1.5 miles. Just before Mitchelltown, turn left on VA 618. Follow this uphill for nearly two miles to the gate. The pavement ends here. Bear left, continuing on Dun's Gap Road (VA 618). This is now a dirt road. Follow Dun's Gap Road a little more than two miles along Cowardin Run. There's a small, gravel parking area on the left. Park here. The ride starts on the right side of Dun's Gap Road, across from the parking area.
DeLorme: Virginia Atlas & Gazetteer. Page 64, D-4

I n this land of bubbling, high-mountain spas, where hot springs well up from the earth at an average temperature of 104 degrees, where diplomats, presidents, world travelers, and tired Virginians come to rejuvenate their weary bodies, and where the luxurious Homestead Resort has resided for more than two centuries, a new kind of recreation has taken shape. Near Hot Springs, Virginia, in the hills of the Allegheny Mountains, lie hundreds of miles of open mountain biking trails.

Mountain bikers throughout the region are making tracks to the Warm Springs Valley of Virginia's western slopes. They come to explore the off-road avenues of pic-

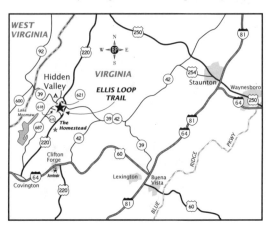

turesque hillsides and pleasant hidden valleys, test their wits on rugged singletrack, or pedal slowly through mountain-rimmed meadows. Then, after trekking exhaustively through the backcountry, these active vacationers can visit one of the area's many hot mineral spas and "take the cure," soaking their tired bodies in naturally heated springs. Does it get any better than this? Well, sure, if you never leave.

There are plenty of places to stay in the Warm Springs Valley. The region has several campgrounds, and primitive camping in the George Washington National Forest is virtually limitless. But why bother sleeping under the stars after a long ride when you can stay where the stars sleep? The Homestead, Virginia's five-star mountain resort pulls out all the stops for weary travelers, and makes a visit to the Warm Springs Valley a world-class event. For cyclists staying at the resort, The Homestead now offers off-road guided tours and rents bikes from the ski lodge.

The Homestead, Virginia's five-star mountain resort.

241

As for the ride itself, this exciting five-mile loop is close enough to Hot Springs that cyclists interested in a nice little pre-ride warm-up can pedal from The Homestead to the ride's start (less than four miles). Get on U.S. Route 220 and head north toward Mitchelltown. After little over one mile, bear left up a narrow, paved road (the only left turn before Mitchelltown)—this is Virginia 618. Follow Virginia 618 uphill for one mile to a gate where Dun's Gap Road (Virginia 618) turns left and changes to dirt. Follow this another one and a half miles along Cowardin Run to the start of the ride. Parking is available if you choose to drive.

Ellis Loop Trail starts at a small, gravel parking area on Virginia 618. From here, turn right on Virginia 618, traveling less than 20 yards, then turn hard left through a gate and ride uphill on an old jeep road. Be sure to look up at the top of this climb to see the view of the Warm Springs Mountain. This jeep road winds through a little valley along mostly flat terrain until a swift descent carries you down toward Jerry Run. Be sure to keep your eyes peeled for a black, wooden arrow that points left into the woods (the trailhead for Ellis Trail). You've gone too far if you cross a creek along the jeep road. Once you locate the trailhead, notice that Ellis Trail is marked with large, wooden, red arrows all the way back to Dun's Gap Road (Virginia 618).

Ride Information

☎ Trail Contacts:
Warm Springs Ranger District
(540) 839-2521

**George Washington
National Forest Headquarters**
(540) 564-8300

⏰ Schedule:
Public land, accessible year-round

❓ Local Information:
**Bath County Chamber of Commerce
& the Forest Place Visitor Center**
1-800-628-8092 or (540) 839-5281

💡 Local Events /Attractions:
The charming town of Warm Springs has a museum called Gristmill Square, restaurants, shopping, and the famous Warm Springs Pools, complete with separate 19th Century bathhouses for men and women.

🛏 Accommodations:
In Warm Springs:
Anderson Cottage B&B
(540) 839-2975

Meadow Lane Lodge
(540) 839-5959

In Hot Springs:
The Homestead (shuttle service available to Roanoke Airport or to the Clifton Forge Amtrak station for registered guests)
1-800-838-1766, (540) 839-1766
or www.thehomestead.com

King's Victorian Inn
(540) 839-3134
or inngetaways.com/va/kingsvic.html

🚲 Local Bike Shops:
There are bike and gear rentals available from The Homestead.

🗺 Maps:
USGS maps: Warm Springs, VA
GW National Forest topo map: Warm Springs District

Because Ellis Trail is a multiple-use trail, you will probably notice lots of horse tracks and possibly some ATV tracks. Chances are, though, you will be alone in this secluded wilderness as you roll along a trail that, at times, should challenge even experienced riders. Just before Ellis Trail ends, there is one last steep climb before a very fast descent to the road. Be careful on this descent; there's a gate at the bottom that's usually closed, which may catch you off-guard.

Turn left on Dun's Gap Road (Virginia 618), and head back along Cowardin Run toward the start of the ride. The soothing sounds of Cowardin Run's cascading water may remind you of the hot mineral baths awaiting you back at the resort.

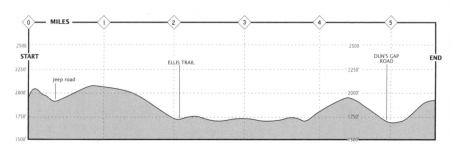

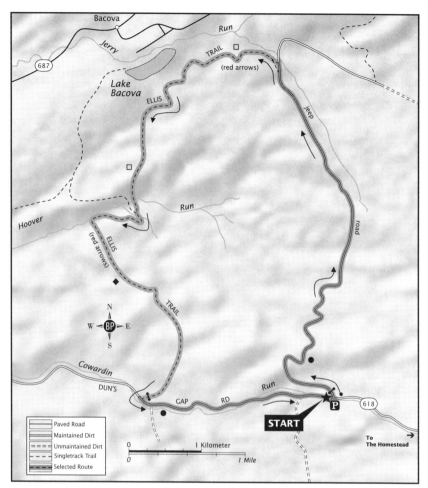

MilesDirections

0.0 START at the parking area on Dun's Gap Road (VA 618). Turn right on Dun's Gap Road.
0.05 Turn hard left through the gate on the Dirt Jeep Road. This dirt road carries you uphill for a spectacular view of the area.
0.3 Reach the top of this climb.
1.0 Great view to the left of the distant mountains. This is a very leisurely, scenic road through this valley.
2.1 Reach the bottom of a fun descent. Turn left on Ellis Trail. *[**Note:** Ellis Trail is marked with a black, wooden arrow nailed to a tree marked*

#20. This arrow points into the woods. Once in the woods, Ellis Trail is marked with large, wooden, red arrows.] If you cross the stream at the bottom of this descent, then you've missed Ellis Trail. Turn around and hunt for these arrows.
2.7 Lake Bacova is visible through the trees on the right.
4.9 Go down a very steep descent, through a gate, then turn left on Dun's Gap Road. Follow Dun's Gap Road upstream along Cowardin Run to the parking area.
5.6 Reach the parking area.

If you consider your mountain bike saddle the most comfortable seat in the house and crave an opportunity to prove your self-sufficiency, try bicycle camping. It does require more planning and preparation than a standard day trip, but the particular satisfaction gained from reaching a campground or a remote outdoor destination on two wheels, knowing you're ready for a cozy night outdoors, makes the extra effort worthwhile.

If you plan on doing a lot of bicycle camping/touring, it's a good idea to invest in quality equipment. Everyone should have a pair of medium-to-large size panniers that can be mounted on a rear rack (if you are planning a long trip, you might consider a front rack). A lightweight backpacking tent, sleeping pad, and sleeping bag can be attached to the rear rack using two or three bungie cords. We all have a tendency to over-pack, but the extra weight of unnecessary equipment may cause you to tire more easily. Here are some tips to help you find the appropriate amount of gear:

- Bring a multi-purpose tool that has a can opener, bottle opener, scissors, knife, and screwdriver.
- Pack only one extra change of clothes, plus any necessary layers such as a polypropylene shirt and tights, polar fleece, wool socks, and rain gear. If you are on a multi-day trip, bring extra shorts and t-shirts, and if it's winter, bring an extra pair of polypropylene tights and shirt, as well as a few extra pairs of wool socks.
- Bring a tin cup and spoon for eating and drinking and one lightweight pot for cooking.
- Invest in a lightweight backpacking stove, tent, and sleeping bag.
- Bring along freeze dried food. You can buy many pre-packaged rice and noodle mixes in the grocery store for half of what you'll pay at backpacking stores.
- Bring the minimum amount of water needed for your intended route. Anticipate if there will be water available. Invest in a water filter that can be used to filter water from water sources along the trail.

Equipment List

Use the checklist of equipment below when you are planning for a single or multi-day trip. You can develop your own equipment list based on the length of your trip, the time of year, weather conditions, and difficulty of the trail.

Essentials
- bungie cords
- compass
- day panniers
- duct tape
- fenders
- pocket knife or multi-purpose tool
- rear rack
- front rack
- trail map
- water bottles
- water filter
- tool kit
- patch kit
- crescent wrench
- tire levers
- spoke wrench
- extra spokes
- chain rivet tool
- extra tube
- tire pump

Clothing
- rain jacket/pants
- polar fleece jacket
- wool sweater
- helmet liner
- bicycle tights
- t-shirts/shorts
- sturdy bicycle shoes/boots
- swimsuit
- underwear
- bike gloves
- eye protection
- bike helmet/liner

First Aid Kit
- bandages (various sizes)
- gauze pads
- surgical tape
- antibiotic ointment
- hydrogen peroxide or iodine
- gauze roll
- ace bandage
- aspirin
- moleskin
- sunscreen
- insect repellent

Personal Items
- towel
- toothbrush/toothpaste
- soap
- comb
- shampoo

Camping Items
- backpacking stove
- tent
- sleeping bag
- foam pad
- cooking and eating utensils
- can opener
- flashlight/batteries
- candle lantern
- touring panniers
- pannier rain covers
- Zip-loc™ bags
- large heavy duty plastic garbage bags
- citronella candles (to repel insects)
- small duffels to organize gear

Miscellaneous Items
- camera/film/batteries
- notebook/pen
- paperback book

Tip:
Zip-loc™ bags are a great way to waterproof and organize your gear. Large, heavy-duty plastic garbage bags also make excellent waterproof liners for the inside of your panniers.

Hidden Valley

Ride Specs

Start: Past campgrounds on FS 241
Length: 11-mile loop
Approximate Riding Time: 1½–2 hours
Difficulty Rating: Moderate
Trail Surface: Jeep trails, singletrack, and dirt roads
Land Status: National forest
Nearest Town: Warm Springs, VA
Other Trail Users: Hikers, equestrians, and ATVs
Canine Compatibility: Dog friendly, but make sure he can swim

Getting There

From Hot Springs: Take U.S. 220 north about 15 miles to Warm Springs and turn left on VA 39 west. Follow VA 39 west about 10 miles and turn right on VA 621 to the Hidden Valley Campgrounds. VA 621 splits in three miles. Bear left, following FS 241. Pass Hidden Valley Campgrounds in five miles. FS 241 turns to dirt. Go another 1.5 miles past the campground until it dead-ends at the cul-de-sac. There is a portable toilet here. The trail starts at the steel gate on the right. *DeLorme: Virginia Atlas & Gazetteer.* Page 64, D-4

D eep in the Allegheny Mountains of Western Virginia there is a quiet little place called Hidden Valley. This peaceful hollow is situated just west of Warm Springs, cradled within the green mountains of the George Washington National Forest.

Warm Springs is renowned for the natural hot springs that well up from deep below the ground on which the town is built. As you drive through Warm Springs notice the large, white spring boxes (bathhouses) containing the relaxing and therapeutic mineral baths. Perhaps this is just the thing you'll need after an arduous mountain bike ride in the hills of the nearby mountains.

If you have the time and money, reserve a night at The Homestead and spend a five-star evening wining and dining at this world-class resort. The Homestead Resort in Hot Springs is less than six miles from the secluded pastures and farmland of Hidden Valley. Hit the trails for an early-morning ride, treat yourself to a five-course lunch and mineral bath back at the resort, then head back to the mountains to explore some of the hundreds of miles of trails and dirt roads that crisscross the area.

The Hidden Valley Loop starts at the end of the road beyond the Hidden Valley

Campgrounds. Just across the Jackson River is the historic Warwick Mansion, which was the site of the motion picture *Sommersby*, starring Richard Gere and Jodie Foster. Some of the buildings from the movie set are still there. The restored mansion is now the Hidden Valley Bed and Breakfast, which may serve you well if The Homestead doesn't fit your budget.

You'll need to ford the Jackson River a number of times along this ride.

249

The loop travels along flat terrain for the first half of the ride and parallels the clear waters of the Jackson River. There are three occasions which call for you to cross the river to continue on the old jeep road. Only once, however, do you have the option of crossing *over* the river (the first crossing can be made by walking across the swinging bridge). Just before the trail leads you to Forest Service Road 241, you must ford the river twice more with your bike over your shoulder. The water is only knee deep and the currents aren't too strong, but be careful during the rainy seasons. The river can swell its banks, becoming too dangerous to cross by foot.

MilesDirections

0.0 START at the cul-de-sac on FS 241 past the Hidden Valley Campground. Go through the steel gate (marked "road closed") on the east side of this parking area and follow the Hidden Valley Trail along the wagon track through the fields of Poor Farm.

0.1 Pass a tree with a brown arrow directing you through the field along the Jackson River.

0.5 Pass another brown arrow directing you away from the Jackson River to the middle of this field. Follow the wagon trail across the field.

0.6 Pass beneath a grove of trees and an overgrown, wooden gateway. The trail continues straight through the field.

0.9 Leave the open fields of Poor Farm and enter into the thick woods on a flat jeep road paralleling the Jackson River. Two wooden posts mark the entrance. This section of the Hidden Valley Trail is blue-blazed.

1.5 There is a trail sign on the left of the jeep road. Turn left at this sign following the Hidden Valley Trail (FS 481) (blue blaze). Cross over a little wooden footbridge toward Jackson River. If you were to continue bearing right on what appears to be the main trail, you

would end up on Muddy Run Trail (FS 481B), which takes you to FS 220.

1.6 Reach the swinging bridge, which spans across the Jackson River.

*[**Note:** You can either ford the Jackson River straight ahead of you and get on the Hidden Valley Trail directly (the wet way), or go the round-about way and walk across the swinging bridge to the other side. Once across the bridge, turn right on a little grassy foot trail that scales the hillside above the river. Follow this overgrown path back toward the river. This little trail takes you to the same spot on the blue-blazed Hidden Valley Trail (FS 481) that you would be on had you waded across the river. Choosing the bridge route keeps you dry, but only for the moment. You will still have two more river crossings where there are no bridges. FS 481 continues along the left side of Jackson River.]*

3.4 FS 481 becomes a grassy doubletrack. Cross a small stream.

3.6 FS 481 returns to a jeep road.

3.8 Cross the Jackson River. You must get wet here! The river is only ankle to knee deep and about 40 to 50 feet across. You can see

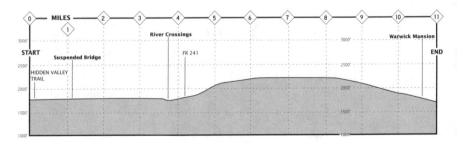

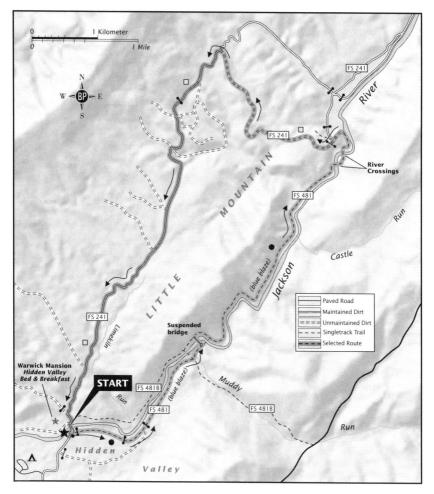

the road continuing on the other side. Walk carefully. The bottom may be slippery.

3.9 Cross the Jackson River again. The river is about knee deep here. Be careful of the slick rocks on the river bottom.

4.0 Follow TR 481 through a small pine forest. Go up a little hill then around a steel gate. The road now becomes FS 241, which will take you all the way back to the start.

4.1 FS 241 comes to a split. Take a hard left around the steel gate. Bearing right on the well-maintained gravel road takes you north. Don't do this! Go under the gate and start climbing this overgrown, dirt road. This road,

at first, may appear to lead nowhere. But once you reach the top of the small incline, the crushed-stone, shale-surfaced road opens up and reveals itself to be very rideable and well maintained.

6.7 Go around a gate.

10.3 Go around a gate. It's all downhill to Hidden Valley from this last gate.

10.8 Reach the bottom of a wild descent along FS 241 and pass the Warwick Mansion (Hidden Valley Bed and Breakfast) on the right. Bear to the left on this road. Cross over the river on a small concrete bridge.

11.0 Arrive back at the parking area.

After crossing the river for the third and final time, you'll follow a jeep road through a thick grove of pines to a well-maintained gravel road with a choice of directions. To continue the Hidden Valley Loop, you must take a hard left off the gravel road around a metal gate. This leads you onto an overgrown dirt road that goes up and around a short incline (Forest Service Road 241 West). The road's appearance improves dramatically as soon as you crest this small hill. From here, follow this rolling dirt road all the way back to Hidden Valley. You'll pass the entrance to the Hidden Valley Bed and Breakfast on your way down the last hill on Forest Service Road 241, then cross over the Jackson River before arriving back at the start of the loop. Consider cycling over to the Warwick Mansion (Hidden Valley Bed and Breakfast) and pedaling through the *Sommersby* movie set before leaving this beautiful valley.

Hidden Valley.

Ride Information

☎ Trail Contacts:
Warm Springs Ranger District
(540) 839-2521

George Washington
National Forest Headquarters
(540) 564-8300

⏱ Schedule:
Public land, accessible year-round

❓ Local Information:
Bath County Chamber of Commerce
& the Forest Place Visitors Center
1-800-628-8092 or (540) 839-5281

💡 Local Events/Attractions:
The charming town of Warm Springs has a museum called Gristmill Square, restaurants, shopping, and the famous Warm Springs Pools, complete with separate 19th century bathhouses for men and women.

🛏 Accommodations:
Hidden Valley Bed and Breakfast
(540) 839-3178

In Warm Springs:
Anderson Cottage B&B
(540) 839-2975

Meadow Lane Lodge
(540) 839-5959

In Hot Springs:
The Homestead (shuttle service available to Roanoke Airport or to the Clifton Forge Amtrak station for registered guests)
1-800-838-1766, (540) 839-1766
or *www.thehomestead.com*

King's Victorian Inn
(540) 839-3134
or *inngetaways.com/va/kingsvic.html*

🚲 Local Bike Shops:
There are bike and gear rentals available from The Homestead.

Ⓝ Maps:
USGS maps: Warm Springs, VA; Sunrise, VA, WVA
GW National Forest topo map: Warm Springs District

Douthat State Park: Stoney Run Trail

Ride Specs

Start: There are multiple trailheads on either side of VA 629 and from the various parking areas throughout the park. One of the more popular starting points is the Stony Run Trail with a small parking area just of VA 629, south of the main office. It is here where this begins.

Length: This is a 3.1-mile loop. However, there are over 40 miles of wooded trails to chose from throughout the year. Nearly all of which are open to bikes.

Approximate Riding Time: 1 hour for this short loop.

Difficulty Rating: Easy to difficult. Several sections throughout the park have fast rocky downhills filled with switchbacks and hidden corners. Other areas, such as creek crossings, can be wide and require patience to cross unless you don't mind getting your feet wet. The easier trail sections tend to be located along or near the lake.

Trail Surface: There are smooth sections, exposed roots, creek crossings, and technical inclines.

Land Status: State park

Nearest Town: Clifton Forge, VA

Other Trail Users: Hikers, back-packers, and anglers

Canine Compatibility: Dog friendly. Dogs love it here, but must be kept on a leash.

There are 25 original CCC cabins available to guests at Douthat State Park.

Getting There

From Lexington: Drive west on I-64 / U.S. 60 toward Clifton Forge. Take Exit 27 and turn right onto VA 629 following signs to Douthat State Park. VA 629 is the only road that leads into the park from Clifton Forge. Follow the brown park signs. Parking for the Stony Run Trail is located on the left. *DeLorme: Virginia Atlas & Gazetteer.* Page 52, A-4

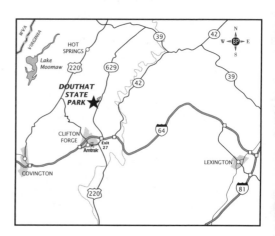

Riding along the high banks of Douthat Lake.

outhat State Park (pronounced "dowthat"), listed on the National Register of Historic Places, opened on June 15, 1936, and continues to be a model for parks across the country. In fact, editors of the *1999 Outside Family Vacation Guide* named Douthat State Park one of the nation's 10 best summer vacation spots (listing it among other top 10 placers in such enviable locations as California and British Columbia).

Douthat was one of the first five parks created under the Civilian Conservation Corps (CCC) and was designed to provide visitors of all types with multiple recreational opportunities. As many as 600 men lived and worked here between 1923 and 1942, building the park's camps and facilities. During this time, nearly everything you'll find at Douthat was constructed by the CCC, including the log cabins, a guest lodge, a full-service restaurant overlooking the lake (open throughout the summer season only), gift shop and camp store, and the lake itself. The CCC

MilesDirections

0.0 START at the trailhead for Stoney Run. There's parking here. This trail is marked by an orange blaze.

0.2 Here is the first creek crossing. There are plenty of stepping-stones at each crossing in case you're not comfortable with riding across.

0.3 The second creek crossing is about three feet wide. Walk upstream a short distance for the narrowest section.

0.4 The third creek crossing is about two feet wide.

0.5 Encounter the fourth creek crossing.

0.6 The fifth creek crossing is quite treacherous.

0.7 Begin a slight incline.

0.8 An exposed drainage pipe will require a "bunny hop."

0.9 This is the beginning of a technical rocky section. This intersection has signs that will direct you throughout the park. Keep a park map on hand for easy reference. At the "T" intersection turn right onto Locust Gap Trail to complete the loop. (You can continue straight to make a six-plus mile loop on Stoney Run Trail. This, however, requires some steep climbing up toward Tuscarora Overlook.)

1.2 Encounter the sixth creek crossing.

1.3 A switchback to the right leads you away from the flatter run-out area.

1.5 A switchback left directs you along the contour of the river.

1.6 Encounter the seventh creek crossing.

1.8 Turning left at this "T" intersection leads to yellow-blazed Locust Gap Trail. Turn right onto Beards Gap Hollow Trail, which follows the loop for this ride.

1.9 There's a switchback left.

2.1 Encounter the eighth creek crossing.

2.2 The ninth creek crossing is usually dry except in the spring.

2.5 The tenth creek crossing is also pretty dry.

2.6 A "T" intersection will slow you down after a fast downhill decent. Turn right and continue downhill on the jeep road. (Left will take you uphill on a dead-end jeep road.)

2.7 The bridge and gate mark the point when you ride to the right to head back to the hardtop.

2.8 Turn right onto VA 629 and head back to the parking site. The visitor's center is located across the road.

3.1 Finish at the parking area.

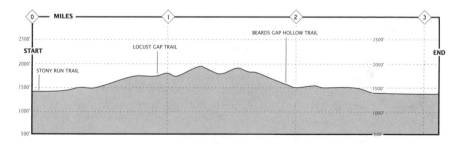

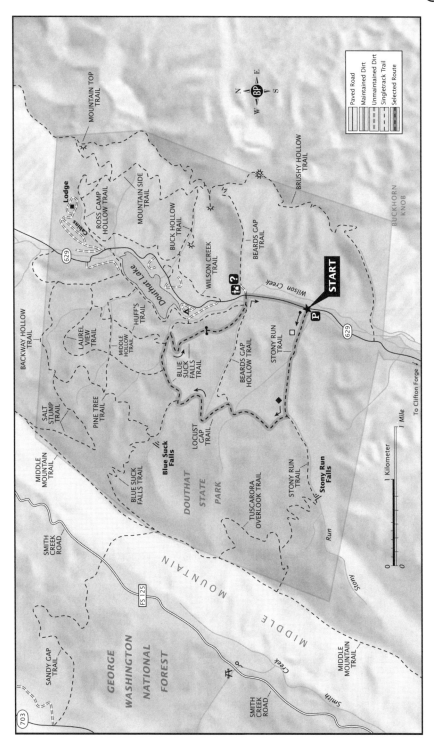

built the dam across the cold mountain waters of Wilson Creek to form Douthat Lake, which covers 50 surface acres and is laden with trout (stocked twice a week from April through September). No motorized boats are allowed on the lake, so about all you might hear is the splashing of paddles on the water from a canoe, paddle boat, or rowboat.

The lake and its mountainous surroundings are sure to entice you to stay a while and camp in one of the three campgrounds or 32 rental cabins so you can explore as much of the 4,493 acres of splendor as possible. There is a centralized bathhouse with hot showers for campers in any of the 77 campsites. And should you chose to stay in one of their 32 rustic log cabins (most of which are original CCC cabins), you'll be treated to just about everything you'll need for an extended stay. The cabins include electricity, central air, a hot shower, fireplace, and fully supplied kitchens (bring your own groceries). The cabins are typically booked solid throughout the year so reserve early.

Douthat is a great place at which to introduce your children to camping, fishing, hiking, and mountain biking. And the park hosts countless programs and special events year-round, including (we're hoping) some upcoming mountain bike clinics. While fishing is still the park's most popular activity, hiking and mountain biking may someday outnumber anglers. Nearly 200,000 visitors came to the park in 1999 and, according to park rangers, more than could be counted rode in on mountain bikes. The remote location of Douthat State Park (surrounded by the George Washington National Forest) makes it a real treasure and a place that you'll want to return to season after season. Whether it's for one of their annual mountain bike races, some scenic hikes, or just an extended stay in one of their fully equipped log cabins overlooking the lake.

There are 24 different trails to choose from in the park, totaling more than 40 miles of rideable terrain. The variety of "magic" mountain bike trails, as some have called them, has lead to the park's nickname, "Mountain Bike Disneyland."

Mountain bikers have access to all but three trails: the Heron Run Trail (blue), the YCC Trail (blue), and the Buck Lick Interpretative Trail (red). The park trail guide, available at the park office, details the distance and difficulty range of each trail in the park. And once you're in the woods, you'll find that each of the trails is clearly marked with an abundance of signs and corresponding color blazes. It'll be tough to get lost and even tougher to decide which trail to take next.

The most popular mountain biking trail in the Douthat trail system is Stony Run. The trail forms a roughly six-mile loop, passing by popular spots such as Tuscarora Overlook Trail, Blue Suck Falls, and Lookout Rock. Stony Run, like all of Douthat's trails, is well marked with clear signs at all of the major intersections. The beginning of the route is flat and fast, and there are exposed roots in several places. Crossing creeks is a regular practice, and the rocks can be quite treacherous—but riding next to the stream keeps you cool as you sweat your way up to Locust Gap. The transfer from Stony Run onto Locust Gap changes your ride from technical to casually meandering inclines and downhills. Locust Gap is much narrower than Stony Run and will require the rider to use more caution when riding through tight sections that have high brush growth.

Along your ride you'll pass under hickory, poplar, and tall oaks and alongside mountain laurel, rhododendron, and huckleberry bushes. Among the wildlife you might see are squirrels, lizards, snakes, rabbits, songbirds, deer, owls, and possibly an occasional black bear. The variety of trails along with the diverse wildlife creates the perfect environment in which to bike.

The spring of 2000 will mark the third annual Middle Mountain Momma Mountain Bike Adventure Race, put on by East Coasters and sponsored by Woods, Water, & Wheels in Lewisburg, West Virginia. This race is usually included in the East Coasters Virginia State Championship Mountain Bike Series. The name of the race was chosen in honor of folk singer John Denver and his song "Country Roads." Mountain bikers treasure Douthat State Park's 40 miles of glorious singletrack, 17 miles of which form the race. The Middle Mountain Momma race covers much more trail than the loop listed in this guide.

Stoney Run is filled with the components to exercise your full spectrum of abili-ties as most of the terrain is consistently challenging. The creek crossings throughout will certainly test your abilities and patience, and expect exposed roots and rocks. Although the featured loop only climbs 755 feet, the mountain bike trails in the park range in elevation from 1,400 to 3,200 feet, which allows for plenty of opportunity to ascend to new and exhausting heights.

Ride Information

Trail Contacts:
Douthat State Park
Millboro, VA
(540) 862-8100

Schedule:
Year-round, weather permitting

Fees/Permits:
$2 per car on the weekend
$1 per car during the week

Local Information:
Virginia Department of Conservation and Recreation
Richmond, VA
(804) 225-3867

Accommodations:
77 campsites with centralized bathhouses are $18 per night year-round.
32 climate-controlled, fully stocked log cabins (minus the food) available year-round. Prices vary depending on size of the cabin and time of year. A single bedroom cabin will cost between $45-$70 per night and can be rented nightly or weekly. Call ahead for current information on prices and for reservations; 1-800-933-PARK

Restaurants:
Lakeview Restaurant—a full-service restaurant overlooking Douthat Lake is open throughout the summer season (Memorial through Labor Day).

Local Events/Attractions:
Middle Mountain Momma Mountain Bike Adventure (field limit 150) held in late May, Douthat State Park
(540) 862-8100

George Washington National Forest
Roanoke, VA
(540) 564-8300

Gift Shop/Camp Store is located next to the Lakeview Restaurant (open seasonally)

Local Bike Shops:
Woods, Water & Wheels
Lewisburg, WV
(304) 645-5200

East Coasters Cycling and Fitness
Blacksburg, VA
(540) 951-2369
or *www.eastcoasters.com*

American Flyers Bicycle Shop
Roanoke, VA
(540) 345-2116
or *www.amflyers.com*

Maps:
USGS maps: Healing Springs, VA; Nimrod Hall, VA
Douthat State Park Mountain Bike Trail Map

Sherando Lake Loop

Ride Specs

Start: From the Turkey Pen Trail parking lot
Length: 18.2-mile loop
Approximate Riding Time: 2–2½ hours
Difficulty Rating: Moderate to difficult with one extreme climb and some lengthy descents.
Trail Surface: Miles of singletrack, some wet and some rocky and dry, with a good section of the Blue Ridge Parkway thrown in for good measure.
Land Status: National forest
Nearest Town: Waynesboro, VA
Other Trail Users: Hikers
Canine Compatibility: Don't bring 'em. You'll be racing down the Parkway on this ride.

Getting There

From I-64 near Waynesboro: Take Exit 96 (Waynesboro-Lyndhurst exit). Follow signs to Sherando Lake. Follow VA 624 2.5 miles to Lyndhurst. At Lyndhurst, bear left on VA 664 south. Go approximately 5.3 miles on VA 664, through Sherando, to FS 42. Turn right on FS 42 (dirt road) and go half a mile to the first parking area on your left. This is the Turkey Pen Trail Parking Area. Park here. The trail starts from the far left corner of the parking lot. When parking here, please don't block the forest service road gate. ***DeLorme: Virginia Atlas & Gazetteer.*** Page 54, A-3

A friendly face at Waynesboro's Rockfish Gap Outfitters pointed at the store-copy topo map and revealed, tapping his finger amidst the thick green contour lines, that this was where he sends off-road riders who come in search of alpine adventure. "You want great trails," he said coolly, "you go here."

"Here" turned out to be one of the largest slabs of mountain I had ridden in Central Virginia. These massive levels of ancient orogeny are just south of the magnificent Shenandoah National Park. They tower above the fertile valley of Shenandoah, nestling the riches of this Eastern breadbasket between its great ridgelines and the slopes of Western Virginia's Allegheny Highlands.

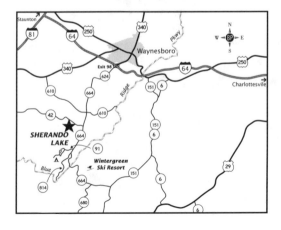

I turned into the gravel parking lot off Forest Service Road 42 and contemplated my ascent into what is commonly known as "Big Levels."

Big Levels has much more to offer than just rugged ridgelines and rocky terrain, however. Between such ominous sounding peaks as Torry Ridge and Devil's Knob lie the peaceful upper and lower lakes of Sherando. The Civilian Conservation Corps built both in the early 1900s for both recre-

ational use and flood control. The CCC built the lower lake, the larger of the two, in 1930. The smaller upper lake was built in 1960s for flood control. The lower lake is used for swimming, boating, and fishing; the upper lake is known primarily for it good fishing. Camping is also popular at Sherando Lake, which has more than 60 units and a large group camping area.

Other nearby scenic wonders include the Blue Ridge Parkway, which rolls along the summits of mountains south of Big Levels; Saint Mary's Wilderness, along the southwest slopes of Big Levels; and the cascades of Saint Mary's Falls.

Sherando's Upper Lake.

The trails around here are clearly marked.

From the parking lot off Forest Service Road 42, Turkey Run Trail begins its slow ascent on an old logging road. The trail narrows just beyond one mile into a thick-foliaged singletrack gaining elevation at such a mild rate you may wonder at times if you're going uphill at all. This changes dramatically, however, at mile 5.5 when the trail lifts off and aims upward to Bald Mountain Overlook. You might not mention to anyone that you needed to push your bike up this section of the trail, but no one will believe you if you say you didn't. The trail is slightly more than handlebar-width with little room for bike handling errors (one side of the trail is a wall of earth, while the other side is an unnerving drop through hundreds of feet of rugged terrain). For some, this poses no challenge, but with more than 1,000 feet of vertical climbing and eight sharp switchbacks in less than one mile, the trail becomes truly an adventure. But please keep the adventure confined to the trail itself and do not short-cut the switchbacks.

The reward? A few aches in the legs, spectacular views, more than 10 miles of furious downhill (all the way back to the ride's start), and the satisfaction of completing a truly rigorous course.

The descent begins at the top of that climb and winds down a rocky fire road to Bald Mountain Overlook and the Blue Ridge Parkway. Turn left on the parkway (rarely any traffic to contend with along this well-maintained, scenic highway), and let gravity pull you for more than three miles past a number of scenic overlooks. Turn left just before the parkway starts climbing and continue downward along White Rock Gap Trail (orange blaze) through an old pine forest. This fun singletrack trail glides downhill for more than two miles before depositing you at Sherando's upper lake.

There are restrooms at the different campground areas in the Sherando Lake area and ice and vending machines adjacent to the beach house pavilion near the lower lake. Outside the park (along Virginia 664, heading back to the start of the ride) there's a general store with food and drinks.

Another point of interest on the way back to the start of the ride is Mount Torry Furnace on Virginia 664. This old iron furnace was built in 1804 to process iron ore mined in the nearby mountains. It was destroyed in 1864 during the Civil War, then rebuilt and operated until 1884.

Ride Information

🕐 Trail Contacts:
Glenwood and Pedlar Ranger Districts
(540) 291-2188

George Washington and Jefferson National Forest Headquarters
(540) 564-5100

🕐 Schedule:
Main gate is open from 6 a.m. to 10 p.m.

💲 Fees/Permits:
Day-use at Sherando Lake: $8.00 per carload for 3+ persons; $6.00 a car if 2 persons; $4.00 a car if 1 person; $1.00 for a person if on bicycle

💡 Local Events /Attractions:
Blue Ridge Parkway—470-mile linear park from Front Royal, VA, to Cherokee, NC

🚲 Local Bike Shops:
Rockfish Gap Outfitters
Waynesboro
(540) 943-1461

Cycle-Recycle Co.
Waynesboro, VA
(540) 949-8973
or *www.cyclerecycle.com*

🅝 Maps:
USGS maps: Sherando, VA; Big Levels, VA
George Washington National Forest map:
Pedlar Ranger District Sportsman's map:
$4.00; $5.00 if ordered by mail—*call the park service for this map.*

MilesDirections

0.0 START at the Turkey Pen Trail parking lot just off FS 42. From the trailhead, follow the jeep trail into the woods heading south toward Bald Mountain Overlook. There will be blue blazes to follow once you reach the rock barricade at the end of Turkey Pen Road, just over one mile into the ride.

1.2 Turkey Pen Trail narrows from an old jeep trail into singletrack. This is a gradual climb. Blue blazes now mark the trail, which is now called Mill Creek Trail.

2.6 Mill Creek Trail appears to split. Turn right, crossing Mill Creek. The trail continues on the other side of the creek, following the blue blazes.

5.5 Begin the switchback ascent up Bald Mountain toward FS 162. There are eight very narrow switchbacks to the top. Good luck!

6.5 Reach the end of this climb! You are now at 3437 feet elevation. The trail exits into a clearing used for primitive camping. Bear right through this grassy field toward FS 162, then turn left onto FS 162 (dirt road).

6.8 Pass the dirt road that goes up to the old fire tower. There is a pit toilet at the end of this road.

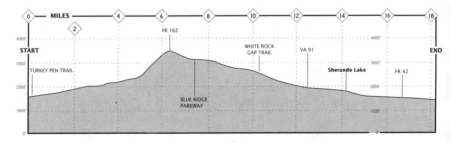

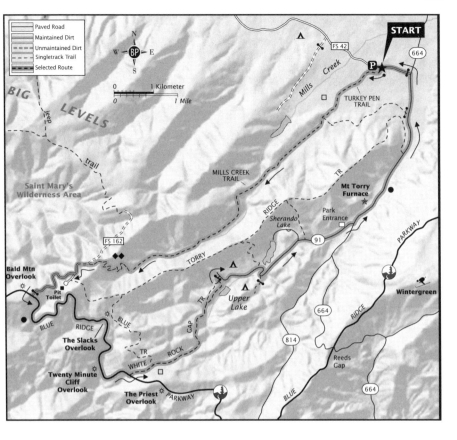

7.3 Reach the Blue Ridge Parkway and Bald Mountain Overlook. Turn left on the Blue Ridge Parkway.

*[**Note:** This section along the Blue Ridge Parkway is downhill all the way to White Rock Gap Trail. If you find yourself climbing any significant climbs, then you've passed the White Rock Gap trailhead.]*

9.7 Pass The Slacks Overlook.

10.6 Pass Twenty-Minute Cliff Overlook.

11.2 Turn left off the parkway onto White Rock Gap Trail. This turn comes just before the Blue Ridge Parkway begins to ascend. You will notice, before this ascent, that there is a small, grassy clearing on the left. Oftentimes, there are cars parked here. At the back of this clearing, there is a large tree with an orange diamond nailed to its trunk. The White Rock

Gap Trail marker is just a few yards into the woods from this tree.

*[**Note:** Along the descent down White Rock Gap Trail, there is an interesting park sign that reads: "The Old Mountain Homesite: Much of the Blue Ridge was settled in the early 1700s and cleared for agricultural purposes. The land was not economically suited for small farms. These farms were abandoned in the 1860s with the opening of western lands and the commencement of the Civil War."]*

13.8 Reach the upper lake of Sherando. Turn right on VA 91. This takes you through the Sherando Lake Campground toward the lower lake and out of the park.

16.5 Turn left on VA 664.

19.2 Turn left on FS 42.

19.7 Reach Turkey Pen Trail parking lot.

Big Levels

Ride Specs

Start: From Sherando's upper lake
Length: 26.8-mile loop
Approximate Riding Time: 4–5 hours
Difficulty Rating: Extremely difficult, thanks to endless, scree-cover climbs (half the ride is uphill), rocky terrain, and overall length.
Trail Surface: Singletrack, jeep, dirt, and paved roads
Land Status: National forest
Nearest Town: Waynesboro, VA
Other Trail Users: Hikers
Canine Compatibility: This is a very dog friendly place, but the ride itself may be too long, rocky, and grueling for your pooch. Also, the ride along VA 664 is no good for a dog. Consider leaving him behind on this one.

Getting There

From I-64 near Waynesboro: Take Exit 96 (Waynesboro-Lyndhurst exit), following signs to Sherando Lake. Follow VA 624 2.5 miles to Lyndhurst. At Lyndhurst, bear left on VA 664 south. Go approximately 7.5 miles on VA 664 to the Sherando Lake entrance. Turn right on the Park Entrance Road (VA 91). Follow the Park Entrance Road past the campgrounds, all the way to the upper lake and group camp parking area. Park here, at the end of the road. *DeLorme: Virginia Atlas & Gazetteer.* Page 54, A-3

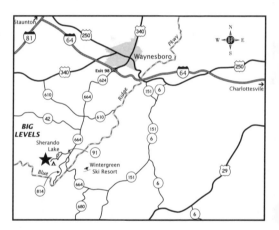

N arrow singletrack trails along rocky ridgelines and steep, barren, sun-baked jeep trails characterize this grueling route, one of the most difficult rides in the book. It's important to remember on a ride like this to bring lots of water and food because there aren't any 7-Elevens out in the woods where you can grab a tasty Big Gulp. Another suggestion before starting this ride is to invest in some type of suspension if you don't already have it. The steep and rocky nature of these trails will probably cause more shock to the body than arms and backs were meant to absorb. Without shocks, you may end this ride quite sore.

The Big Levels ride begins at the Sherando Lake Campground near Sherando's upper lake. *[Note: It can also begin at the Turkey Pen Trail parking area off Forest Service*

Oh no, Bryan! I think your wheel's hung up…

Road 42 and follow this route in reverse. A lot of folks prefer this ride starting from Forest Service Road 42 so they can climb up Kennedy Ridge (as difficult as that may sound), then descend White Rock Gap Trail back to the park. This is another great way to travel this route, so take your pick.] To get to Sherando's upper lake, follow the park access road through the park toward the group campgrounds. Immediately after the final turn, before the group camping area, there is a grassy meadow next to the upper lake dam. The White Rock Gap trailhead is on the far side of this meadow at the gate. You may leave your car in the parking area just past the trailhead.

White Rock Gap Trail crosses the meadow and heads into the woods, following small plastic orange blazes tacked to the trees. The trail splits almost immediately, heading either straight on the jeep road paralleling the lake or right, climbing into the woods. Take the trail to the right off the dirt road, which leads down to the lake. This trail leads back to White Rock Gap Trail.

MilesDirections

0.0 START from the parking area at the group campgrounds near Sherando's upper lake. Follow White Rock Gap Trail (orange blaze) across the upper lake meadow into the woods. *[**Note:** The trail starts at the gate on the lake side of the park entrance road.]* There is a large wooden trail post with an orange marker at the wood's edge. The trail splits just within the woods. Follow the upper trail, which meets back at White Rock Gap Trail.

Ouch! Meet Bryan. He made the maps in this book.

2.2 Reach another trail split, marked with a wooden trail post. Bear right at this split, following The Slacks Trail (blue blaze) uphill toward Torry Ridge. White Rock Gap Trail continues left toward the Blue Ridge Parkway.

3.0 Reach the top of the steep ascent. The rest of The Slacks Trail rambles along the contours of the mountain's ridgeline.

4.3 The Slacks Trail passes below Slacks Overlook on the Blue Ridge Parkway. The overlook can easily be reached by a short path on the left marked with an orange blaze. Continue on The Slacks Trail. There are two rockslides ahead that you must walk across.

4.8 Reach a three-way intersection where The Slacks Trail runs into Torry Ridge Trail. Turn left at the sign, following into Torry Ridge Trail (yellow blaze) up to Bald Mountain.

5.2 Shoulder your bikes up this rock slab. Torry Ridge Trail continues at the top.

5.3 Overlook on the right. Nice view of Kelly Mountain.

5.8 Reach the summit of Bald Mountain (3,587 feet). The site of the old fire tower is on the left. Turn right down this dirt road toward FS 162.

5.9 Turn right on FS 162 (Big Levels Primitive Road). This dirt road travels along Bald Mountain Ridge to Flint Mountain, then to Big Levels.

7.8 Reach the top of Flint Mountain. Begin the descent to Big Levels.

8.7 Arrive at a four-way intersection with a large clearing. Kennedy Ridge Trail is on the right of this clearing. On the left is a small wooden gate leading into Saint Mary's Wilderness (bikes not allowed). Continue straight on FS 162 (Big Levels Primitive Road).

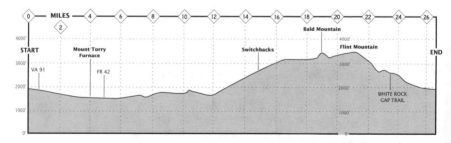

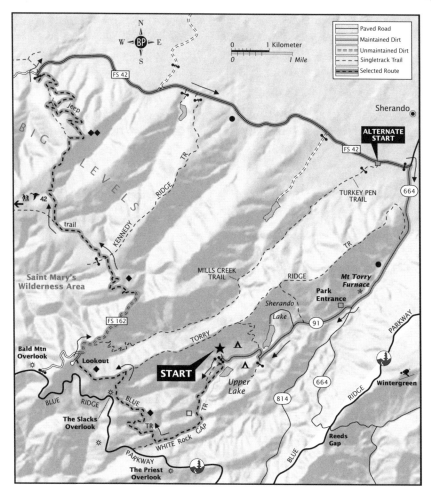

9.8 Bear right (north) at this large, sandy intersection, following a rocky jeep trail down Big Levels. Turning left (west) takes you along Bald Mountain Trail for 3.5 miles to FS 42.

10.3 Cross a small creek (John's Run).

11.3 The trail becomes very rocky and steep. Follow the switchback route rather than the straight route.

14.5 Reach the bottom of this treacherous descent! Go around the gate and turn right on FR 42 (unpaved).

21.8 Turn right on VA 664 (paved), heading back to Sherando Lake.

22.4 Convenience store on the right. Ahh, refreshments!

22.8 Mount Torry Furnace on the right.

24.2 Turn right into Sherando Lake Park on VA 91. Remember to carry your receipt with you so you don't have to worry about paying a second time to get back into the park.

26.1 Pass the lower lake.

26.8 Reach the group campground. Is your body devastated?

Alternate Start: *Start from Turkey Run Trail parking area and travel this route in reverse, heading along FS 42 to Kennedy Ridge. You'll climb Kennedy Ridge first and finish your ride flying down White Rock Gap Trail back into the park at Sherando's upper lake. This is a great way to approach this trail, so give it a try.*

Ride Information

🕐 Trail Contacts:
Glenwood and Pedlar Ranger Districts
(540) 291-2188

George Washington and Jefferson National Forest Headquarters
(540) 564-5100

🕐 Schedule:
Main gate is open from 6 a.m. to 10 p.m.

💲 Fees/Permits:
Day-use at Sherando Lake: $8.00 per carload for 3+ persons; $6.00 a car if 2 persons; $4.00 a car if 1 person; $1.00 for a person if on bicycle

💡 Local Events /Attractions:
Blue Ridge Parkway—470-mile linear park from Front Royal, VA, to Cherokee, NC

🚲 Local Bike Shops:
Rockfish Gap Outfitters
Waynesboro
(540) 943-1461

Cycle-Recycle Co.
Waynesboro, VA
(540) 949-8973
or *www.cyclerecycle.com*

Ⓝ Maps:
USGS maps: Sherando, VA; Big Levels, VA
George Washington National Forest map:
Pedlar Ranger District Sportsman's Map:
$4.00; $5.00 if ordered by mail—*call the park service for this map.*

At mile two, White Rock Gap Trail junctures with the Slacks Trail, marked by a wooden milepost. Turn right, following the blue-blazed Slacks Trail toward Torry Ridge. The trail is a vertical climb through this first section, and you may have to walk. It soon levels out, however, threading its way along a scenic ridgeline and crossing a small ravine and two rockslides before intersecting with Torry Ridge Trail. Turn left here on the yellow-blazed trail and follow the sign toward Bald Mountain Overlook on the Blue Ridge Parkway.

The real challenge begins here, as the route becomes extremely steep and rocky at this point. Turning the pedals up this trail may result in futility. Then, as you've convinced yourself that the trail can't get any steeper, you must shoulder your bike and scramble on foot up a rock wall to connect with the trail on top. Fortunately, only a few yards past the top of this wall is a small rock outcrop with a breathtaking view of Kelly Mountain. Roll along this trail, before the final grassy climb, which heads uphill to an open area that was formerly Bald Mountain Lookout Tower. Turn right onto Forest Service Road 162 (Big Levels-Bald Mountain Primitive Road) and battle the hot, scrubby terrain toward Big Levels. At this point, you have conquered a mere quarter of the battle.

You receive a well-deserved break from the past 1.5 hours of climbing with a quick and exhilarating downhill along Forest Service Road 162 (Big Levels Primitive Road). Dirt, holes, rocks, and mud make for an exciting downhill. But soon you'll be ascending again to the top of Flint Mountain. Much of this fire road is unforgiving, as the path repeatedly switches toward the top. With little shade from trees, the sun typically beats on this dusty, barren route, giving the road an unforgiving character.

Once at the top of Flint Mountain, continue along Big Levels Primitive Road until reaching a four-way intersection with a fairly large clearing. You will notice a small wooden gate on the left, marking the trail into Saint Mary's Wilderness (bikes are not allowed past this gate). On the right is Kennedy Ridge Trail, which travels sharply downhill to Forest Service Road 42. Take this trail if you wish to cut the ride short and avoid the extremely difficult descent down Big Levels Primitive Road. Kennedy Ridge, however, is still very difficult in its own right.

You'll encounter one more intersection along Big Levels Primitive Road (Forest Service Road 162) before making the descent down Big Levels. Loose dirt and sand make up the surface cover at the spot where you must bear right and begin criss-crossing down the ridge to Forest Service Road 42. This section of switchbacks down to the bottom can be extremely difficult and will take some time to maneuver. Large rocks, steep grades, and the elements of fatigue combine to make this a true mountain biker's challenge. Do not follow the trail that heads straight down—a straight-line descent through the switchbacks does not always make for a faster descent. This deteriorating jeep trail is little more than a two-lane rockslide clear to the bottom of the mountain.

At last, you'll reach the bottom, pass through a gate, and be rewarded with a mostly downhill ride on Forest Service Road 42's well-maintained gravel and hard-packed dirt road. Once you reach Virginia 664, turn right and enjoy the feel of smooth pavement. Remember to keep some money on hand in case you need to stop at the convenience store (along Virginia 664 on your way back to Sherando).

This ride sequentially combines all types of mountain-bikeable terrain imaginable. It begins with smooth singletrack up White Rock Gap, then changes to a rocky trail along the slopes of Torry Ridge. Rocky, barren, forest roads pick up where the trails leave off, as you travel along the mountain tops of Big Levels. Once at the bottom, you ride on Forest Service Road 42, a well maintained gravel road. This leads you to pavement, and you're back to where you started from.

Big Levels isn't all hard work. Just mostly...

Henry Lanum Memorial Trail

Ride Specs

Start: From the AT parking area on VA 775
Length: 5.3-mile loop
Approximate Riding Time: 1–1½ hours
Difficulty Rating: Difficult due to length and extreme climbs combined with rugged single-track
Trail Surface: Singletrack and jeep trails
Land Status: National forest
Nearest Town: Buena Vista, VA
Other Trail Users: Hikers and equestrians
Canine Compatibility: Dog friendly

Getting There

From I-81 near Lexington and Buena Vista: Take U.S. 60 east through Buena Vista to VA 634 (Daris Mill Creek Road) and Ham's County Store, near Oronoco. Turn left on VA 634. In approximately 1.5 miles, bear right at the split on VA 755 (Wiggin's Springs Road), which changes to gravel. Follow this approximately three miles to Hog Camp Gap, where the Appalachian Trail crosses. Park in the parking area on the left side of the road or continue a short distance ahead, taking the gravel road to the right, which becomes a trailhead parking lot for Henry Lanum Memorial Trail. *DeLorme: Virginia Atlas & Gazetteer.* Page 54, B-2

ormerly known as the Pompey and Mount Pleasant Loop Trail, this five-mile loop is well worth the trip to its somewhat remote location.

The Henry Lanum Jr. Trail has the reputation of being a "somewhere else to go" trail for outdoors people weary of the state's major trail systems and eager for a change of scenery. This well-marked course from start to finish is a loop not so heavily traveled, and consequently it offers people a bit more solitude.

However, for off-road cyclists, the Henry Lanum Jr. Trail is not *just* a place to go when Virginia's trails prove mundane. For daring and eager mountain bikers, this is a first-class loop of trails with more challenges and greater rewards than many trails more conveniently located and twice its size.

The trail is located nine miles east of Buena Vista, off U.S. Route 60. Its remoteness is apparent after driving along a number of backroads north of U.S. 60 to the trailhead parking lot where this ride begins.

The loop is something of a spur to the Appalachian Trail (hikers need simply to follow the Mount Pleasant National Scenic Area signs to find this loop), which crosses the dirt road at the trailhead parking lot. The lot itself is intended to be an access

point for the Appalachian Trail. However, when Henry Lanum designed the Pompey and Mount Pleasant Loop, developing it for public use, his vision was to create a beautiful diversion from the popular Appalachian Trail. He succeeded in doing so, personally maintaining this loop year-round. In July 1991, Lanum died while working on the Hidden Lake Trail in Idaho's Panhandle National Forest. In memory of Henry Lanum Jr., the Pompey and Mount Pleasant Trail was renamed and dedicated in his name. Because the Henry Lanum Jr. Trail is not actually a part of the Appalachian Trail, cyclists are welcome to ride here.

This ride begins at the same trailhead parking lot that intersects with the Appalachian Trail. You could begin the loop by parking farther down the road at the Henry Lanum Trail parking area, but there is more space in this lot, and the ride to the loop's start is recommended.

Follow the dirt road downhill momentarily until you see a grassy trail on the right that zips up into the woods. Follow this to another trail sign, where you'll turn left and find yourself at the parking area and trailhead for the Henry Lanum Jr. Trail.

After riding this loop, it becomes apparent that unbearably steep climbs can be avoided if you travel in a counterclockwise direction. Follow the trail on the right side of the parking area (marked "Mount Pleasant") around the wooden trail gate and pedal into the woods on a flat, old logging road. This trail gradually ascends until it reaches the North Fork Creek and Cascades. At this point, the trail climbs rather abruptly toward Mount Pleasant. This climb lasts nearly one mile before you reach the top and pedal through a small meadow. You'll ascend another one-half mile of steep, rocky terrain in order to reach the summit of Mount Pleasant (4021 feet). This prominent peak offers an outstanding view of the Appalachian Mountains, and its

Moo...

Ride Information

📞 Trail Contacts:
Glenwood & Pedlar Ranger Districts
(540) 291-2188

George Washington & Jefferson National Forest Headquarters
(540) 564-5100

🕐 Schedule:
Public land, accessible year-round

❓ Local Information
Historic Lexington Visitor Center
Lexington, VA
(540) 463-3777
or *www.lexingtonvirginia.com*

🍸 Local Events /Attractions:
Virginia Military Institute
Washington & Lee University

🚲 Local Bike Shops:
The Lexington Bicycle Shop
Lexington, VA
(540) 463-7969

🅽 Maps:
USGS maps: Montebello, VA; Forks of Buffalo, VA
George Washington National Forest map:
Pedlar Ranger District Sportsman's Map:
$4.00; $5.00 if ordered by mail—*call the park service for this map.*

3,000-foot drop-off yields a mostly unimpaired view. Traveling to the top of this peak adds an extra mile to the loop. *[Note: the park service recently relocated one mile of this trail due to resource damage, so call ahead for the status on this trail should you be interested in hiking it.]*

The loop continues along the ridgetop upward to Pompey Mountain. No startling views or sweeping panoramas are visible from this mountaintop, but the thrilling descent on the other side compensates nicely. Ride this descent with extreme caution—the trail is extremely narrow and steep and is loaded with obstacles that can throw you from your bike. As soon as this descent ends, you'll climb a bit before hitting a wild and deliriously fast downhill run to the trailhead parking lot at the beginning of this loop. Please be extra careful on this last descent that you don't collide with other trail users. Much of this descent is quick and bumpy and is known to have some blind corners. From this trailhead parking area, follow the same route back to the parking area.

If you're more interested in muscling this loop at a slower pace to capture its scenery, watch for patches of wildflowers, mountain laurel, blueberries, rhododendron, oak, hickory, and yellow birch. The trail winds through a garden of colorful flora.

[Attention: The park service is beginning to see a good deal of resource damage as a result of mountain bike use along this loop. Trail damage is caused primarily by bikers "braiding" the tread to avoid rocks. This results in the trail widening, which causes increased erosion. They are monitoring the situation. A worst case scenario would be that the trail could be closed to bikes sometime in the future if damage increases to unacceptable levels. But, thankfully, it hasn't gotten to that point yet. Please do your best to help maintain this trail if you ride here. We don't want this trail closed to bikes.]

If you make the extra one-mile hike to Mount Pleasant, you won't be disappointed.

MilesDirections

0.0 START from the trailhead parking area next to the Appalachian Trail. Go east on VA 48.

0.2 Just before VA 48 and VA 635 split, there is a little grass trail that zips up the hill on the right side of the road. Marking this trail are three wooden posts with a blue square. Bear right off VA 48 on this Grassy Trail, and follow it into the trees.

0.3 Come to a trail sign and a small wooden trail gate. Turn left, continuing to follow the Grassy Trail to the start of the Henry Lanum Jr. Trail.

0.35 Cross VA 635 and enter a small parking area at the start of the Henry Lanum Jr. Trail.

Note there are two trailheads from this parking area. Both trails lead into the woods. Take the trail on the far right marked "Mt. Pleasant 2.6 miles." This will take you around the loop in a counterclockwise direction. You can go either way. However, traveling in the counterclockwise direction helps make this loop much more manageable and fun. The loop starts off as a flat wagon trail along the creek. Go around the wooden trail gate to begin.

1.6 Arrive at the cascades. The trail continues up from here.

1.9 Start climbing toward Mount Pleasant.

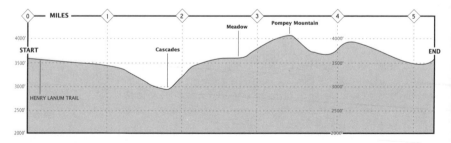

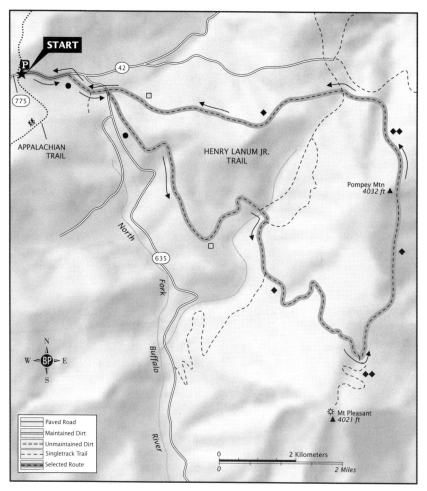

START

P

42

775

APPALACHIAN
TRAIL

HENRY LANUM JR.
TRAIL

Pompey Mtn
4032 ft ▲

North

635

Fork

Buffalo

N
W ⊕ BP E
S

Mt Pleasant
▲ 4021 ft

River

Paved Road
Maintained Dirt
Unmaintained Dirt
Singletrack Trail
Selected Route

0
2 Kilometers
0
2 Miles

2.7 The trail becomes level, crosses through a thick meadow, and reaches a wooden trail sign. From this sign you may either continue this loop toward Pompey Mountain or detour a half mile to the summit of Mount Pleasant. If you wish to make the one-mile, round-trip effort to the top of Mount Pleasant, be aware that the trail is very steep and rocky. From 4021 feet, however, the view is well worth the trouble, revealing an incredible panoramic view of the surrounding mountains.

3.4 Crest Pompey Mountain (4032 feet). There's no real view from this mountaintop,

but the climb is rewarded with a wild descent down a challenging, narrow trail.

3.8 This descent ends. Start climbing again. This climb is moderate compared with those before it.

4.3 Reach the top of this climb. The trail levels off, then begins a final, fast descent to the beginning of the loop. This descent is very quick. Watch out for other trail users on your way down.

5.0 Return to the Henry Lanum Jr. Trail trailhead. Ride back to the car the way you came.

5.3 Arrive at the parking area.

Blue Ridge Dirt Ride

Ride Specs

Start: From the Buena Vista Overlook

Length: 15.3-mile loop

Approximate Riding Time: 2 hours

Difficulty Rating: This is a fairly easy to moderate ride along unpaved forest roads and the paved Blue Ridge Parkway. The climbing is moderate, but the non-technical trail surface tempers the climbs well.

Trail Surface: Forest roads and the Blue Ridge Parkway

Land Status: National forest

Nearest Town: Buena Vista, VA

Other Trail Users: Motorists

Canine Compatibility: Not good. Too much road riding.

Getting There

From I-81 near Lexington and Buena Vista: Take U.S. 60 (Buena Vista exit) east. Pass through Buena Vista on U.S. 60 east and enter the George Washington National Forest. Climb up to the Blue Ridge Parkway. Cross beneath the parkway, then turn left on the entrance ramp to access the Blue Ridge Parkway. Turn left on the Blue Ridge Parkway heading south. Go approximately 0.5 miles to the Buena Vista Overlook on the right. *DeLorme: Virginia Atlas & Gazetteer:* Page 54, C-1

The Blue Ridge Parkway and Skyline Drive together form a scenic byway of some 470 miles of quiet, beautifully designed road, rolling atop the mountain peaks of the Appalachian Mountain Range. Construction began on the project in 1935 near the Virginia-North Carolina border and continued north to Front Royal, Virginia. The parkway changes names at the top of Afton Mountain near Waynesboro, Virginia. The route south into North Carolina is the Blue Ridge Parkway (which is free to ride on) and the route north, which winds through the Shenandoah National Park all the way to Front Royal, is Skyline Drive (which currently costs $10 per car, $5 per bike). The first segment of the grand parkway opened in April of 1939, while the final section opened in 1987 with the completion of the Grandfather Mountain segment in North Carolina. Throughout its short history, nearly 600 million visitors have visited Skyline Drive and the Blue Ridge Parkway. That's almost 11 million visitors per year or more than 30,000 per day.

From Front Royal, Virginia, to the Cherokee Indian Reservation near Cherokee, North Carolina, Skyline Drive and the Blue Ridge Parkway are the scenic links between the Shenandoah National Park in

Sights along the Parkway.

Virginia and the Great Smokey Mountains of North Carolina and Tennessee. They follow the Appalachian's highest ridges, attaining altitudes of more than 6,000 feet while averaging between 3,000 and 4,000 feet. This magnificent national treasure was designed specifically for a leisurely and scenic route through this prominent mountain region.

The moderately difficult and extremely scenic loop included in this guide is meant to illustrate to mountain bikers an obvious but often overlooked asset of the Blue Ridge Parkway.

The Parkway, from Front Royal to Cherokee, is well suited for both bicycling tourists and day-cyclists alike. However, the smooth pavement and long, leisurely climbs may not appeal quite as much to the off-road rider. What many folks fail to realize is that along certain sections of the Parkway off-road cyclists can access hundreds of miles of both well maintained and abandoned forest roads, all of which are open to the public. Virginia's main access is through the Glenwood and Pedlar Ranger Districts of the George Washington and Jefferson National Forests. The Blue

Ride Information

📞 Trail Contacts:
Glenwood and Pedlar Ranger District
(540) 291-2188

George Washington and Jefferson National Forests Headquarters
(540) 564-5100

Friends of the Blue Ridge Parkway
1-800-228-PARK

🕐 Schedule:
Public land, accessible year-round
Parkway may be closed to vehicle traffic
during heavy snow

🚲 Local Bike Shops:
The Lexington Bicycle Shop
(540) 463-7969

🗺 Maps:
USGS maps: Buena Vista, VA
George Washington National Forest map:
Pedlar Ranger District Sportsman's Map:
$4.00; $5.00 if ordered by mail—*call the park service for this map.*

Ridge Parkway extends over more than 100 miles through this 147,000-acre section of public land and offers countless points of access into the national forest.

In addition to the dramatic change of scenery, from skyline views along the Parkway to dense, old-growth forests surrounding the dirt roads, these forest routes afford cyclists the luxury to abandon their traffic woes and concentrate on nothing but the ride itself. There are seldom any vehicles to worry about, either in view or in earshot, and wildlife is often visible from every point of the ride. The lush green of the forest's thick undergrowth and splashy array of colorful wildflowers could hardly exist along the paved roads of the busy world beyond.

This loop starts from the Buena Vista Overlook on the Blue Ridge Parkway. Like most overlooks and access points, there's plenty of room to park the car. Pedal north up the Parkway a bit, then exit west on U.S. Route 60. This takes you right down to Forest Service Road 315 (Panther Falls Road).

Through the gate, this well maintained dirt road descends the mountain toward Pedlar River, for which this district of the forest is named. After a few ups and downs and more than seven miles of forested serenity, Forest Service Road 315 comes to an end at Forest Service Road 311. Unfortunately, most of these dirt roads don't have any signs or road names, so it's important to follow the maps closely, know your distances, and carry a compass. There are so many miles of dirt roads back here that a wrong turn can get you completely spun around and heading in the wrong direction.

At Forest Service Road 311, pass through a gate and begin climbing the slow but steady grade back toward the Parkway. At the top of this climb, pass through another gate and come to another intersection (Virginia 607). Turn right on this dirt road and notice the Blue Ridge Parkway on your left. Virginia 607 travels along the ridge for just over one mile, then ducks under the Parkway and heads down the west side of the mountain to Buena Vista. Unfortunately, at this point Virginia 607 doesn't directly access the Parkway. You will have to walk your bike up the embankment at the underpass to get on the road. Once up the embankment, turn right and ride along the mountain peaks for more than four miles back to the car. Much of this section is downhill.

This ride is but one of the countless opportunities the Blue Ridge Parkway offers mountain bikers as it passes through this large segment of the George Washington National Forest. Please remember, of course, that while the Blue Ridge Parkway becomes Skyline Drive and travels through the Shenandoah National Park just north of Afton Mountain, mountain bikes are not allowed within the Park's boundaries. Only national forest land is open in Virginia to cyclists.

MilesDirections

0.0 START at the Buena Vista Overlook on the Blue Ridge Parkway. Head north on the Blue Ridge Parkway to U.S. 60.

0.1 Cross over U.S. 60.

0.2 Exit the Blue Ridge Parkway to U.S. 60 East.

0.3 Turn left on U.S. 60 East through Humphreys Gap.

0.4 Turn right on FS 315 and go through the gate (this gate is usually open year-round). This dirt road winds up and down through the valley of Pedlar River.

3.4 Cross over Roberts Creek. An unnamed dirt road intersects with FS 315 at this point. Continue straight on FS 315. Reach the low point along FS 315 (1390 feet).

4.5 Cross over Shady Mountain Creek. This, like Roberts Creek, is a fairly small tributary of Pedlar River.

6.9 Turn right on FS 311. Turning left would take you to the Lynchburg Reservoir. FS 311 travels along Little Irish Creek up the mountain to the Blue Ridge Parkway.

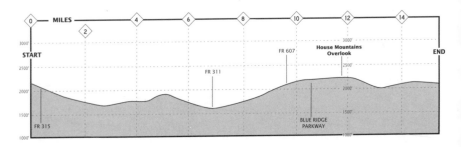

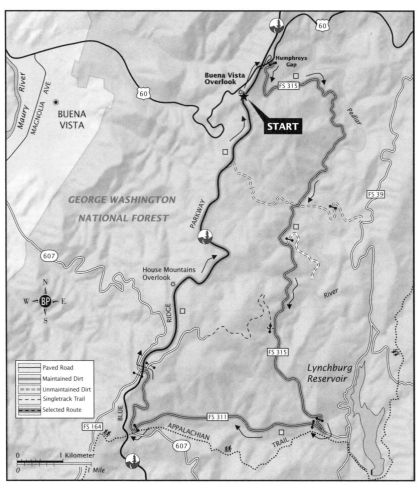

9.5 Reach the top of this climb, go through the gate, and turn right on VA 607. This dirt road climbs a little farther to reach the Blue Ridge Parkway.

10.5 Arrive at the Blue Ridge Parkway through Robinson's Gap (2412 feet). Unfortunately, when VA 607 meets up with the parkway, it doesn't actually connect with it. Rather, VA 607 goes underneath the parkway to the other side, then descends all the way to Buena Vista. To get on the parkway, climb the embankment from FS 607 with your bike on your shoulder. This easy little hike gets you on the Parkway. Turn right, heading north on the Blue Ridge Parkway. *[**Note:** An alternative to climbing the embankment is to cross underneath the Blue Ridge Parkway heading west to Buena Vista where there is a dirt road to the left. Turn left on this road and follow it for about one mile. Turn left again over a steep bank. Less than a quarter-mile ahead through the gate is the Blue Ridge Parkway.]*

11.7 House Mountains Overlook on the left.

15.3 Arrive at Buena Vista Overlook on the left.

Western Virginia

Compiled here is an index of great rides in the Western Highlands region that didn't make the A-list this time around but deserve recognition. Check them out and let us know what you think. You may decide that one or more of these rides deserves higher status in future editions or, perhaps, you may have a ride of your own that merits some attention.

Ⓛ Duncan Hollow Trail

As I may have noted in the Massanutten Mountain Chapter (see Ride 25), there are countless routes of singletrack, doubletrack, and forest roads along which mountain biking is superb. Most of the mountain is within the George Washington National Forest and is open to the public for multiple uses. This route, known as Duncan Hollow, leaves right from the Massanutten Visitor Center and takes cyclists through the heart of Massanutten Mountain. Located just five miles east of New Market, folks are encouraged to stop in at the Visitor Center and walk the quarter-mile Massanutten Story Trail to learn more about the history of the mountain. This ride head north from the Visitor Center along FS 274 taking you along Passage Creek all the way up to Camp Roosevelt. At camp Roosevelt, you'll turn back around and follow the orange-blazed Duncan Hollow Trail, climbing your up Middle Mountain to Scothorn Gap. From Scothorn Gap, follow the yellow-blazed trail all the way downhill back to FS 274. Turn left onto FS 274 and make your way back to the Visitor Center. This is a fairly long loop at just over 17 miles, so plan to bring along enough water and food, or even consider camping overnight at Camp Roosevelt.

To get to Massanutten Visitor Center and the start of this ride, travel on I-81 to the town of New Market. From New Market, turn east on U.S. 211 and head up the mountain through New Market Gap to the Massanutten Visitor Center. The trail starts from here. *DeLorme: Virginia Atlas & Gazetteer:* Page 73 C-D7

Ⓜ Edinburg Gap ORV Trails: Massanutten Mountain

The George Washington National Forest Service has, over the past number of years, recognized operating off-road vehicles in the national forests as a valid use of forest land, and consequently, has identified and constructed a number of All-Terrain Vehicle (ATV) or Off-Road Vehicle (ORV) trails for 4WD vehicles, motorcycles, and motorbikes. These ORV trails also provide excellent mountain biking, as cyclists will find miles of narrow, twisting routes coupled with wide, inviting paths, all of which are clearly labeled and easy to follow. Cyclists just want to beware that there are motorized vehicles back here and should ride with their heads on a swivel in case a 4WD truck or motorcycle comes out of nowhere and needs to be avoided at an emergency's pace. Don't fool yourself that you'll be alone back here and find a peaceful place in which to ride. It can sometimes be noisy and downright crowded with traffic. But you will find tons of tough, rugged trails on which to ride, and an afternoon back here won't be hard to fill. Just stay away after a big rain as the ruts and ridges created by the ORVs will get really nasty and full of mud.

In the Lee Ranger District at Edinburg Gap, there are two such ORV trail systems: Peters Mill Run ORV Trails and Tasker Gap ORV Trails. Both systems can be accessed from Virginia 675 southeast of Edinburg. Signs will direct you from Virginia 675 onto the ORV trails. To get there, take Interstate 81 to the Edinburg / Virginia 675 exit. Go east (left) on Virginia 675 through Edinburg. When you see the Chrysler dealer, stay on Virginia 675 by turning right onto Edinburg Gap Road. Follow Virginia 675 up the mountain about three miles. The trailhead is at the very top on your right, just after a hairpin turn to your right. For more information on the ORV trails in the GW, visit www.fs.fed.us/gwjnf/orvtrails.html. For a detailed trail map of the Tasker Gap ORV Trails go to the Northern Virginia Trail Rider's web site at www.nvtr.org/taskers.html. *DeLorme: **Virginia Atlas & Gazetteer:*** Page 73 B-7

(N) McDowell Battlefield Trail

Here's a great little ride for history buffs if you happen already to be in the neighborhood for the Williamsville Loop ride (see Ride 32). This ride is located right next to the town of McDowell, just north of Williamsville. You can start at either the west end or the east end of this point-to-point ride, which take you up Bullpasture Mountain to the top of Sittlington Hill and the core of the McDowell Battlefield. Fought on May 8, 1862, this battle was the Jackson's Valley Campaigns' first victory. The trail isn't very long (just a little over one mile each way), but takes you uphill to over 2500 feet. To start from the eastern end of this trail, park at the Battlefield parking area along U.S. 250, approximately one mile from the top of Bullpasture Mountain. If you want to start from the western end of this trail, part at the Presbyterian Church at the junction of VA 678 right outside McDowell. To learn more about this trail and the area visit the Sugar Tree Country Store in McDowell for interpretive information and details of the Civil War Trail. For more information, call 1-800-396-2445. *DeLorme: Virginia Atlas & Gazetteer:* Page 65, B-7

(O) South Pedlar ATV Trail

Situated on the Pedlar Ranger District of the George Washington National Forest, this is a looping network of nearly 20 miles of trails designed for the recreational all-terrain vehicle rider (ATV). The routes here are open to ATV's, motorbikes, and mountain bikes and follow narrow, twisting trails through the hilly terrain of the Blue Ridge Mountains. The South Pedlar ATV Trail system (also known as Terrapin and Rattlesnake Trails) is popular among mountain bikers from Lynchburg, Buena Vista, and Lexington and boasts some of the most difficult terrain around. Cyclists interested in heading out here should consider coming in the spring when the mountain laurel, thick around here, are in spectacular bloom. The forest is pretty dense in the summer sheltering you from most of the summer heat. Located one-half mile west of the Blue Ridge Parkway off VA 130. Signs for the Terrapin and Rattlesnake Trailhead Parking in posted along VA 130. Once you arrive, there's a pay-as-you-park honor system in place, so please don't hesitate to drop in your $5 parking fee to support the forest service. For more information go to www.fs.fed.us/gwjnf/orvtrails.html. *DeLorme: Virginia Atlas & Gazetteer*: Page 54, D-1

(P) North Mountain Trail near Roanoke

This is a trail that Roanoke's hard-core mountain bikers often frequent when they're feeling aggressive. Fewer than 10 miles west of Roanoke on VA 311, you can access this trail in the New Castle Ranger District of the Jefferson National Forest from the road. Narrow, rugged singletrack follows the North Mountain ridge nearly 12 miles north. There are some smaller trails that fall down the west side of North Mountain to FR 224, a forest road that may give you the relief you need to get back to the start of this ride. *DeLorme: Virginia Atlas & Gazetteer:* Page 42, A-2

South west

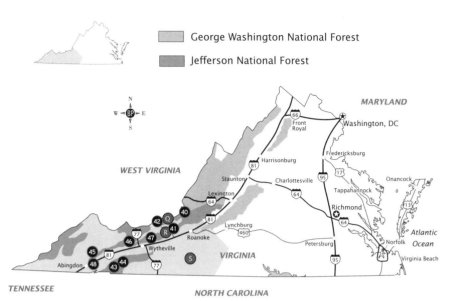

40

Potts Mountain

Ride Specs

Start: From the Hanging Rock parking area
Length: 8.6-mile loop
Approximate Riding Time: 1–2 hours
Difficulty Rating: Difficult. There's one very fast, technical descent that requires a good deal of skill, and the climbs on the backend make for an additional challenge physically.
Trail Surface: Forest roads and hilly singletrack
Land Status: National forest
Nearest Town: Roanoke, VA
Other Trail Users: Hikers, equestrians, and motorists (very few)
Canine Compatibility: Dog friendly

Getting There

From Roanoke: Take Exit 141 off I-81 to VA 311 North toward New Castle (18 miles). Continue on VA 311 approximately 10 miles farther to the top of Potts Mountain. Turn right off VA 311 on FS 177 at the picnic area. Travel on FS 177 for about 4.5 miles to the Hanging Rock parking area. Park here. *DeLorme: Virginia Atlas & Gazetteer.* Page 52, D-1

o get to Roanoke, the state's largest city west of Richmond, just follow the great star perched atop Mill Mountain. Roanoke, the self-proclaimed "Star City of the South," lies on the banks of the Roanoke River at the southern end of the Shenandoah Valley and is flanked by both the Blue Ridge and Allegheny mountains.

In earlier days Roanoke was just a small village known as Big Lick—named for the deer that sought out the area's salt deposits. With the arrival of the railroad industry, Big Lick grew into a sizable town, and in 1882 two large railroads, the Shenandoah Valley Railroad and the Norfolk & Western built junctions along the Roanoke River. In 1884 Big Lick's population had grown to more than 5,000, and this Western Virginia crossroads was chartered as the city of Roanoke.

The city thrived on coal, timber, and limestone from the nearby mountains until manufacturing railroad cars, textiles, and furniture, as well as building hardware, proved more profitable and enduring. Today Roanoke makes its claim as the capital of the Blue Ridge, enjoying all the wonders of a modern city. Unlike Virginia's other hubs, though, Roanoke is the only one fortunate enough to be nestled between the Blue Ridge and the Allegheny mountains. What this means for people who enjoy both urban and rural lifestyles is that 4,000-foot peaks are only minutes from the

Museum of Fine Arts. Just west of downtown Roanoke, the Appalachian Trail passes by such natural wonders as Dragons Tooth and McAfee's Knob. For mountain bikers in the region, hundreds of miles of trails and forest roads network through the endless acres of national forest land only a short drive away.

Potts Mountain is one such place near Roanoke that is regarded by off-road cyclists as a match made in heaven. Its scenic forest roads and steep singletrack descents are only a short drive from Roanoke, and its forested terrain can entrance you for hours on end. Situated in the heart of the Jefferson National Forest, Potts Mountain rises to nearly 3800 feet above sea level, with a ridgeline nearly as sharp as nearby Dragons Tooth. The ride begins from the Hanging Rock parking area on Forest Service Road 177 atop Potts Mountain ridge. There is a short trail from this parking lot to Hanging Rock Overlook. The overlook offers an incredible view of Hanging Rock Valley and is worth the extra time to make the hike.

From the parking area head north on Forest Service Road 177 (Potts Mountain Road). The ride along Forest Service Road 177 brings you along the eastern boundary of the Shawvers Run Wilderness Area. This wilderness area extends from the top of Potts Mountain down to the lower Hanging Rock Valley. Forest Service Road 177 runs along the ridge of Potts Mountain past an old radio facility resembling a con-

Ride Information

🕐 Trail Contacts:
New Castle Ranger District
(540) 864-5195
Jefferson National Forest Headquarters
(540) 265-6054

🕐 Schedule:
Public land, accessible year-round

Local Bike Shops:
American Flyers Bicycle Shop
Roanoke, VA
(540) 345-2116
or *www.amflyers.com*

Cardinal Bicycle
Roanoke, VA
(540) 344-2453

Valley Bicycles
Roanoke, VA
(540) 389-2453

East Coasters Cycling and Fitness
Blacksburg, VA
(540) 951-2369
or *www.eastcoasters.com*

Ⓝ Maps:
USGS maps: Potts Creek, VA, WVA
Jefferson National Forest topo map:
New Castle District Sportsman's Map:
$4.00; $5.00 if ordered by mail—*call the park service for this map*

MilesDirections

0.0 START at the parking area for Hanging Rock Overlook on FS 177. Travel northeast along FS 177 toward Cove Trail.

1.1 Pass the old Radio Facility on the left. This resembles a large concrete bunker. Keep your eyes peeled for the trailhead sign on the right pointing to Cove Trail.

1.6 Turn right on Cove Trail. There should be a sign on the right with a hiker on it at this trailhead. Be ready for a steep descent into Potts Cove.

3.5 Reach the bottom of the descent and travel through Potts Cove.

3.6 Cross a small wooden bridge from the trail onto a gravel road. This road leads you up to FS 176.

4.2 Turn left on FS 176. This leads you uphill back to the top of Potts Mountain. Start climbing.

5.4 Reach the top. Turn left on FS 177 at this intersection. There are some wonderful views from this road on either side of the mountain.

7.2 Pass the trailhead for Cove Trail.

7.6 Pass the concrete radio "bunker" on the right.

8.6 Reach the Hanging Rock parking area.

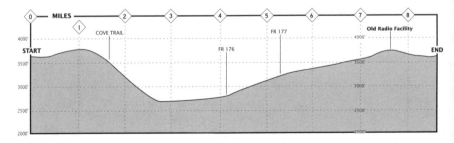

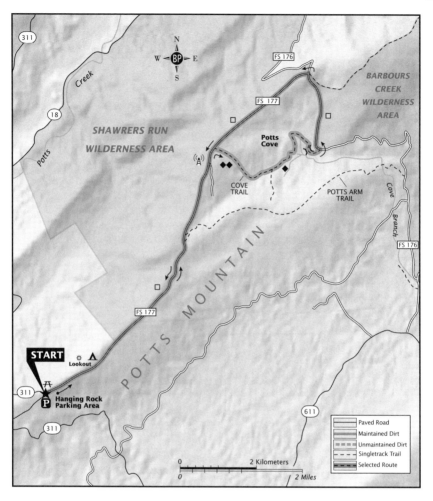

crete bunker. One-half mile past this radio facility you'll come upon a trail sign on the right. This is the sign for Cove Trail. Turn right on this trail and be ready for an incredibly quick and steep descent into Potts Cove. Be sure to follow the yellow blaze trail all the way. Cove Trail will lead you through Potts Cove for two miles, then cross over a small, wooden bridge and end up on a gravel road. This gravel road travels a half mile to Forest Service Road 176. Turn left on Forest Service Road 176 and start climbing. Forest Service Road 176 used to be the old stagecoach route from Fincastle to Sweet Springs, West Virginia. It was known back then as the "Sweet Springs Turnpike." It is still locally known as the turnpike road. This gravel forest road takes you back to the top of Potts Mountain. Turn left on Forest Service Road 177 at the top and follow this all the way back to Hanging Rock.

This ride is just a sample of the many different rides possible in this region. Ask the New Castle District Rangers about which trails are appropriate for riding. All of the forest roads are open to bicycling, but recently they have lost the right-of-way along a number of trails to private ownership.

41

Brush Mountain

Ride Specs

Start: From FS 188.2 off U.S. 460
Length: 8.3-mile loop
Approximate Riding Time: 2–2½ hours
Difficulty Rating: Both physically and techni-cally, this ride is tough. There are long, fast singletrack descents and equally long, tough climbs. It's not all bad, but be prepared for a good workout.
Trail Surface: Singletrack and gravel road
Land Status: National forest
Nearest Town: Blacksburg, VA
Other Trail Users: Hikers and equestrians
Canine Compatibility: Dog Friendly

Getting There

From Blacksburg: Take Main Street (Business U.S. 460) west toward Brush Mountain. Continue on U.S. 460 west for about four miles. At the top of the climb over Brush Mountain, turn left on FS 188.2 (dirt road). Park wherever you can along FS 188.2 or go two miles along FS 188.2 to the old lookout tower and park. *DeLorme: Virginia Atlas & Gazetteer.* Page 41, B-6

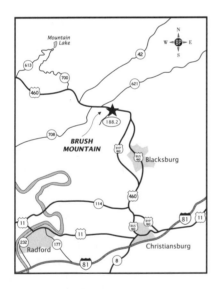

P icture in your mind the *perfect* mountain biking spot. Chances are, you'd be thinking of some-thing that is, in fact, very similar to a place called Brush Mountain, located just north of the small Virginia college town of Blacksburg.

Brush Mountain has become, for nearly all off-road cyclists in this area, the quintes-sential mountain biking haven. Its proximity to town and campus—the mountain is cycling distance from the Virginia Tech cam-pus—makes Brush Mountain an ideal place for busy students to ride. They can easily spend an afternoon riding around the moun-tain's trails and still get back with plenty of time to hit the books at day's end (yeah, like that'll happen). The mountain's convenient location, though, is not the only reason Brush Mountain is included in this guide. This mountain is also home to some of the finest off-road bicycling trails in the state of Virginia.

The Brush and Gap Mountain multiple-use trails have not gone under-appreci-ated. Local clubs practice regular trail maintenance to preserve this mountain bik-ing mecca. There are numerous waterbars strategically placed along the steep descents that protect the trails from excessive run-off and erosion. Trail courdoroy-ing, a method of repairing wet or muddy trails, is also evident throughout the moun-tain's trail system, further maintaining the trail's integrity from so much use. If you

want to become more involved with trail maintenance, or just want some fun people to ride with, contact the friendly family at the East Coasters Bike Shop, down the road from Brush Mountain.

The closest access to the trails on Brush Mountain is from Forest Service Road 188.2, just off U.S. Route 460. Take U.S. Route 460 west out of Blacksburg and start climbing (this is the east side of Brush Mountain). At the top of this climb, on the left, is Forest Service Road 188.2. Follow this gravel-surfaced road up the steep hill and along the ridge of Brush Mountain. This leads you all the way to the site of the old fire tower, a circular drive at the end of the state-maintained service road.

Ride Information

📞 Trail Contacts:
Jefferson National Forest
Roanoke, VA
(540) 265-6054

Blacksburg Ranger District
Blacksburg, VA
(540) 552-4641

🕐 Schedule:
Year-round—*weather permitting*

❓ Local Information:
For information on the area go to the website *www.blacksburg.va.us*

💡 Local Events/Attractions:
Smithfield Plantation
Smithfield Plantation Drive
Blacksburg, VA
(540) 231-3947

Virginia Museum of Natural History at Virginia Tech
Blacksburg, VA
(540) 231-3001

🚲 Group Rides:
Saturday mornings weather permitting, start at 10:30 a.m. (540) 951-2369—*sponsored by East Coasters a local bike shop*

🚲 Local Bike Shops:
East Coasters
Blacksburg, VA
(540) 951-2369
or *www.eastcoasters.com*

🅝 Maps:
USGS maps: Blacksburg, VA; Newport, VA
Jefferson National Forest topo map: Blacksburg District

From this circular drive, continue along the ridge of Brush Mountain, on what is now an unmaintained jeep trail. Follow this trail along the ridge for one half mile before reaching a three-way split. Notice, at this point, the red paint blazes on the trees. Turn right, following the red blazes into the woods, and begin your first wild descent down "The Beast" toward Poverty Creek. Hold onto your brake pads as you descend through four very tight switchbacks, then straight down the west side of Brush Mountain.

At the bottom of the descent, this red-blazed trail comes to a "T," intersecting with the orange-blazed multiple-use trail. Turn right at this "T" and follow the smooth, flat single-track trail alongside Poverty Creek. Be aware of hikers and equestrians who may also be using this trail, and always yield the right-of-way. The orange blazes will lead you all the way back to Forest Service Road 188.2 if you choose to complete this loop.

In just under one mile along the secluded Poverty Creek Multiple-Use Trail, you'll reach a small opening. To follow this loop, you need to bear right into the woods, following the orange blazes. Bearing to the left will lead you to Gap Mountain, which has an entirely different network of great trails. To continue this loop, though, turn right and follow the orange blazes. These lead you toward Pandapas Pond. Please note that bicycles are not allowed within 300 feet of Pandapas Pond. There are a number of trails bordering the pond designed *exclusively* for hikers. Be careful not to stray too far on the Poverty Creek Multiple-Use Trail and wind up at Pandapas Pond.

The orange trail turns right before the pond and crosses over Poverty Creek into a thick growth of rhododendron. From this point, all the way back up to the ridge of Brush Mountain and Forest Service Road 188.2, the trail weaves through heavy foliage, rolling up and down the mountain's western slope. This section is exciting enough to turn around at the jeep trail and grind it out a second time. Once at the jeep trail, turn right and climb your way back up to Forest Service Road 188.2.

Because Brush Mountain is so close to town, the easiest way to get there may be by bicycle. There are few places to park aside from the circular drive at the old fire tower or along Forest Service Road 188.2. Unfortunately, parking is severely limited on the mountain's peak. And Forest Service Road 188.2, while accessible to cars, is a gravel road with some large potholes. You may prefer to leave your car near the East Coasters Bike Shop, then ride the four miles uphill to the start. Another option is to park at the Pandapas Pond parking lot and walk your bike over to the main trail. This option will, of course, start you in a different place than the featured ride, but it will nevertheless lead you to the same trails.

There are also no camping facilities at the park, so plan to make reservations in Blacksburg if you decide to stay in the area. The numerous trails here at Brush Mountain provide more than one day of riding, and staying overnight will allow you to explore all that Brush Mountain, Poverty Creek, and Pandapas Pond has to offer. Each switchback, incline and singletrack has the potential of opening a new avenue of trails to explore. Enjoy the other trails like Snake Root, Jacobs Ladder, Queen Anne, Prickley Pear, Skullcap, Trillium, and Indian Pipe. All of these trails lead to each other at some point along the ride, so pick up an outlined map and some local advice from the East Coasters. Each trail here at Brush Mountain is guaranteed satisfaction as well as the opportunity for cyclists to ride premium singletrack.

Be sure to visit the folks at East Coasters, just down the road from Brush Mountain—especially if you park in their lot to get to the trail.

MilesDirections

0.0 START at FS 188.2, just off U.S. 460. Head up the steep climb to the top of the ridge.

0.9 Pass the first orange-blazed trailhead for the Brush Mountain Multiple-Use Trail. Continue on FS 188.2. This forest road is a well maintained, gravel service road with some steep, rolling hills.

1.9 Reach the remains of the old lookout tower. This is a large circular drive where the tower once existed. State maintenance ends at this point. Go straight through this circular drive to the old jeep trail which continues into the woods.

2.5 The trail splits in a number of different directions. Turn right into the woods, following the red blazes. This leads to an incredible, singletrack descent called The Beast. Watch out, it's fast!

*[**Note:** Along the trail between the old lookout tower and this turn, you will ride through two semi-permanent mud holes before reaching this trail split. If you turn left at this split, you will drop down the south side of Brush Mountain through private property. Going straight takes you all the way to Boley Fields. Make sure to turn right (west) on the red-blazed trail.]*

3.7 Reach the bottom of this descent.

3.75 Cross over Poverty Creek. This is a fairly dry creek crossing.

3.8 Turn right on the Poverty Creek Multiple-Use Trail (orange blaze). This is a well maintained, flat, smooth singletrack trail that parallels Poverty Creek. The thick growth of rhododendron on either side of this trail gives the trail a deep, remote quality. You may feel very removed from the outside world along this peaceful trail.

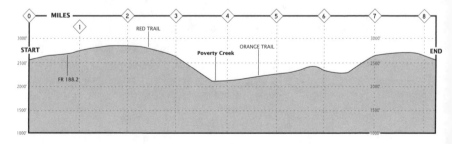

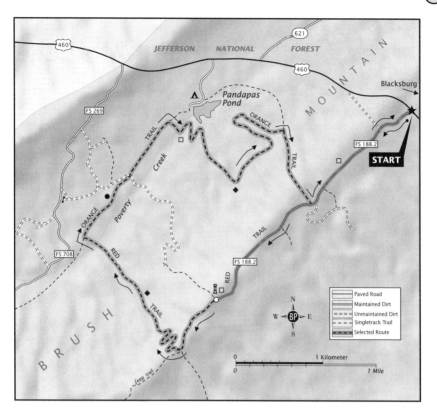

4.6 Reach a small clearing. Bear right on the trail that leads into the woods and follow the Orange Blaze. If, at this point, you bear left into the open area, you will end up following trails that lead to Gap Mountain and FS 708 on the west side of Poverty Creek.

4.7 Arrive at a four-way trail intersection after a quick, muddy section. Go straight through this trail intersection, following the Orange Diamond Blazes nailed to the trees in front of you.

5.2 Turn right (southeast) across Poverty Creek on a narrow singletrack trail that winds through trees and a thick grove of rhododendron. There are two orange paint squares nailed to a tree at this turn, but both are slightly hidden. If you reach Pandapas Pond, 0.2 miles away, you've gone too far. *[Caution: Mountain bikers and equestrians are not allowed to ride within 300 feet of the*

Pandapas Pond, so try not to miss the turn.]

5.6 Just past the thick grove of rhododendron, start climbing a steep hill with switchbacks.

5.85 This orange-blazed trail comes to a "T" intersection. Stay left, following the double orange blazes.

5.85 The trail almost immediately comes to another "T" intersection. There are four orange blocks painted on a tree on the left. Take a hard right at this "T" intersection. Start climbing.

6.2 Descend a short but very steep hill with warning labels posted on the trees. The uphill on the other side is equally as steep.

6.5 Turn right on a wide jeep trail. This takes you uphill all the way back to FS 188.2.

7.4 Turn left on FS 188.2.

8.3 Reach U.S. 406.

Mountain Lake

Ride Specs

Start: From Mountain Lake Resort

Length: 21.4-mile loop

Approximate Riding Time: 2½–3 hours

Difficulty Rating: Moderate to difficult due to the length of the ride and some long, gradual climbs. Technically, this ride doesn't pose a great a challenge.

Trail Surface: Hilly dirt roads and jeep trails, some of which can get rocky

Land Status: National forest

Nearest Town: Blacksburg, VA

Other Trail Users: Hikers and motorists

Canine Compatibility: Dog friendly, although it may be a little long for the pooch

Getting There

From I-81 near Blacksburg: Take Exit-118 to U.S. 460 west to Blacksburg. Take U.S. 460 Bypass (left fork) around Blacksburg to VA 700. Turn right on VA 700, going seven uphill miles to Mountain Lake. **DeLorme: Virginia Atlas & Gazetteer:** Page 41, B-5

Mountain Lake, one of only two natural lakes in the state of Virginia (the other is Lake Drummond in the Great Dismal Swamp) and one of the highest lakes in the East, is home to the renowned Mountain Lake Resort. This romantic, sandstone resort has been a luxurious, year-round mountaintop getaway for nearly 200 years.

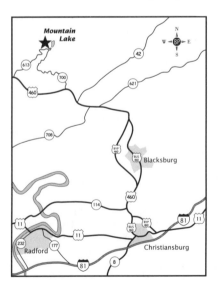

In 1986, the majesty of this grand old resort hotel was captured forever on film as the setting for the major motion picture *Dirty Dancing*, starring Patrick Swayze.

At nearly 4,000 feet above sea level, Mountain Lake's summers are cool and pleasant and its winters can often register some of the coldest temperatures in the state. This helps make Mountain Lake ideal for outdoor recreation year-round, from mountain biking in the summer to cross-country skiing in the winter. Autumn brings with it an explosion of fall colors, such that few places compare. During the winters, when the mountains are filled with heavy snow, cross-country skiing and horse-drawn carriage rides keep guests busy and entertained.

Mountain Lake.

Mountain Lake is one of only two natural lakes in Virginia. The other is Lake Drummond in the Great Dismal Swamp.

MilesDirections

0.0 START at Mountain Lake Resort. From the resort, follow the paved road (VA 613) around the west side of the lake.

0.6 VA 613 changes to a dirt road.

1.5 Pass the Mountain Lake Biological Station on the right. The University of Virginia sponsors this biological station. Bear left, continuing on VA 613.

3.2 Pass the parking area on the right for the War Spur and Chestnut Trail. These trails make a 4.5-mile loop through the Mountain Lake Wilderness of the Jefferson National Forest along Salt Pond Mountain Ridge. War Spur Overlook is less than two miles into this loop. Continue north on VA 613.

4.0 Start climbing Minnie Ball Hill.

5.3 Reach the top of this climb (3972 feet). Turn left on Rocky Mountain Road at this intersection and follow the rocky jeep trail along the ridge of Big Mountain. There is a dirt parking area at this intersection for the Appalachian Trail.

8.6 Go through Bailey Gap (3637 feet).

10.9 Go through Lybrook Gap (3794 feet).

13.0 Reach Butt Mountain Overlook (4210 feet). Check out the incredible view of the New River Valley. Continue following the main dirt road, now FS 714. Get ready for a long, fast descent down to Little Meadows.

15.6 On the right is the trailhead for the Cascades Trail. Continue on FS 714.

16.0 Cross over Laurel Creek.

16.9 Pedal through Little Meadows.

17.1 Cross over Little Stony Creek. Get ready to start climbing again.

19.2 Go through Pacers Gap (3635 feet).

20.1 Turn left on VA 613 (Paved). This is a very steep section of road that takes you back to the summit at Mountain Lake Resort.

21.4 Arrive at Mountain Lake Resort. What a ride!

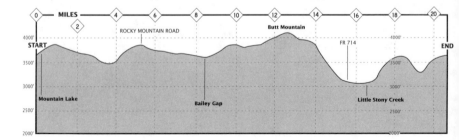

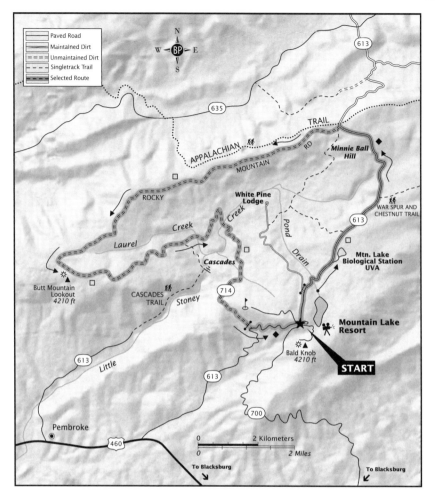

The resort offers many guest activities on its 2,600-acre lot, and recently designated several miles of its wooded trails for mountain bikes. Tangent Outfitters of Dublin, Virginia, occupies a small shop at the resort and rents mountain bikes from the Lakeview Cottage. Guided mountain bike trips are also scheduled from the resort for those interested in exploring some of the area's more scenic spots. Maps detailing their trail systems are available from Mountain Lake Resort.

This fairly large loop, from Mountain Lake Resort to Butt Mountain, doesn't actually use any of the trails on the Mountain Lake Resort property. Instead, it leads cyclists on a more strenuous off-road journey deep into the Jefferson National Forest. This is a great ride for anyone interested in spending an afternoon mountain biking, who isn't afraid of a few hefty climbs along the way.

305

The terrain is hilly and the surface is, at times, rather rocky. Be prepared for a long ride. When you arrive at Butt Mountain Overlook, though, you're greeted with a panoramic view of the New River Valley and the vast stretches of land nearly 2,000 feet below, making all the effort worth your while. Perhaps the only lookout comparable in the entire region is the fabled McAfee's Knob, located north of Roanoke on the Appalachian Trail.

Ride Information

🕐 Trail Contacts:
Blacksburg Ranger District
(540) 552-4641

Jefferson National Forest Headquarters
(540) 265-6054

🕐 Schedule:
Open year-round

🍴 Accommodations:
Mountain Lake Resort—prices range from $75-$335 per night
1-800-346-3334

💡 Local Events /Attractions:
German Oktoberfest, September and October at Mountain Lake Resort

🚲 Local Bike Shops:
Tangent Outfitters
Dublin, VA and Mountain Lake
(540) 674-5202

East Coasters Bike Shop
Blacksburg
(540) 951-2369

🗺 Maps:
USGS maps: Eggleston, VA; Interior, VA, WVA; Pearisburg, VA; Lindside, VA
Jefferson National Forest topo map: Blacksburg District

If you have any remaining energy after Butt Mountain, take time to depart from the main route and check out the cascading falls along Cascades Trail. Otherwise, continue along the jeep road down through Little Meadows, then climb uphill toward Virginia 613. This incredibly steep road heads back to Mountain Lake and was used as a brutal climb in the mountainous Stage Four of both the 1994 and 1995 editions of the Tour DuPont professional bicycle race. Many of the world's greatest cyclists struggled up Virginia 613 before making the harrowing, high-speed descent back down Virginia 700. American, world champion, and Tour de France winner Lance Armstrong was first to crest this Category-1 climb over Salt Pond Mountain at Mountain Lake Resort both years running, and in 1995 won the 141-mile stage from Lynchburg to Blacksburg with a solo break-away.

Chances are, after this ride, you may want to pedal directly into the 72-degree water of Mountain Lake. Afterward, taste the superb cuisine in Mountain Lake's formal stone dining room. If you're visiting in autumn, help celebrate a traditional German Oktoberfest, held the last two Saturdays in September and each Friday and Saturday in October. So if you're interested in mountain biking on top of the world, Mountain Lake is, without question, the place to go.

Mount Rogers Loop

Ride Specs

Start: From the pull-off on FS 90
Length: 8-mile loop
Approximate Riding Time: 2 hours
Difficulty Rating: This is a fairly difficult ride due to the elevation gains along the route. Cyclists will have to be ready to climb quite a bit and still be fresh enough to handle the technical descents on the other end.
Trail Surface: Hilly fire roads and singletrack
Land Status: National forest
Nearest Town: Damascus, VA
Other Trail Users: Hikers and equestrians
Canine Compatibility: Dog friendly. Just watch out for the horses.

Getting There

From Abingdon: Take U.S. 58 east to Damascus. From Damascus, continue on U.S. 58 for approximately six miles to FS 90. Turn left on FS 90 (dirt road) and park along the side of the road at the small pull-off. *DeLorme: Virginia Atlas & Gazetteer:* Page 22, C-3

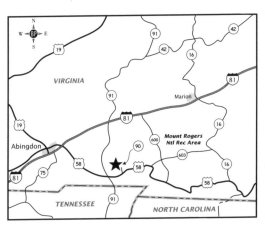

I was not the first to discover this ride. In fact, long before I arrived, countless hours had already been spent clearing the trails and marking this route. It's no accident, therefore, that this loop, used as the official race course for the Virginia Highlands Mountain Bike Club's Mountain Bike Challenge is one of the finest mountain bike rides in Virginia.

Smooth singletrack, fast descents, spectacular overlooks and mountain meadows, winding dirt roads, and trails that grip the edges of steep ridges combine to form an extraordinary ride in the highlands of Southwest Virginia worthy enough to attract Virginia's best off-road cyclists.

But this should come as no surprise since this loop is located within the boundaries of Mount Rogers National Recreation Area. Mountain biking is both welcome and encouraged inside this 115,000-acre mountain wilderness. Over 400 miles of open trails in the Mount Rogers National Recreation Area wind over high mountain peaks, across wind-beaten meadows and along rushing highland streams. This is one of the East Coast's wildest and most rugged regions and includes a number of Virginia's loftiest mountains. It's no wonder mountain biking is taken seriously down here.

Whitetop Mountain dominates the landscape.

Mount Rogers National Recreation Area is named for Virginia's highest peak (Mount Rogers), which stands at 5729 feet. Whitetop Mountain, a close second, stands nearby at 5520 feet and was so named because it is often covered with snow long after the snow has melted away in the valleys. The summit of Whitetop Mountain is also home to the highest vehicular road in the state. Virginia 89 takes cars from Virginia 600 on a spectacular uphill drive to the "balds," or open meadows, at the top of this lofty mountain.

Ride Information

🕐 Trail Contacts:
Mount Rogers National Recreation Area
(540) 783-5196

Jefferson National Forest Headquarters
(540) 265-6054

🕐 Schedule:
Open daylight to dark all year-round

❓ Local Information:
Abingdon Convention & Visitors Bureau
Abingdon, VA
1-800-435-3440

Mount Rogers National Recreation Area
1-800-628-7202

💡 Local Events /Attractions:
Appalachian Trail Days, in May
Damascus, VA—visit www.damascus.org

🛏 Accommodations:
Maxwell Manor Bed and Breakfast,
Abingdon, VA 1-888-851-1100

Summerfield Inn, Abingdon, VA
1-800-668-5905

Silversmith Inn, Abingdon, VA
1-800-533-0195

Victoria and Albert Inn, Abingdon, VA
1-888-645-5636

🚲 Local Bike Shops:
(All listed shops offer rentals and shuttles.)
Highlands Ski & Outdoor Center
Abingdon, VA
(540) 628-1329
or www.adventuresports.com/shops/
highlands/bike_rentals.htm

Blue Blaze Bike and Shuttle
Damascus, VA
1-800-475-5095 or (540) 475-5095
or http://blueblaze.naxs.com

Adventure Damascus
Damascus, VA
1-888-595-BIKE or (540) 475-6262
or www.adventuredamascus.com

🅝 Maps:
USGS maps: Konnarock, VA
**Mount Rogers National Recreation Area
topo map**

Also near this loop is the Virginia Creeper Trail. This rail-trail travels 34 miles through the rugged landscape of Mount Rogers, from Abingdon to the Virginia-North Carolina border. If you're looking for a low-difficulty ride that passes over high-river gorges, travels past waterfalls and rolling pastures, and crosses more than 100 bridges and trestles, then stay an extra few days and fit this unique trail into your schedule.

This particular loop in the Mount Rogers National Recreation Area, just off U.S. Route 58, takes you up and over Iron Mountain. It begins on a well maintained dirt road and eventually becomes complete singletrack. Though most of the dirt roads you will encounter on this loop travel uphill, there will be occasions of extreme speed on white-knuckled descents. The loop's singletrack stretches up and down the mountain's ridges and, at times, grips the side of the mountain with barely a bike-width of trail. Equestrians frequent these trails as well, so use caution when pedaling along these tight routes.

You'll also notice along the route many different trails, all of which branch farther into the National Recreation Area. Detailed area maps, useful for exploring the many trails in this vast, off-road playground can be found at Highland Ski and Outdoor Center in Abingdon. Perhaps even set up a base camp at one of Mount Rogers National Recreation Area's many campsites and spend the weekend riding as many new trails as possible. Because of this area's inspiring scenery and its hundreds of miles of rideable trails, very few places in the state can compare to this mountain biking wonderland.

MilesDirections

0.0 START from the pull-off on the right-hand side of FS 90, just off U.S. 58. Begin climbing this hard-packed, dirt road.

0.5 To the right is a great view of Whitetop Mountain. Just up the road is a gated fire road.

Share the trail.

0.6 Turn left, pedaling around the gate on this grassy Forest Service Road. This jeep trail slowly winds uphill.

0.9 Turn right on a slightly hidden singletrack trail that climbs a short, steep hill. *[Note: To find this trailhead, follow the grassy forest service road uphill for 0.3 miles from FS 90. As*

you round the third curve (this will be curving left), there is a large hickory tree and a small creek at the apex on the right side of the road. The hickory tree marks the singletrack trailhead. The climb up this trail is very steep, but is less than a tenth of a mile.]

1.0 Reach the top of the steep, singletrack climb and turn right on a wide, singletrack trail.

1.4 Small clearing on the right. Continue straight (bear left) on this wide, singletrack trail.

1.5 Arrive at an intersection of trails. There is a shelter and picnic area on the left. To the right is a trail with man-made steps that heads up the mountain. Continue straight on the trail you're already on and descend toward FS 90.

1.6 Arrive at an intersection between FS 90 and FS 615. FS 90 crosses from right to left. FS 615 bears a soft right and heads downhill. Turn left on FS 90 and follow this uphill to Iron Mountain Trail (yellow blaze). Note the Feathercamp Branch Trail on the far left, past the gate. Feathercamp Branch Trail will take you downhill along its grassy terrain for nearly two miles to U.S. 58.

1.7 Turn left on Iron Mountain Trail (yellow blaze). This trail gently climbs Feathercamp Ridge, skirting the ridgeline. The surface of this trail is smooth and well maintained.

2.4 Reach the top of the climb and begin a fun, quick descent.

2.7 Arrive at a "T" intersection. Turn right, continuing to loop clockwise around this route. A left turn would take you west along

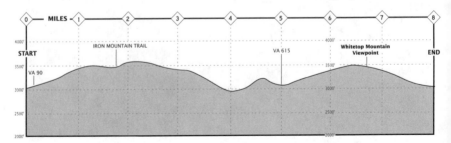

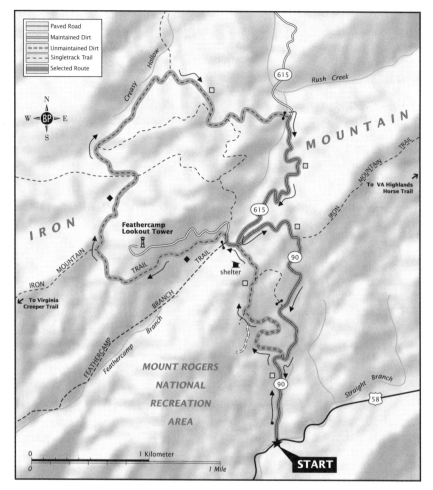

Iron Mountain Trail, traveling along the crest of Feathercamp Ridge. Note the large oak tree marked with a yellow blaze.

3.2 Cross Buzzard Den Branch. This section of trail at the bottom of the descent is often very muddy. Equestrians also use this trail, and you will notice the deep imprints of horseshoes in the wet soil.

3.3 Reach the low point along this loop. Bear right up a very short trail. This takes you to a larger trail intersection.

3.35 At this trail intersection, turn hard-left on the Forest Service Road.

3.8 Overview on the left.

4.6 Pedal across a small meadow.

5.0 Cross through a steel gate and turn right on FS 615. Start climbing.

6.1 Turn hard-left on FS 90. This takes you back to the start of the ride. Not done climbing yet!

6.5 Reach the summit of this climb on FS 90. Get ready for a fast descent!

6.8 Spectacular view of Whitetop Mountain to the south.

8.0 Reach the start of the ride at the bottom of FS 90.

313

Grayson Highlands State Park

Ride Specs

Start: From Massie Gap parking area

Length: 8-mile loop

Approximate Riding Time: 2 hours

Difficulty Rating: Difficult. The excessive water crossings, teeth rattling down hills, and length create for a very challenging journey.

Trail Surfaces: Flat sections, smooth up hills, and wet rocky down hills

Land Status: State park

Nearest Town: Volney, VA

Other Trail Users: Equestrians, hikers, backpackers, and anglers

Canine Compatibility: Dog friendly

Getting There

From Marion: Follow VA 16 south for approximately 33 miles. Then turn right onto U.S. 58 in Volney. Follow U.S. 58 for eight miles, then turn right into Grayson Highlands State Park and onto VA 362. Park at the Massie Gap parking area, which is on the right, past Campground Road. *DeLorme: Virginia Atlas & Gazetteer:* Page 23, C-5

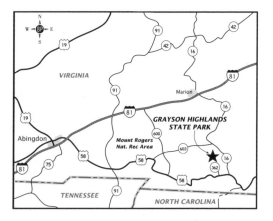

Virginia's highest state park, Grayson Highlands, lies adjacent to Mount Rogers (5729 feet), Virginia's highest point, and ties together a unique collection of flora and fauna. A highly versatile recreational area, the park is one of the most picturesque spots you'll find in Southwestern Virginia. You're likely to encounter some of the wild ponies that live and roam in the park year-round or catch the blooming of the Catawba rhododendron in the middle of June. Visitors are encouraged not to feed or spook the ponies, but they are relatively calm and will gladly pose for a photo. The large light pink blooms of the Catawba explode during the hot summer months and are accentuated by their cluster of shiny oval shaped leaves. The aroma alone is worth the trip. Most of the Catawbas are around four feet high, but they can grow in excess of eight feet.

The boreal forests in Grayson Highlands are the same as those found in Nova Scotia. This unique environment provides the perfect climate for moss, which has the ability to retain water almost all year. The presence of moss causes the area to be moist year-round. When combined with the elevation, this moisture makes the air temperature even cooler.

A park sign at the trailhead reminds hikers and cyclists to take a sufficient supply of water if venturing into the backcountry. Within Grayson Highlands are a number of trails that connect with nearby landmarks like Whitetop Mountain and Mount Rogers. The park provides full camping facilities that make visiting the area a pleasure. Plan to spend some time here and explore the extensive trail system.

When you ride to Wilburn Ridge in the distance you'll notice the Frasier firs, which are popular as Christmas trees. There are many fir tree farms in this region and some allow you to pick your own Christmas tree, while others are cut and sent throughout the nation for sale.

The first uphill section takes you through a short section of pines and a boulder filled jeep trail. As you pass through the metal horse gate you'll notice an adjoining trail to the right, which is your return path on this journey. This section has erosion logs to help decrease the amount of erosion

Don't be surprised to be greeted by one of the local residents while you're here.

on its steep slope. Entering the Horse Trail you'll notice the adverse effects of not having erosion control, which makes this first section challenging. Wilburn Ridge is an important landmark because it marks the intersection of the Appalachian Trail and the continuation of the Horse Trail. Make sure not to venture onto the Appalachian Trail because only foot traffic is allowed.

As you continue to ride north and northwest you increase your chances of meeting the small population of wild ponies. There are several metal gates throughout the ride that you'll have to go through. The second gate at mile 1.3 contains a mileage sign and an Appalachian Trail register. This begins a glorious section of rocky fast switchback filled with downhill runs. Tighten your suspension and dial-in your brakes. The remaining six miles consists of repetitious creek crossings, switchbacks, and gradual elevation changes. Endurance plays a key part in completing the entire eight miles.

Most of the terrain after the second gate is wooded. One area that extends into the valley is the last section without tree cover. As you begin the last leg that runs parallel to Campground Road the "Country Store" will greet you with Southern hospitality. It is visible from the trail and makes a wonderful intermission before completing your journey. When you can see Massie Gap you know that you're close to the finish. Take a hot shower, enjoy a campfire, and do it all again in the morning.

MilesDirections

0.0 START from the Massie Gap parking lot and ride west toward the fence line. Several signs will inform you of which trails are mountain bikes are not permitted.

0.2 Go through a metal horse gate and follow signs up to Wilburn Ridge.

0.3 Ride up the first incline.

0.4 The first plateau places you in the middle of the joining horse and jeep access.

0.5 This is Wilburn Ridge and a spectacular view.

0.7 The sign and intersection mark a crucial landmark. Continue straight ahead but note the following landmarks: the Appalachian Trail (AT) north goes right, the AT south goes left,

Scales is five miles straight, Old Orchard Shelter is 8.1 miles straight, Mount Rogers is 3.8 miles.

1.0 A steady incline and likely place for a wild pony encounter.

1.2 The footpath for the AT goes directly uphill toward the fence line. You'll want to stay on the gravel road. This also marks the spot of the first creek crossing.

1.3 Dismount and open the gate manually. The trail register for the AT is on the facing side. The mileage sign is on the opposite side.

1.9 This is a section of technical traverses.

2.0 Encounter a very tight switchback right.

2.1 Encounter a steep downhill then a switchback left.

2.2 Encounter a technical switchback left.

2.9 This marks a downhill traverse.

3.0 A flat section takes you into a valley.

3.1 The steep downhill is fairly treacherous.

3.2 Come to a large creek crossing (10 feet wide and one foot deep). This section opens up to a scenic part of the valley.

3.4 Another flat section allows you to catch your breath.

4.2 Encounter a creek crossing before a steady incline.

4.3 The extensive ridgeline is a great spot for photos of the valley.

4.4 Veer right downhill at the sign and intersection.

4.7 This creek crossing is very wide (about 15 feet) but can be crossed with care.

5.0 A large ravine requires you to gain a lot of speed.

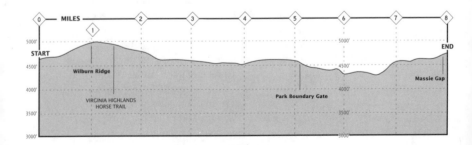

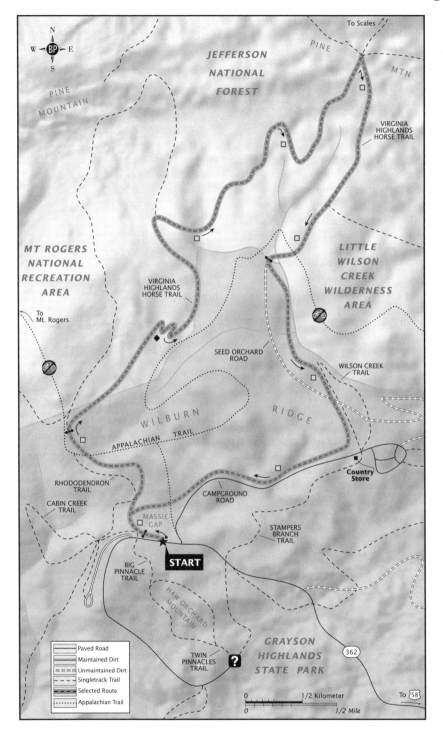

N
W—BP—E
S

JEFFERSON
NATIONAL
FOREST

PINE

To Scales

MTN

PINE

MOUNTAIN

VIRGINIA
HIGHLANDS
HORSE TRAIL

MT ROGERS
NATIONAL
RECREATION
AREA

LITTLE
WILSON
CREEK
WILDERNESS
AREA

To
Mt. Rogers

VIRGINIA
HIGHLANDS
HORSE TRAIL

SEED ORCHARD
ROAD

WILSON CREEK
TRAIL

WILBURN
RIDGE

APPALACHIAN TRAIL

RHODODENDRON
TRAIL

Country
Store

CABIN CREEK
TRAIL

CAMPGROUND
ROAD

MASSIE
GAP

STAMPERS
BRANCH
TRAIL

START

BIG
PINNACLE
TRAIL

HAW ORCHARD MOUNTAIN

GRAYSON
HIGHLANDS
STATE PARK

362

TWIN
PINNACLES
TRAIL

?

To 58

	Paved Road
	Maintained Dirt
	Unmaintained Dirt
	Singletrack Trail
	Selected Route
	Appalachian Trail

0   1/2 Kilometer
0   1/2 Mile

MilesDirections (Continued)

5.2 A large steel gate marks the park boundary (Sign: State Park Horse Camp – 2.5 miles.)

5.5 Come to another large creek crossing.

5.7 This spot marks a sign that directs you toward the campground.

5.9 A "Y" intersection is the pivotal point on the trail. Straight ahead is private property. Ride uphill to the right and continue along the Virginia Horse Trail.

6.3 Reach a gravel parking lot and the "Country Store" across the paved road. The road left will take you toward the camping area. Continue right on the trail that runs parallel to the road.

6.5 Continue up the steep incline before you

reach the parking lot. This will take you along the camp road and back to the Massie Gap parking area.

6.6 Cross the access road and continue straight.

7.1 You will be in sight of Massie Gap Peak.

7.8 Continue straight toward Massie Gap parking area. A foot-trail to the left and marked by a blue blaze takes you back to Campground Road.

7.9 This is the intersection of the first incline. Turn left here and the gate to reach Massie Gap parking area will be in plane sight.

8.0 Arrive at your car and a descriptive park sign.

Feral ponies help keep the balds of Mount Rogers and the Grayson Highlands area brush free, maintaining the open meadows of Virginia's high peaks.

Ride Information

○ Trail Contacts:
Grayson Highlands State Park
Mouth of Wilson, VA
(540) 579-7092

◔ Schedule:
April through November

⑤ Fees/Permits:
$2 at the gate

♀ Local Events/Attractions:
Jefferson National Forest
Roanoke, VA
(540) 265-6054

Whitetop Mountain Maple Festival
late March
Mount Rogers Fire Hall
(540) 388-3257

Grayson Highlands Fall Festival
late September
Grayson Highlands State Park
(540) 579-6423

☹ Local Bike Shops:
Highlands Ski & Outdoor Center
Abingdon, VA
(540) 628-1329

Ⓝ Maps:
USGS maps: Troutdale, VA

Hidden Valley Lake

Ride Specs

Start: From the Hidden Valley Lake parking area and boat launch

Length: 3.8-mile loop

Approximate Riding Time: 1 hour

Difficulty Rating: Moderate due to the technicality of existing surface rocks and uneven trail transitions

Trail Surface: Most of the trail is smooth and flat with sections of surface rocks

Land Status: National forest

Nearest Town: Abingdon, VA

Other Trail Users: Hikers, backpackers, rock climbers, anglers, and hunters (in season)

Canine Compatibility: Dog friendly

Getting There

From Abingdon: Drive U.S. 19/U.S. Alt. 58 for 15 miles. Turn right onto Hidden Valley Drive/VA 690. Warning! This paved road is very steep so make sure that your brakes and transmission aren't going to fail you. Use low gears going uphill and downhill. There are two switchbacks toward the top so try not to loose momentum. When you reach the top the road turns to gravel. (Rock climbers park here.) Continue straight until you reach the first right turn. Turn right here and park. **DeLorme: Virginia Atlas & Gazetteer.** Page 21, B-7

T he Hidden Valley Lake loop will charm you and invite you back for more. A lazy roll through a section of Virginia's highlands has been known to make visitors want to stay forever. Anglers will rejoice at the great fishing to be had in the lake, species such as bass, northern pike, sunfish, and crappie. Rock climbing is another popular attraction. The land is privately owned but as long as you sign in, respect the rock, and don't bring your dog, you're gladly welcome. The exposed walls of limestone and sandstone are clearly visible as you drive up toward the top of the

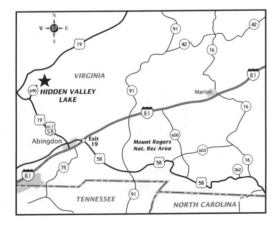

ridge. The climber or visitor and not the landowner assume all risk. Even if you don't climb, this trail offers a breathtaking view just the same.

Pass the peak of the ridge and continue onto the gravel jeep road straight ahead. There is ample parking at lakeside and the ride should begin at this point. The beginning will consist of a well-maintained jeep road until you reach the dam. At the dam the jeep road goes into tree cover and becomes

slightly rocky. Some of the sharper edges of the sandstone rocks that are exposed can be potential hazards to your wheels. Consider staying in the worn path in order to avoid any mishaps. Extra tubes and tools are recommended on this trail.

After you finish several switchbacks and the two major inclines, the trail will plane out and the jeep road comes into sight. There's not much room for navigating around the boulder barrier that connects with the jeep road. A quick sprint back to the parking area is in order once you reach the road. Trail selection and

MilesDirections

0.0 START at the first parking area on the right. Go back up the road as if you were leaving. Turn right at the "T" intersection.

0.2 Continue straight and past the second gravel road on the right, which takes you to the camping area.

0.7 Follow the switchback to the right. The dam and lake are visible at this point.

0.8 Two steel gates are located at either end of the dam. Go down the concrete overflow and direct yourself right, toward the jeep road.

1.0 A switchback right begins a series of uphill sections.

2.1 There is a steady incline for the next 0.2 miles.

2.5 This flat section is overgrown and contains several surface rocks.

2.9 A steel barrier and entrance road are visible at this point. The barrier is straight ahead and the entrance road will run from left to right. Continue right onto the gravel road.

3.0 Cross a stone barrier and ride right at the "Y." Follow the road back to the parking area and beginning of the ride.

3.8 Arrive at the parking area.

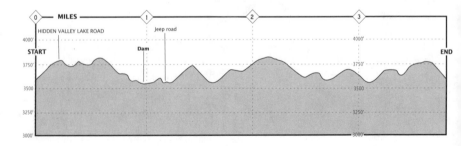

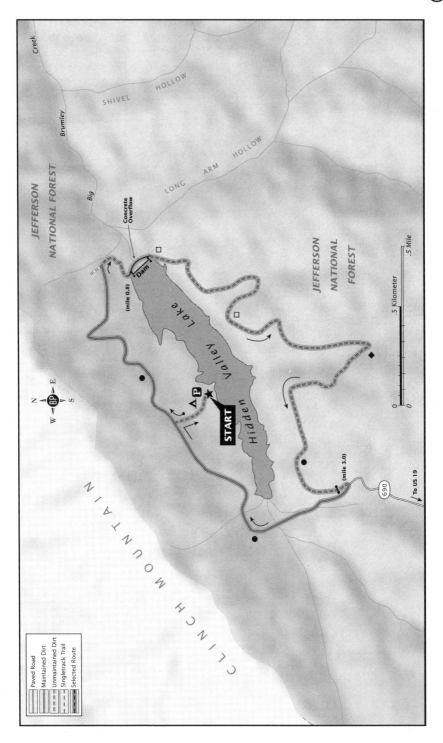

Sidebar

- Locals will tell you that the proper pronunciation of Appalachian is with equal stress on the first and third "a": **A**ppal**a**chian.

variation is virtually non-existent, but the run is short enough to be done in multiples. Facing east, toward the lake in the parking lot, provides the visitor with a dramatic sunset. Since you're so deep into rural Virginia, you have the freedom of viewing stars and night swimming without the distractive glare of city lights.

Ride Information

📞 Trail Contacts:
Jefferson National Park
Roanoke, VA
(540) 265-6054

🕐 Schedule:
May through November

❓ Local Information:
Abingdon Convention & Visitors Bureau
Abingdon, VA
(540) 676-2282

**Washington County
Chamber of Commerce**
Abingdon, VA
(540) 628-8141

💡 Local Events/Attractions:
Virginia Highlands Festival
mid August
Abingdon, VA
1-800-435-3440
or www.va-highlands-festival.org

Barter Theatre
Abingdon, VA
(540) 628-3991
or www.bartertheatre.com

🛏 Accommodations:
Camberley's Martha Washington Inn
Abingdon, VA
(540) 628-3161
or www.camberleyhotels.com

🍴 Restaurants:
The Tavern
Abingdon, VA
(540) 628-1118
reservations recommended

The Starving Artist Café
Abingdon, VA
(540) 628-8445

🚲 Local Bike Shops:
Highlands Ski & Outdoor Center
Abingdon, VA
(540) 628-1329

🗺 Maps:
USGS maps: Brumley, VA

Plan to camp but bring plenty of water. Even though the lake is always high, you'll need to bring potable water, unless you boil what you take from the lake. The drive back down is rougher than going up. Remember to use low gears while going both ways. This is a friendly area and has seen major improvements in recent years. Keeping the park clean has become an important part of the Forest Service's mission.

If you don't care to camp, this ride is a mere 30 minutes from Abingdon. Book a room early and try to catch the Virginia Highlands Festival in mid August. The festival is acclaimed nationwide and provides an assortment of crafts, food and music. This weeklong extravaganza could be the perfect ending to a sweet ride at Hidden Valley.

Seven Sisters Trail

Ride Specs

Start: From the first gravel lot on the left as you head toward Stoney Fork campsite on VA 717
Length: 7.3- mile loop
Approximate Riding Time: 2 hours
Difficulty Rating: Difficult due to a strenuous series of ascents
Trail Surface: Older established trail is well maintained and quite challenging
Land Status: National forest
Nearest Town: Wytheville, VA
Other Trail Users: Hikers, backpackers, and hunters (in season)
Canine Compatibility: Dog friendly

Getting There

From Wytheville: Drive I-77 North toward Bland. Take the exit for VA 717. Head south on VA 717 and park in the first marked lot on the left. A small, square brown sign will mark the parking area. *DeLorme: Virginia Atlas & Gazetteer.* Page 39, D-7

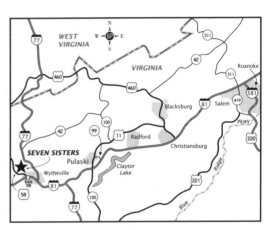

S even Sisters is not as kind as it sounds. This traverse will demand the very best of you. It is challenging from the very beginning. The seven peaks on Little Walker Mountain can surprise you and tantalize you. The series of gradual inclines in the beginning pump your legs so much they'll feel like rocks. Take the chance to refuel as you go down the backside of each peak. The last major incline at mile 2.6 is the climb of all climbs.

The delicious 1.7-mile downhill will leave you drooling for more, along with the spectacular view of Walker and Brushy mountains. The Stoney Fork camping area is a full-service facility that's a wonderful place to rest before you do it all again. If you are not fortunate enough to be able to stay, make sure to bring a camera and keep the ridge on Walker Mountain in mind. You won't be disappointed.

The trail begins with a subtle set of switchbacks before the sign at mile 1.0. This is a great warm-up for the next seven miles. Rock exposure is not a great concern except for one section when beginning the downhill at the end. This large bed of loose slate can prove to be tricky due to the steep drop on the right that follows you all the way down. Most of the terrain obstacles consist of fallen trees crossing the path and jagged turns through the trees. Navigating through vertical posts is kind of like skiing slalom on snow—you have to keep your rhythm.

Most of the trees are oak, red and yellow maple, pine, and white spruce. Common wildlife inhabitants are deer, squirrels, owls, red-tailed hawks, and the occasional black bear. As you enter the camping area you pass through a fortress of hand-planted pines. These rows of symmetric pines appear to be a finishing gate as you blast through the last flat of Seven Sisters. There is one final manmade jump to clear when you reach the pine grove—perfect for pictures or a speed check. You may find that some of the tracks after the jump get uncomfortably close to the trees, ouch. By starting your ride from the first gravel lot on the left, the rider is granted a wonderful cooldown by taking the hardtop back to the parking area. The hardtop section is approximately two miles and is slightly inclined. From the road you can see the Seven Sisters and Little Walker Mountain to the right and Walker Mountain to the left.

Seven Sisters is just minutes away from Wytheville. The rugged terrain has a reputation of making its visitors love it or hate it. After you are done it's recommended that you unwrap yourself from the pines and join everyone at the Pure Country Steak House and Saloon for some true Southern soul food. Wytheville also hosts the historic Millwald Theatre, which is Virginia's oldest motion picture theater still in operation. Hospitality is as plentiful as the good food.

Ride Information

Trail Contacts:
Jefferson National Forest
Roanoke, VA
(540) 265-6054

Schedule:
All year, weather permitting

Fees/Permits:
$2 at Stony Fork campground. No fee for parking or biking at the parking area.

Local Information:
Wytheville-Wythe-Bland
Chamber of Commerce
Wytheville, VA (540) 223-3315

Local Events/Attractions:
Big Walker Lookout
Wytheville, VA
(540) 228-4401

Millwald Theatre
Wytheville, VA
(540) 228-5031

Restaurants:
Pure Country Steak House and Saloon
Wytheville, VA
(540) 223-7303

Maps:
USGS maps: Big Bend, VA; Bland, VA

MilesDirections

0.0 START at the gravel parking lot and trailhead.
0.1 You can cross the creek by either going through it or walking over the bridge.
0.3 The tight switchback left begins a steady incline.
0.6 Another switchback takes you to the right and up the ridge.
1.0 A sign and intersection mark a new direction. Turn right and uphill at the "T" intersection.
1.6 Come to the first major incline.
1.8 The second incline is steep but can be completed.
2.2 This begins the first of a series of tight tree sections and downhills.

2.6 A very challenging incline will most likely cause you to walk uphill.
3.2 A sign directing you to the campsite is located here at the highest point on the trail (3310 feet).
3.6 Ride carefully through this technical rock section and extremely fast downhill.
5.3 Reach the campsite. Turn right onto the hardtop (VA 717) to return to the parking area.
7.3 Return to the parking area after two miles of hardtop.
Alternate Starts: *Continue to Stony Fork campsite, park, pay, and ride to trailhead two miles back as a warm up.*

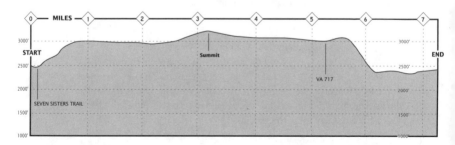

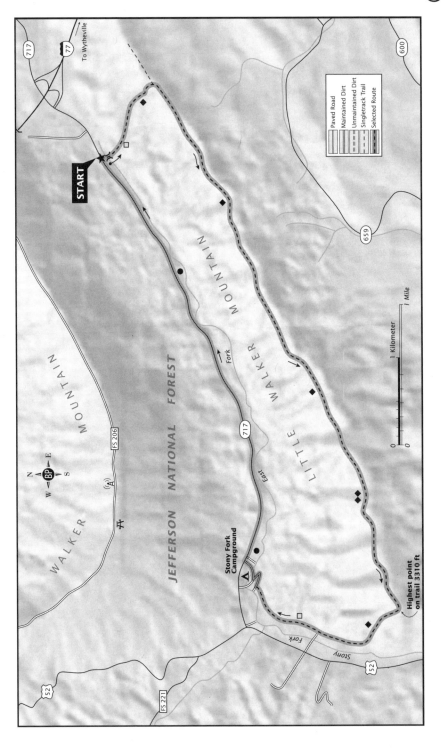

START

To Wytheville

717
77

600

659

Paved Road
Maintained Dirt
Unmaintained Dirt
Singletrack Trail
Selected Route

1 Mile
1 Kilometer
0

MOUNTAIN

WALKER

LITTLE

JEFFERSON   NATIONAL   FOREST

WALKER   MOUNTAIN

FS 206

FS 221

Fork

East

717

Stony Fork
Campground

Stony   Fork

52

52

N
W   E
S

Highest point
on trail 3310 ft

The mission of Rails-to-Trails Conservancy is to "enhance America's communities and countryside by converting thousands of miles of abandoned rail corridors and connecting open spaces into a nationwide network of public trails."

Every large city and small town in America, by the early 20ᵗʰ Century, was connected by steel and railroad ties. In 1916, the United States had laid nearly 300,000 miles of track across the country, giving it the distinction as having the world's largest rail system. Since then, other forms of transportation, such as cars, trucks, and airplanes, have diminished the importance of the railroad and that impressive network of rail lines has shrunk to less than 150,000 miles. Railroad companies abandon more than 2,000 miles of track each year, leaving unused rail corridors overgrown and idle.

It wasn't until the mid 1960s that the idea to refurbish these abandoned rail corridors into useable footpaths and trails was introduced. And in 1963, work began in Chicago and its suburbs on a 55-mile stretch of abandoned right-of-way to create the Illinois Prairie Path.

It took nearly two decades for the idea of converting old railways into useable footpaths to catch on. Then in 1986 the Rails-To-Trails Conservancy was founded, its mission specifically to help communities see their dreams of having a useable rail corridor for recreation and non-motorized travel a reality. At the time the Conservancy began operations, only 100 open rail-trails existed. Today, more than 500 trails are open to the public, totaling more than 5,000 miles of converted pathways. The Rails-To-Trails Conservancy is currently working on more than 500 additional rails-to-trails projects.

Ultimately, their goal is to see a completely interconnected system of trails throughout the entire United States. If you're interested in learning more about rails-to-trails and wish to support the Conservancy, please write to:

Rails-To-Trails Conservancy
1400 16th Street, NW, Suite 300
Washington, DC 20036-2222
or call (202) 797-5400

New River Trail State Park

Ride Specs

Start: From the Pulaski Station
Length: 51.5 miles long
Approximate Riding Time: Varies with distance
Difficulty Rating: Technically easy due to a flat gravel surface. Physically easy to moderate depending on length of ride.
Trail Surface: Rail trail. Flat, hard-packed gravel surface.
Land Status: State park
Nearest Town: Pulaski, VA
Other Trail Users: Hikers and equestrians
Canine Compatibility: Dog friendly

Getting There

From Roanoke: Take I-81 south to Exit-94 and head north on VA 99 approximately two miles into Pulaski. Just before the first red light there is a sign for the Northern Terminus, Dora Junction. Parking is available. *DeLorme: Virginia Atlas & Gazetteer.* Page 40 D-4

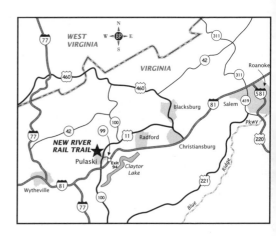

Virginia has always been a leader in park development. On June 15, 1936, for example, Virginia became the first state to open an entire park system on the same day. When Norfolk Southern Corporation donated a 57-mile section of railroad right-of-way between Pulaski and Galax to the Virginia Department of Conservation and Recreation in December 1986, the state again took the lead in park development and created its first linear greenway and certainly one of its most unique parks.

Southwestern Virginia's New River Trail follows the 57-mile abandoned railroad bed from Pulaski to Galax with a branch trail that leads to the town of Fries. For nearly 40 miles, this rail trail parallels the banks of the New River, the great grandfather of rivers. The New River is much older than its name might suggest. Flowing south to north, as very few rivers in North America do, the New River has the distinction of being the world's second oldest river.

Along the trail, cyclists will cross more than 30 bridges and trestles and cycle through tunnels nearly 200 feet long. The longest bridge in the park, located at Fries Junction, is more than 1,000 feet long and offers dramatic views of the ancient

Some of the tunnels reach up to 200 feet long.

river which courses more than 40 feet below. Scenery unique to Southwest Virginia is visible along the way. The area's rich history of an era long past, with the departure of the railroad, lives on whole-heartedly in the towns and communities that line the trail.

The railroad was built in the late 1800s by the Norfolk & Western Railway Company to transport what was believed to be a wealth of quality minerals in Wythe County, a cache larger than any other in the United States. Work on the railway began in Pulaski on December 10, 1883, and in 1890 much of the rail line reached well into Carroll County near Galax.

Blast furnaces were erected, massive supplies of minerals mined, thousands of tons of iron ore produced, and "boom towns" developed in numbers along the railroad as the industry prospered. Most of these towns still exist today.

As the hills emptied and the mines played out their last supplies, the railway became less and less profitable for the Norfolk Southern Corporation. Finally, in 1986, the decision came to abandon this stretch of railroad and donate the right-of-way to the state for a new purpose.

With the help of volunteer groups throughout Virginia, the park was able to open four miles of trail in May of 1987. Today all 57 miles of this rails-to-trails park is open to the public. With so many places along the route to park your car and access the trail, there's no need to attempt riding the entire trail in one day. Pick different sections with each visit and explore the beauty and history of one of Virginia's finest rail trails and most unique state parks.

Other Trail Entrances: See Route Map on Page 339

Draper Station *(mile 6.2) – From I-81, take VA 658 east through Draper. Parking is available across from Bryson's Store, less than one mile from I-81.*

Shot Tower Historical State Park *(New River Trail Headquarters, mile 25.2) – From I-77, take Exit 24, go east on VA 69 to U.S. 52 and follow signs to Shot Tower.*

Buck Dam *(mile 34.7) – Take VA 602 to Byllesby, then go north on VA 737 to the dam.*

Byllesby Dam *(mile 37.3) – Go east on VA 602 off VA 94. Park at the dam.*

Gambetta and Chestnut Yard *(mile 45.2) – Take VA 721 north past Cliffview.*

Cliffview Station *(mile 49.5) – Take U.S. 58 to Galax, then go north on VA 887 to Cliffview Road (VA 721). Parking is on the left, across from Cliffview Mansion and Cliffview Trading Post.*

Galax Station *(mile 51.5) – Parking is available where VA 58 crosses Chestnut Creek.*

Ride Information

📞 Trail Contacts:
New River Trail State Park Headquarters
(540) 699-6778
or *www.newrivertrail.org*

🕐 Schedule:
Open daylight to dark all year-round

💡 Local Events/Attractions:
Wythe County Heritage Days, in June
Wythe County Parks & Recreation
(540) 223-6022
or *www.wytheville.org*

🛏 Accommodations:
Hosteling International
Blue Ridge Mountains
Blue Ridge Parkway
Galax, VA
(540) 236-4962
or *www.hiayh.org*

🚲 Local Bike Shops:
New River Bicycles
(540)-980-1741—*offers shuttle service
to various points of the New River Trail*

New River Riders Bike Shoppe
Galax, VA
1-877-510-2572
or *www.ls.net/~nrtbikes*

🅽 Maps:
USGS maps: Radford South, VA; Dublin,
VA; Hiwassee, VA; Fosters Falls, VA; Max
Meadows, VA; Sylvatus, VA; Austinville,
VA; Galaz, VA

The New River is one of the oldest rivers in North America.

MilesDirections

[0.0 The New River Trail actually starts at the Pulaski Station, but due to parking issues, you'll be picking up the trail at mile 2.0, Dora Junction, where there is ample parking. I've adjusted the cues here so that this book agrees with the official mileage cues. In short, ignore this cue.]

2.0 START from Dora Junction, just off VA 99.

2.5 Peak Creek Trestle.

3.6 I-81 Overpass.

3.8 McAdam Trestle.

6.2 Draper Station. Parking, food, ranger station, restrooms available.

6.5 Sloan Creek Trestle.

8.0 Delton Trestle.

8.1 Site of Clarks Ferry. Stopped operating in 1939.

9.0 Delton. Convenience store and campgrounds available.

10.2 Cross Hiwassee River Bridge (951 feet long) to the east side of the New River.

12.6 Allisonia Station. Convenience store located along trail.

12.8 Gauging station to measure the depth of the river.

13.2 Big Reed Trestle over Big Reed Island Creek.

14.2 Reed Junction.

17.4 Barren Springs Furnace. Built in 1883, it produced more than five tons of pig iron each day.

17.8 Barren Springs Station.

19.0 Lone Ash.

20.3 Bertha.

22.7 Pass over the stone arch. This was built over a local farmer's spring box so that he could continue refrigerating his food and milk.

24.3 Fosters Falls.

25.2 Shot Tower. New River Trail Sate Park Headquarters. Parking, information, and restrooms. Shot Tower was built in the early 1900s to make shot for guns used by local hunters and soldiers in the Civil War. Molten metal was dropped 150 feet from the top of the tower into a kettle of cooling water below. It was thought that 150 feet was the distance necessary to shape falling molten lead into shot.

28.9 Reach Austinville, named after Moses Austin. Moses was the father of Stephen Austin for whom Austin, Texas, is named.

31.6 Ivanhoe Depot. Convenience store near to trail. (Ivanhoe Bridge is 670 feet long.)

32.6 Jubilee Park.

34.0 Junction with the Virginia Highlands Horse Trail

34.7 Buck Dam.

35.5 VA 737 and New River Campground (16 sites)

37.3 Byllesby Dam.

38.6 Grayson sulfur springs, once a health resort touting its natural spa. The waters here were once thought to cure ailments and skin diseases. The site of the old-time spa is now under water.

39.4 Grayson. Nearby restrooms and picnic area available.

39.8 Fries Junction. The New River Trial splits here and heads to either Fries or Galax. (Longest bridge along this trail at

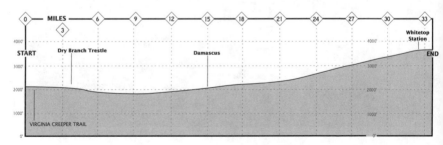

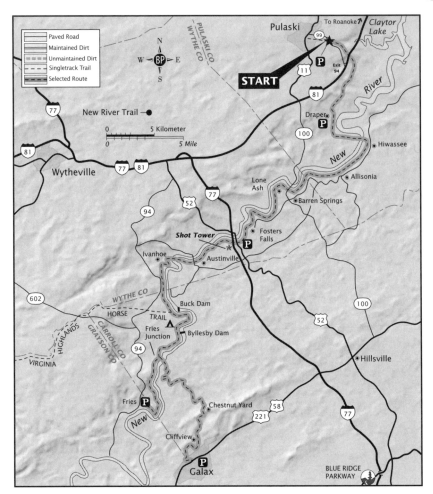

1,089 feet long.)

43.3 VA 721. (Fries Branch)

45.3 Fries. Parking, information, and picnic area available. (Fries Branch)

40.1 Site of 1928 train wreck that killed three people and injured nine.

40.3 Pass through a tunnel 229 feet long.

42.3 Gambetta.

45.1 Turntable site. The railroad line once ended here before being extended all the way to Galax. The turntable was used to turn trains around so that they may head north again toward Pulaski.

45.2 Chestnut Yard.

46.3 Chestnut Creek Falls.

49.5 Cliffview Station. Parking, restrooms, information, horse and bicycle rental, ranger station, and food available.

51.5 Galax Station. Located off the main trail. Parking available.

Virginia Creeper Trail

Ride Specs

Start: From the Abingdon Station

Length: 33.4 miles total

Approximate Riding Time: Varies with distance

Difficulty Rating: Technically easy due to flat gravel surface. Physically easy to moderate depending on distance.

Trail Surface: Rail-trail. Flat, hard-packed, gravel surface.

Land Status: Linear right of way jointly owned by Abingdon and Damascus. Eastern segment is within Mount Rogers National Recreation Area.

Nearest Town: Abingdon, VA

Other Trail Users: Hikers and equestrians

Canine Compatibility: Dog friendly

Getting There

From Roanoke: Take I-81 South to Exit 8 in Abingdon. Go north on VA Alt. 58 to Main Street and turn right. Pass Martha Washington Inn and the historic Barter Theater before turning right on Pecan Street. The trail begins at the old locomotive on display at the trailhead. *DeLorme: Virginia Atlas & Gazetteer.* Page 22, C-1

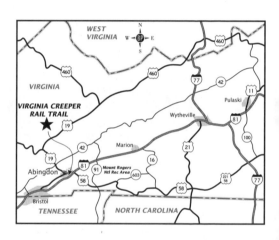

For hundreds of years, this ancient route was used by Native Americans as a footpath through the high mountains of the Appalachians. In 1900 the first locomotive chugged along this course from Abingdon Station to Damascus. By 1914, the railroad extended over even more of this ancient foot trail, all the way to Elkland, North Carolina. For over 75 years the Virginia Creeper (Locomotive #433) crept its way across rivers and gorges and up the steep grades of Virginia's highlands to collect timber, iron ore, passengers, and supplies. By 1977, due to economic hardships incurred as far back as the Great Depression, Locomotive #433 could not survive. Salvage rights for the rail line were subsequently sold to willing bidders. A year later, after the U.S. Forest Service purchased the right-of-way from Damascus to the Virginia-North Carolina border, work began to restore this scenic pathway. A few years later, Damascus and Abingdon bought the rest of the old railway. Today, 34 miles of this ancient Native American footpath have come full-circle and are, once again, open as a public trail open for all to enjoy.

The Virginia Creeper Trail begins in Abingdon, in Southwest Virginia, and stretches its 34 miles across striking scenery and over some of the state's most rugged land before ending at the Virginia-North Carolina border. The trail's waterfalls, deep river gorges, wildlife, rolling pastures, and 100 bridges and trestles make it one of America's premier rail-trails.

MilesDirections

0.0 START at the Abingdon Trailhead. There is limited parking here.

1.0 Cross under I-81.

1.3 Pass the Glenrochie Country Club.

2.9 Cross VA 677 in Watauga. Limited parking available here.

3.7 Walk or ride across the Dry Branch Trestle.

7.2 Walk or ride across the South Holston Trestle. This is a very scenic trestle. It spans the northern point of South Holston Lake where the south and middle forks of the Holston River converge. This is the lowest point on the Virginia Creeper Trail (1900 feet).

8.5 Arrive in the town of Alvarado. Limited parking available here.

15.5 Arrive in the town of Damascus. The big, red caboose is a U.S. Forest Service information station. Limited parking available here. Restrooms in the town park.

16.9 Cross VA 91. Be careful. Traffic is fast on this highway.

17.5 Ride across the Iron Bridge. Enter Mountain Rogers National Recreation Area.

19.5 Reach the Straight Branch parking lot on the right. The Appalachian Trail goes off to the left. The Beech Grove Trailhead is across U.S.

58 for those who wish to access the Iron Mountain Trail.

21.0 Arrive in Taylor's Valley. There is a vending area on the left. Go through the gate. The river is on your right. Limited parking available here.

21.4 Walk or ride across this trestle.

24.0 Pass through Konnarock Junction. Limited parking available here.

25.0 Walk or ride across High Trestle. Crossing this 550-foot-long trestle can be a bit unnerving as it is more than 100 feet above the ground!

25.4 The Appalachian Trail joins the Virginia Creeper Trail.

25.8 The Appalachian Trail goes left, deep into the Mount Rogers National Recreation Area.

27.2 Walk or ride across a small trestle.

29.3 Arrive at the old Green Cove Station. There is a seasonal U.S. Forest Service information station located here. There is also a portable toilet and limited parking available.

32.3 Arrive at Whitetop Station. This is the highest point on the trail at 3576 feet. There is limited parking available.

33.4 Virginia-North Carolina border. This is the end of the Virginia Creeper Trail.

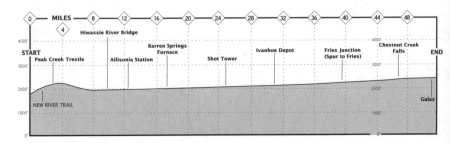

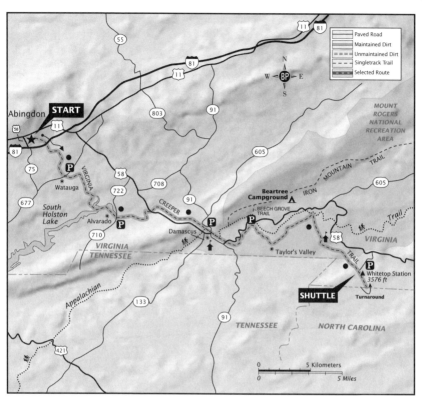

Other Trail Entrances: See Route Map on Page 343

Damascus (mile 15.5) - *Take U.S. 58 east from Abingdon to Damascus. Once in Damascus, follow U.S. 58 through the town to the red caboose on the right. Parking available at this trailhead.*

Green Cove Station (29.3) - *From the intersection of U.S. 58 and VA 91 outside Damascus, take U.S. 58 east. Stay right on U.S. 58 at the intersection with VA 603 and go 4.2 miles to Green Cove Road (FS 600). Turn right on Green Cove Road and follow this to Green Cove Station. Parking available.*

Whitetop Station (mile 32.3) - *Follow the above directions on U.S. 58 to VA 603. Stay right on U.S. 58 and go 6.2 miles to Fire House Road (FS 755). Turn right on Fire House Road and go approximately two miles to the Whitetop parking area.*

Mountain biking happens to be one of the most popular activities on the trail. The surface is smooth and cinder-covered, with a terrain that never exceeds a grade of more than six percent. The trail only becomes steep when it crosses Whitetop Mountain, Virginia's second highest peak, and heads to its highest point of 3600 feet at the Whitetop Station. One way to avoid this demanding aerobic workout is to take the Blue Blaze Shuttle Service *[see Ride Information]* from Abingdon up to the Whitetop parking area. The shuttle will transport both you and your bike, and allows cyclists a carefree and easy downhill ride from Whitetop Station all the way back to Abingdon. More information is available at Highland Ski & Outdoor Center in Abingdon, which also rents bikes.

One point to remember when cycling the Virginia Creeper is that the right-of-way passes through some areas of private property. Local landowners ask that you shut gates behind you and respect their property as you ride along the trail.

Ride Information

● Trail Contacts:
Mount Rogers National Recreation Area
(540) 783-5196

Rails-to-Trails Conservancy
(202) 797-5400

● Schedule:
Open daylight to dark all year-round

● Local Information:
Abingdon Convention & Visitors Bureau
Abingdon, VA
1-800-435-3440

Mount Rogers National Recreation Area
1-800-628-7202

● Local Events /Attractions:
Appalachian Trail Days, in May
Damascus, VA—visit *www.damascus.org*

● Local Bike Shops:
Highlands Ski & Outdoor Center
Abingdon, VA
(540) 628-1329
or *www.adventuresports.com/shops/highlands/bike_rentals.htm*

Blue Blaze Shuttle Service
Damascus, VA
1-800-475-5095 or (540) 475-5095
or *http://blueblaze.naxs.com*

Adventure Damascus
Damascus, VA
1-888-595-BIKE or (540) 475-6262
or *www.adventuredamascus.com*

● Maps:
USGS maps: Abingdon, VA; Damascus. VA; Konnarock, VA; Whitetop Mountain, VA; Grayson, TN, VA; Park, NC, VA
Virginia Creeper Trail map

Connections: It's a word you'll hear from rails-to-trails advocates over and over. Connections could mean a trail connecting a neighborhood to a park, or it could mean a trail connecting the suburbs to a subway line. On a larger scale it may refer to connecting trails to create long traffic free corridors. For example volunteers are nearing completion on a series of trails that will connect Washington to Pittsburgh. Plans also call for an East Coast Greenway to extend from to Maine to Florida.

In Southwest Virginia the connection has been made! Not long after the completion of the New River Trail, trail builders finished a connection to the trail network in the Mount Rogers National Recreation Area, which already connected with the Virginia Creeper Trail to the west. This distance, from Pulaski to Abingdon, is 134 miles. The bald mile-high peaks and rugged terrain of Mount Rogers give this ride the feel of a Western odyssey, rather than an Eastern rail trail ramble.

Before you start your journey, remember that it's important to contact the Mount Rogers Recreation Area for a comprehensive trail log, as there are four detours along parallel roads and trails that mountain bikers will need to follow. Starting at Pulaski you proceed on the New River Trail [see Ride 47]. At mile 32.8 of the New River Trail you reach a new extension of the Virginia Highlands Horse Trail (orange diamond blazes). Eventually the trail connects with the Iron Mountain Trail (yellow blazes) near Virginia 16. The Iron Mountain Trail will take you to Beech Grove Trail, which takes you one mile farther to the Virginia Creeper Trail near Damascus [see Ride 48]. Follow the Virginia Creeper Trail for 19.7 miles, finishing your ride in Abingdon where you have arranged a shuttle.

Allow four complete days for this trip, more if you plan on side trips or hikes in the Wilderness Areas. Numerous campgrounds exist convenient to the ride are located in the Mount Rogers Recreation Area and on the New River Trail. More traditional lodgings are also available in Galax as well as Abingdon and Pulaski. Greyhound offers one bus trip daily in each direction between Pulaski and Abingdon, [see Getting Around Virginia]. It may also be possible to utilize one of the bike shuttle services listed below; although none of the companies currently publish rates between the two cities.

Getting There
See rides 47 and 48 for trailhead directions

The Virginia Highlands Trail Network

Ride Information

Trail Contacts:
Mount Rogers National Recreation Area (540) 783-5196—*Publishes a trail log for the entire route and trail brochures for each segment.* • **New River Trail State Park** (540) 699-6778

Shuttle Services:
New River Trail: New River Bicycles, Draper, VA (540) 980-1741

VA Creeper Trail: Blue Blaze Bike and Shuttle, Damascus, VA 1-800-475-5095 or (540) 475-5095 or *http://blue-blaze.naxs.com* •**Adventure Damascus,** Damascus, VA 1-888-595-BIKE or (540) 475-6262

Maps:
DeLorme: Virginia Atlas & Gazetteer. Pages 22 C-1, 40 D-4

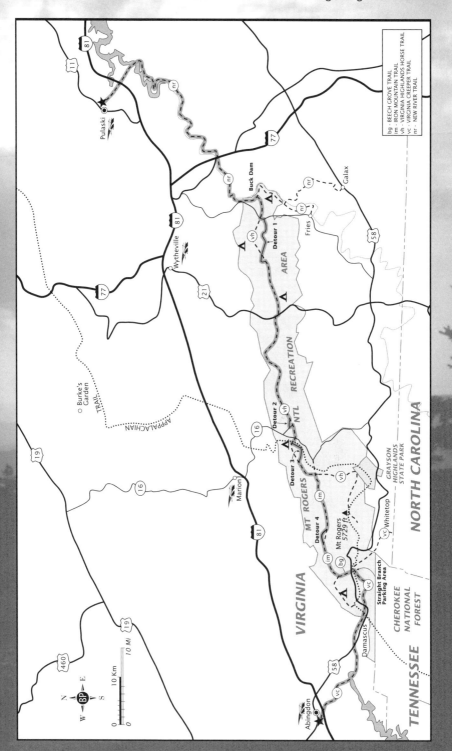

Southwest Virginia

Compiled here is an index of great rides in Southwest Virginia that didn't make the A-list this time around but deserve recognition. Check them out and let us know what you think. You may decide that one or more of these rides deserves higher status in future editions or, perhaps, you may have a ride of your own that merits some attention.

(Q) Mountain Lake Mountain Bike Trails

In 1994, Mountain Lake Resort (see Ride 44) designated nearly 10 miles of its trails for use by mountain bikes. Guests can rent mountain bikes from the Lakeview Cottage on a half-day and full-day rental basis and take guided trips to some of the Mountain Lake region's most scenic areas. All cyclists interested in riding the trails must get trail passes from the recreation office before heading out into the woods. A trail map is also available. For more information, call Mountain Lake at 1-800-346-3334. *DeLorme: Virginia Atlas & Gazetteer:* Page 41, B-5

®︎ Poverty Creek

The established nature and diversity of the trails between Gap and Brush Mountains just west of Blacksburg is what makes riding at Poverty Creek so enjoyable. It's a virtual playground of terrain and intersections for cyclists around the area to enjoy for the better part of a day. The trails and roads are open to everyone. However, mountain bikers and equestrians are not allowed to ride within 300 feet of Pandapas Pond. The reason I'm including this ride as an Honorable Mention (you'll note I've already got a full-featured ride called Brush Mountain - Ride 41) is to highlight the diversity of what else exists just west of town. The Brush Mountain Ride sends folks on a pretty hilly course up and down the western slopes of Brush Mountain. However, in the middle of the course, the ride follows the Basin Trail along Poverty Creek. This trail continues along Poverty Creek for nearly seven miles to a loop around Boley Fields, offering cyclists and chance to go well beyond the Brush Mountain area. So the next time you head out to Brush Mountain, consider following Poverty Creek east for a while and see what else this area has to offer. Many local volunteers from the town of Blacksburg and Virginia Tech contribute to the maintenance of these trails, giving Poverty Creek and Pandapas Pond the distinction of being considered "scenic assets" by the National Forest Service.

To get there from Blacksburg, drive northwest on U.S. 460 for three miles. You will pass over Brush Mountain. After you pass VA 621 on your right, turn left into the park entrance. Park signs mark the turn and there is no fee for parking or biking. The large gravel parking lot is on your immediate left as you pass the sign. *DeLorme: Virginia Atlas & Gazetteer:* Page 41, B-6

ⓢ Fairy Stone State Park

If you think Douthat State Park sounds great (see Ride 36) then check out Fairy Stone State Park located in the foothills of the Blue Ridge Mountains down near Martinsville, Virginia. The park is a little out of the way for most people, but those who find their way here always come home with pleasant memories. Fairy Stone State Park is one of six original state parks established in Virginia back in 1933. The 4,868 acres of land were donated by Roanoke newspaper publisher Julius B. Fishburn, and to this day remains one of the state's largest parks. The CCC built the 24 cabins and most of the facilities you'll find here back in the early 1930s, giving this park a sense of history not found in many other parks in Virginia. Nine of the park's 14 miles of trails are designated as multi-use trails and are open to horses, hikers, and mountain bikers. The rest are hiking-only trails. Similar in many ways to Douthat State Park, Fairy Stone is a great place to spend a weekend, bunking in one of the fully equipped rustic cabins, mountain biking during the day, and enjoying a Blue Ridge sunset over the 168-acre lake. For more information, call (540) 930-2424 or to reserve cabins or campsites call 1-800-933-PARK. *DeLorme: Virginia Atlas & Gazetteer:* Page 26, B-2.

Appendix

Bicycle Clubs and Organizations

Charlottesville Albemarle Bicycling Association
Advocating bicycle safety education and bicycle lanes on city streets.
www.cycling.org/lists/chaba/

Virginia Bicycling Federation
A state-wide bicycling advocacy organization composed of clubs.
PO Box 5621
Arlington, VA 22205

Recreational

Blue Ridge Bicycle Club
A recreational and road racing club based in Roanoke.
Box 13383
Roanoke, Virginia 24033
www.roava.net/~bike/

Charlottesville Bike Club
Charlottesville's bike touring club.
2570 Kendalwood Lane
Charlottesville, VA 22901
www.mindspring.com/~sgdowell/cbc.htm

Eastern Shore of Virginia Bicycle Club
5248 Willow Oaks Rd
PO Box 882
Eastville, VA 23347
cbes@esva.nets

Eastern Virginia Mountain Bike Association
Concerned with trail access issues in the Tidewater region
PO Box 7553
Hampton, VA 23666

Fredericksburg Cyclists Bicycle Touring Club
Encourages cycling for recreation, sport, fitness, and transportation in and around Fredericksburg.
PO Box 7844
Fredericksburg, VA 22404
(540) 373-1451
www.bikefred.com

Mid-Atlantic Off Road Enthusiasts
An off-road cycling group based in the DC area.
14846 Basingstoke Loop
Centerville, VA 22020
scudaman@erols.com
www.more-mtb.org

Milepost Zero Bicycle Club
Road bike club based in Waynesboro.
P.O. Box 1693
Waynesboro, VA 22980-2118
cfw.com/~ringgold/mpzero.htm

Mountain Bike Club of Virginia Tech
An off-road collegiate club at Virginia Tech in Blacksburg.
www.vt.edu:10021/org/mtnbike

Nelson Bicycle Alliance
Bicycle advocacy organization.
9994 Rockfish Valley
Afton, VA 22920
(540) 456-6746

New River Valley Bike Club/Rock 'n' Road Riders
Based in southwestern Virginia (Blacksburg, Christainsburg, Radford, Pulaski).
PO Box 488
Blacksburg, VA 24063
www.montgomery-floyd.lib.va.us/compages/nrvbc/

Potomac Pedalers Touring Club
A large recreational club in the DC area with approximately 5000 members.
6878 Fleetwood Rd, Suite D
McLean, VA 22101
(202) 363-TOUR
www.bikepptc.org/

Peninsula Bicycling Association
PO Box 12115
Newport News, VA 23612
(757) 875-1594

Rappahannock Bicycle Club
PO Box 682
Bowling Green, VA 22427
(804) 633-6500

Richmond Area Bicycling Association
For recreational cyclists of all abilities in the
Richmond area.
Betsy Blevins c/o RABA
409-H North Hamilton St.
Richmond, VA 23221
(804) 266-BIKE
www.erols.com/debraj/raba/

Shenandoah Valley Bicycle Club
For recreational cyclists of all abilities, also an
advocacy organization
PO Box 1014
Harrisonburg, VA 22801
www.math.jmu.edu/~vanwyk/svbc/

University of Virginia Mountain Bike Club
A recreational and racing club at the University
of Virginia in Charlottesville.
www.virginia.edu/~bikeclub/

Wheel Power Christian Cyclists
A road and off-road recreational club based in
Lynchburg.
PO Box 4791
Lynchburg, VA 24502
(804) 525-9552
wheelpwr1@aol.com

Williamsburg Area Bicyclists
Road cycling club based in Williamsburg.
PO Box 2222
Williamsburg VA 23187

Winchester Wheelmen
Road and off road club based in Winchester.
PO Box 1695
Winchester, VA 22604

Racing

Arlington Masters Velo Club / GS Foster
Norm Woodley
2000 N Calvert St Apt 4
Arlington, VA 22201
(703) 528-7194

Beltway Bicycle Club/Golds-Saturn-Dominoes
A road racing club based in Alexandria with approximately 30 members, from Cat 1 through 5.
Skip Foley
sfoley@erols.com

Blue Ridge Bicycle Club / Team Josta
A recreational and road racing club based in
Roanoke.
Box 13383
Roanoke, VA 24033
www.roava.net/~bike/

Chronos Racing/Plow & Hearth
A road racing club based in Charlottesville.
Matthew Butterman
2514 Fontaine Ave., Apt A
Charlottesville, VA 22903
(804) 979-7145

CyCor/Richbrau Cycling Team
A road and off-road team focusing on races in
the East.
Tom Doyle
3202 Hunts Bridge Ct.
Midlothian, VA 23112
www.cycor.org/

East Coasters Bicycle Race Team
A small, grassroots road and off-road racing
team based in Blacksburg, Virginia, and focusing on events in Virginia, West Virginia, North
Carolina, and Maryland.
Mike Matzuk
1001 North Main St.
Blacksburg VA 24060
(540) 774-7933
www.g3.net/rowdydawg/

Hilton Cycling Club/Conte's Bike and Fitness
Contact Hilton Cycling Club
PO Box 1056
Newport News, VA 23612
(757) 595-1333

James River Velo Sport/HDK-Sentara
A road racing club based in Newport
News/Hampton
P.O Box 12072
Newport News, VA 23612
reality.sgi.com/billh/jrvs/

Monticello Velo Club/Powerbar
A road racing club headquartered in
Charlottesville VA.
Ruth Stornetta
19 Elliewood Ave.
Charlottesville, VA 22903
rs3j@virginia.edu
www.bluewheel.com./html/mvc.htm

Old Dominion University Cycling Club
The collegiate racing club at Old Dominion University.
111 Constant Hall
ODU MBA Office
Norfolk, VA 23529
(757) 683-3585

PDO Velo
The majority of the club are USCF Cat 4 and 5 riders, with many racing Masters as well (thus, Pretty Darn Old).
Randy Meadows
category4@home.com

Potomac Velo Club/A-1 Cycling
A road and off-road racing club based in Dumfries.
Ben Williams
15611 Rhame Dr
Dumfries, VA 22026
703) 670-2665
www.nv.cc.va.us/~nvportg/pvc2.htm

Prince William Elite Racing
Brian Hackett
12312 Mulberry Ct.
Lake Ridge, VA 22192
(703) 497-1671

Regulators Elite Cycling Team
A road racing club based in Clifton.
Marcel Bengston
12441 Popes Head Rd.
Clifton, VA 20124
(703) 803-2815

Reston Bicycle Club
A road and off-road racing club based in Reston.
Mark Kukulich
PO Box 3389
Reston, VA 20195
(703) 848-5370

Squadra Coppi/Java Shack
A road racing club based in Arlington, also known as Unione Sportiva Coppi.
Pete Laszcz
(703) 524-5834
pjlaszcz@ix.netcom.com.
www.squadracoppi.com/

TBA Race Team
A road racing club based in Norfolk.
TBA Race Team
PO Box 12254
Norfolk, VA 23541

Team Anarchy
A road racing club based in Warrenton.
Steve Chalke
748 Cherry Tree Lane
Warrenton, VA 20186
(540) 349-8612

Team Bean Cycling
John Huth
125 King William Dr.
Williamsburg, VA 23188
(757) 565-0203

Team Gold
Adam Coon
1175 Herndon Parkway
Suite 500; Herndon, VA 20170
(703) 435-2001

Team Hampton Roads
A USCF racing team based in Hampton VA. 30+ members, mostly Masters. Members race primarily local crits and promote many events, including a Thursday night crit series, Winning Edge crits, and the Lawyer Ashe Dash for Cash.
Dave Venable
17 N Greenfield Ave.
Hampton, VA 23555
(757) 838-7127

Team Richmond/White House Apple Juice
A road racing club based in Richmond.
Thomas J Sweeney
PO Box 11495
Richmond, VA 23230

Team Ultimate Edge
Emily Wilson
1720 Elmsere Ave.
Richmond, VA 23227
(804) 355-7994

Tidewater Bicycle Association
PO Box 12254
Norfolk, VA 23541
(804) 490-1831
www.vabch.com/tbapage/INDEX.HTM

University of Richmond Cycling
Eneas Freyre
310 North Shields Ave., Apt #2
Richmond, VA 23220
(804) 353-1164.

University of Virginia Cycling Team
The collegiate road racing club at the University
of Virginia in Charlottesville.
cycling@virginia.edu.
www.student.virginia.edu/~cycling/

University of Virginia Mountain Bike Club
A recreational and racing club at the Unviersity
of Virginia in Charlottesville.
www.virginia.edu/~bikeclub/

Valley Bicycles
Craig Cooper
1236 West Main St.
Salem, VA 24153
(540) 389-2453

Virginia Beach Velo/Fitness Works Racing
A road racing club based in Virginia Beach.
Bill Collins
1993 Southaven Dr.
Virginia Beach, VA 23464
Billbikes2@aol.com

Virginia Tech Cycling Team
The road collegiate cycling team at Virginia
Tech in Blacksburg.
125 G War Memorial Hall
Blacksburg, VA 2406
(540) 231-7005
www.vt.edu:10021/org/cycling/

Whole Wheel Velo Club
A road racing club based in Arlington.
Duwayne Frank
6124 Edsall Road, #103
Alexandria, VA 22304
www.monumental.com/wwvc/WWVCPAGE.HTM

William & Mary Cycling Team
Ryan McKinney
CSU 4391 PO Box 8793
Williamsburg, VA 23186
(757) 221-4533

National

American Trails
The only national, nonprofit organization working on behalf of ALL trail interests. Members
want to create and protect America's network of
interconnected trailways.
P.O. Box 200787, Denver, CO 80220
(303) 321-6606, *www.outdoorlink.com/amtrails*

International Mountain Bicycling Association
IMBA - Works to keep public lands accessible to
bikers and provides information of trail design
and maintenance.
P.O. Box 7578, Boulder, CO 80306
(303) 545-9011, *www.greatoutdoors.com/imba*

National Off-Road Bicycling Association
NORBA - National governing body of US moun-
tain bike racing.
One Olympic Plaza
Colorado Springs, CO 80909
(719) 578-4717, *www.usacycling.org/mtb*

Outdoor Recreation Coalition of America
ORCA - Oversees and examines issues for outdoor recreation, Boulder, CO
(303) 444-3353, *www.orca.org, info@orca.org*

Rails-to-Trails Conservancy
Organized to promote conversion of abandoned
rail corridors to trails for public use.
1400 16th Street, NW, Suite 300
Washington, D.C. 20036-2222, *www.railtrails.org*

League of American Wheelmen
190 West Ostend Street #120
Baltimore, MD 21230-3731. (410) 539-3399

United States Cycling Federation
Governing body for amateur cycling.
Colorado Springs, CO
(719) 578-4581, *www.usacycling.org*

Dear Reader: *It's the very nature of print media that the second the presses run off the last book, all the phone
numbers change. If you notice a wrong number or that a club or organization has disappeared or that a new one
has put out its shingle, we'd love to know about it. And if you run a club or have a favorite one and we missed it;
again, let us know. We plan on doing our part to keep this list up-to-date for future editions, but we could always
use the help. You can write us, call us, e-mail us, or heck, just stop by if you're in the neighborhood.*

Outside America
300 West Main Street, Suite A
Charlottesville, Virginia 22903 (804) 245-6800
editorial@outside-america.com

Ski Resorts
[...for mountain biking?]

Massanutten
Harrisonburg, VA
(703) 289-9441

Wintergreen
Waynesboro, VA
(804) 325-2200

The Homestead
Hot Springs, VA
(703) 839-5500

Bryce
Basye, VA
(703) 856-2121

Wisp
McHenry, MD
(301) 387-4911

Timberline
Davis, WV
1-800-843-1751

Canaan Valley
Davis, WV
(304) 866-4121

Snowshoe
Marlinton, WV
(304) 572-1000

Whitetail
Mercersburg, PA
(717) 328-9400

Ski Liberty
Carroll Valley, PA
(717) 642-8282

Ski Roundtop
Lewisberry, PA
(717) 432-9631

Blue Knob
Claysburg, PA
(814) 239- 5111

Hidden Valley
Somerset, PA
(814) 443-6454

Seven Springs
Somerset, PA
1-800-452-2223

Ski resorts offer a great alternative to local trail riding. During the spring, summer, and fall, many resorts will open their trails for mountain biking and, just like during ski season, sell lift tickets to take you and your bike to the top of the mountain. Lodging is also available for the weekend mountain bike junkies, and rates are often discounted from the normal ski-season prices. Some resorts will even rent bikes and lead guided mountain bike tours. Call ahead to find out just what each resort offers in the way of mountain bike riding, and pick the one that best suits your fancy.

The following is a list of many of the ski resorts in the Mid-Atlantic area that say **yes!** to mountain biking when the weather turns too warm for skiing.

Fat Tire Vacations

[Bicycle Touring Companies]

There are literally dozens of off-road bicycling tour companies offering an incredible variety of guided tours for mountain bikers. On these pay-as-you-pedal, fat-tire vacations, you will have a chance to go places around the globe that only an expert can take you, and your experiences will be so much different than if seen through the window of a tour bus.

From Hut to Hut in the Colorado Rockies or Inn to Inn through Vermont's Green Mountains, there is a tour company for you. Whether you want hardcore singletrack during the day and camping at night, or you want scenic trails followed by a bottle of wine at night and a mint on each pillow, someone out there offers what you're looking for. The tours are well organized and fully supported with expert guides, bike mechanics, and "sag wagons" which carry gear, food, and tired bodies. Prices range from $100-$500 for a weekend to more than $2000 for two-week-long trips to far-off lands such as New Zealand or Ireland. Each of these companies will gladly send you their free literature to whet your appetite with breathtaking photography and titillating stories of each of their tours.

Selected Touring Companies

Elk River Touring Center
Slatyfork, WV
(304) 572-3771

Vermont Bicycling Touring
Bristol, VT
1-800-245-3868

Backroads
Berkley, CA
1-800-BIKE TRIP

Timberline Bicycle Tours
Denver, CO
(303) 759-3804

Roads Less Traveled
Longmont, CO
(303) 678-8750

Blackwater Bikes
Davis, WV
(304) 259-5286

Bicycle Adventures
Olympia, WA
1-800-443-6060

Trails Unlimited, Inc.
Nashville, IN
(812) 988-6232

Repair and
Mainte

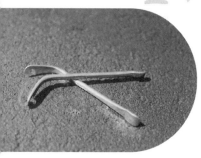

Repair and Maintenance

FIXING A FLAT

TOOLS YOU WILL NEED

- Two tire irons
- Pump (either a floor pump or a frame pump)
- No screwdrivers!!! (This can puncture the tube)

REMOVING THE WHEEL

The front wheel is easy. Simply open the quick release mechanism or undo the bolts with the proper sized wrench, then remove the wheel from the bike.

The rear wheel is a little more tricky. Before you loosen the wheel from the frame, shift the chain into the smallest gear on the freewheel (the cluster of gears in the back). Once you've done this, removing and installing the wheel, like the front, is much easier.

REMOVING THE TIRE

Step one: Insert a tire iron under the bead of the tire and pry the tire over the lip of the rim. Be careful not to pinch the tube when you do this.

Step two: Hold the first tire iron in place. With the second tire iron, repeat step one, three or four inches down the rim. Alternate tire irons, pulling the bead of the tire over the rim, section by section, until one side of the tire bead is completely off the rim.

Step three: Remove the rest of the tire and tube from the rim. This can be done by hand. It's easiest to remove the valve stem last. Once the tire is off the rim, pull the tubeout of the tire.

CLEAN AND SAFETY CHECK

Step four: Using a rag, wipe the inside of the tire to clean out any dirt, sand, glass, thorns, etc. These may cause the tube to puncture. The inside of a tire should feel smooth. Any pricks or bumps could mean that you have found the culprit responsible for your flat tire.

Step five: Wipe the rim clean, then check the rim strip, making sure it covers the spoke nipples properly on the inside of the rim. If a spoke is poking through the rim strip, it could cause a puncture.

Step six: At this point, you can do one of two things: replace the punctured tube with a new one, or patch the hole. It's easiest to just replace the tube with a new tube when you're out on the trails. Roll up the old tube and take it home to repair later that night in front of the TV. Directions on patching a tube are usually included with the patch kit itself.

INSTALLING THE TIRE AND TUBE
(This can be done entirely by hand)

Step seven: Inflate the new or repaired tube with enough air to give it shape, then tuck it back into the tire.

Step eight: To put the tire and tube back on the rim, begin by putting the valve in the valve hole. The valve must be straight. Then use your hands to push the beaded edge of the tire onto the rim all the way around so that one side of your tire is on the rim.

Step nine: Let most of the air out of the tube to allow room for the rest of the tire.

Step ten: Beginning opposite the valve, use your thumbs to push the other side of the tire onto the rim. Be careful not to pinch the tube in between the tire and the rim. The last few inches may be difficult, and you may need the tire iron to pry the tire onto the rim. If so, just be careful not to puncture the tube.

BEFORE INFLATING COMPLETELY

Step eleven: Check to make sure the tire is seated properly and that the tube is not caught between the tire and the rim. Do this by adding about 5 to 10 pounds of air, and watch closely that the tube does not bulge out of the tire.

Step twelve: Once you're sure the tire and tube are properly seated, put the wheel back on the bike, then fill the tire with air. It's easier squeezing the wheel through the brake shoes if the tire is still flat.

Step thirteen: Now fill the tire with the proper amount of air, and check constantly to make sure the tube doesn't bulge from the rim. If the tube does appear to bulge out, release all the air as quickly as possible, or you could be in for a big bang.

When installing the rear wheel, place the chain back onto the smallest cog (furthest gear on the right), and pull the derailleur out of the way. Your wheel should slide right on.

LUBRICATION PREVENTS DETERIORATION

Lubrication is crucial to maintaining your bike. Dry spots will be eliminated. Creaks, squeaks, grinding, and binding will be gone. The chain will run quietly, and the gears will shift smoothly. The brakes will grip quicker, and your bike may last longer with fewer repairs. Need I say more? Well, yes. Without knowing where to put the lubrication, what good is it?

THINGS YOU WILL NEED
- One can of bicycle lubricant, found at any bike store.
- A clean rag (to wipe excess lubricant away).

WHAT GETS LUBRICATED
- Front derailleur
- Rear derailleur
- Shift levers
- Front brake
- Rear brake

- Both brake levers
- Chain

WHERE TO LUBRICATE

To make it easy, simply spray a little lubricant on all the pivot points of your bike. If you're using a squeeze bottle, use just a drop or two. Put a few drops on each point wherever metal moves against metal, for instance, at the center of the brake calipers. Then let the lube sink in.

Once you have applied the lubricant to the derailleurs, shift the gears a few times, working the derailleurs back and forth. This allows the lubricant to work itself into the tiny cracks and spaces it must occupy to do its job. Work the brakes a few times as well.

LUBING THE CHAIN

Lubricating the chain should be done after the chain has been wiped clean of most road grime. Do this by spinning the pedals counterclockwise while gripping the chain with a clean rag. As you add the lubricant, be sure to get some in between each link. With an aerosol spray, just spray the chain while pedalling backwards (counterclockwise) until the chain is fully lubricated. Let the lubricant soak in for a few seconds before wiping the excess away. Chains will collect dirt much faster if they're loaded with too much lubrication.

Index

Index

Y

Euphoria...
in many different states.

The most beautiful, challenging and exhilarating rides are just a day-trip away.

Visit **www.outside-america.com** to order the latest guides for areas near you – or not so near. Also, get information and updates on future publications and other guidebooks from Outside America™.

For more information or to place an order, Call **1–800–243–0495.**

OUTSIDE AMERICA GUI

Mountain Bike
AMERICA

Meet the Author

When not conquering fiery new trails on his mountain bike or racing from town to town on his road bike, Scott Adams is hard at work on his next guidebook, cleaning up after his dogs, or exploring the backcountry and unique corners of this planet with his wife, Amy. Scott is a native of Virginia who lives his life to be outdoors, but finds much of his time spent behind the monitor of a computer preparing the next set of maps or arranging for the next book in the series. Few things reward him more than a long hike to the top of a mountain or an early-morning bike ride with no particular place to go.

Author